DEAFENING MODERNI

*Cultural Front*

GENERAL EDITOR
Michael Bérubé

*Manifesto of a Tenured Radical*
Cary Nelson

*Bad Subjects: Political Education for Everyday Life*
Edited by the Bad Subjects Production Team

*Claiming Disability: Knowledge and Identity*
Simi Linton

*The Employment of English: Theory, Jobs, and the Future of Literary Studies*
Michael Bérubé

*Feeling Global: Internationalism in Distress*
Bruce Robbins

*Doing Time: Feminist Theory and Postmodern Culture*
Rita Felski

*Modernism, Inc.: Body, Memory, Capital*
Edited by Jani Scandura and Michael Thurston

*Bending Over Backwards: Disability, Dismodernism, and Other Difficult Positions*
Lennard J. Davis

*After Whiteness: Unmaking an American Majority*
Mike Hill

*Critics at Work: Interviews 1993–2003*
Edited by Jeffrey J. Williams

*Crip Theory: Cultural Signs of Queerness and Disability*
Robert McRuer

*How the University Works: Higher Education and the Low-Wage Nation*
Marc Bousquet
Foreword by Cary Nelson

*Deaf Subjects: Between Identities and Places*
Brenda Jo Brueggemann

*The Left at War*
Michael Bérubé

*No University Is an Island: Saving Academic Freedom*
Cary Nelson

*Fantasies of Identification: Disability, Gender, Race*
Ellen Samuels

*The Disarticulate: Language, Impairment, and the Narratives of Modernity*
James Berger

*Deafening Modernism: Embodied Language and Visual Poetics in American Literature*
Rebecca Sanchez

# DEAFENING MODERNISM

Embodied Language and Visual Poetics
in American Literature

REBECCA SANCHEZ

New York University Press
NEW YORK AND LONDON

NEW YORK UNIVERSITY PRESS
New York and London
www.nyupress.org

© 2015 by New York University
All rights reserved

LIBRARY OF CONGRESS CATALOGING-IN-PUBLICATION DATA

Sanchez, Rebecca.
Deafening Modernism : embodied language and visual poetics in American literature / Rebecca Sanchez.
pages cm. — (Cultural front)
Includes bibliographical references and index.
ISBN 978-1-4798-2886-9 (cloth : acid-free paper)
ISBN 978-1-4798-0555-6 (pbk : acid-free paper)
1. Modernism (Literature)—United States. 2. Visual poetry, American—History and criticism. 3. Language and languages in literature. I. Title.
PS228.M63S26 2015
810.9'112—dc23

2015015624

References to Internet websites (URLs) were accurate at the time of writing Neither the author nor New York University Press is responsible for URLs that may have expired or changed since the manuscript was prepared.

New York University Press books are printed on acid-free paper, and their binding materials are chosen for strength and durability. We strive to use environmentally responsible suppliers and materials to the greatest extent possible in publishing our books.

Manufactured in the United States of America

10 9 8 7 6 5 4 3 2 1

Also available as an ebook

A book in the American Literatures Initiative (ALI), a collaborative publishing project of NYU Press, Fordham University Press, Rutgers University Press, Temple University Press, and the University of Virginia Press. The Initiative is supported by The Andrew W. Mellon Foundation. For more information, please visit www.americanliteratures.org.

# Contents

| | | |
|---|---|---|
| | Acknowledgments | vii |
| | Introduction | 1 |
| 1 | Impersonality: Tradition and the Inescapable Body | 35 |
| 2 | Primitivism: Communicative Norms and the Ethics of the Story | 62 |
| 3 | Difficulty: Juxtaposition, Indeterminacy, and the Linguistics of Simultaneity | 91 |
| 4 | The Image: Cinematic Poetics and Deaf Vision | 121 |
| | Epilogue: The Textual Body | 147 |
| | Notes | 153 |
| | Bibliography | 181 |
| | Index | 195 |
| | About the Author | 199 |

Acknowledgments

I have had the immense good fortune to be surrounded throughout my academic career by mentors who are just as generous and kind as they are brilliant. I am thankful to everyone who worked, taught, or studied at the sorely missed Barat College of DePaul University for creating such a magical environment, especially Missy Bradshaw, who introduced me to modernism and showed me that I could do this with my life. At the University at Buffalo, Randy Schiff, Michael Sayeau, and Damien Keane provided incredibly helpful advice and feedback on my work. I am grateful to Ramón Soto-Crespo for pushing me to find the thesis and to Tim Dean for your invaluable guidance at every stage of this project. For so many reasons, this book would not exist without the two of you and all of your support.

My colleagues at Fordham University have created a warm academic home for which I am deeply grateful. I am also appreciative and humbled by the amazing community of disability scholars, activists, and students it has been my privilege to interact with at conferences, in classrooms, in print, and online.

Thank you to those who read the manuscript in its latter stages and helped me to shape it, especially Stephanie Kerschbaum and my reviewers, Rachel Adams and Brenda Jo Brueggemann; and to everyone at New York University Press, especially Eric Zinner and Alicia Nadkarni, who helped guide me through this process.

It has taken a lot to get this book written, and throughout I have been sustained by the most amazing friendships. Thank you to Nicole Coover-Thompson for being there, always, for all these years; and to Sonya Brockman and Lorna Pérez, for Bollywood dance parties, Sunday hiking expeditions, and your willingness to cross international borders, even when only to acquire bubble bath. Having such brilliant women as interlocutors has enhanced my work, and having you all as friends has immeasurably enriched my life.

And finally, thank you to my mother, Linda, for teaching me to read and making everything possible. This is for you.

\* \* \*

A portion of chapter 2 appeared as "Shattering Communicative Norms: The Politics of Embodied Language in *Winesburg, Ohio*," in *Modern Language Studies* 43.2 (2014): 25–39. Reprinted with permission.

# Introduction

The image on the front cover is a detail of Randy Garber's 2011 *Made in Translation* from her series of the same name. The piece consists of a five-foot-eighteen-inch rectangular copper panel, above which coil bits of copper wire. At times resembling pieces of mesh and at others organic shapes—leaves, branches, buds—the intricate twists of the wires create both depth, which is heightened by the variegated tones of the copper background, and a sense of something coming alive, reaching outward toward the viewer. The translation of the copper into these various textures and dimensions results in the creation of something complex and difficult to decipher but nonetheless vibrant and vital. Like much of the modernist work I discuss, rather than transmitting a "message," the piece highlights the communicative processes through which we are accustomed to receiving information. One of these is alluded to through the use of the wires, which evoke the copper telecoils found in hearing aids and cochlear implants that boost magnetic signals from telephones and hearing loops, translating sound waves into magnetic signals so that users can access specific sounds more directly. The tangles of copper appear to be messages caught in the middle of this process, information translated into another form but not yet decoded.

In "Conversing and Reversing," Garber explains, "I suggest this liminal state in my work by creating ambiguous abstract forms, open-ended narratives and unsettling spaces and figures that hover between the volumetric and flat. Thus the imagery expresses not only my particular experience of navigating through auditory distortion, but also reveals the elusive nature of communication."[1] As the twisted wires of *Made in Translation* reach out past the frame of the background, refusing to be pinned down or straightened into coherent meaning, they connote both the specific difficulties of an individual attempting to make sense of an oral utterance she cannot process aurally and the universal experience of the way meaning is transformed as it is passed between media, languages, and minds. Garber's embodied experience of deafness, that is, opens onto broad questions about the processes through which we signify, the relationship between different forms and modalities of language, and what is artistically made (rather than lost or even just found) in recognizing these diverse types of communication by attempting to translate between them.

This sense of the deep intersections between deafness and artistic and linguistic experimentation around sites of indeterminacy, embodiment, translation, and trace drives my exploration of the connections between critical Deafness and modernist studies throughout *Deafening Modernism*. In developing a Deaf theory that engages with but is not restricted to identity-based understandings of deafness, I draw on Lennard Davis's work on Deaf critical insight. In his influential *Enforcing Normalcy*, Davis explores the potential of "deafness as a critical modality," as a series of metaphors and assumptions pertaining to both bodies and languages. Rather than operating solely as a biological fact, or even a social construction, he suggests, deafness can also function as a lens through which we gain new appreciation of issues such as silence and voice that are central to literary works.[2] To deafen is to "deprive of the power of hearing, to stun with noise," a definition that is itself revealing of some of the valuable critical work such a concept might perform.[3] So deeply enmeshed in our language use is the concept of sound that even the ways we describe the absence of audition cannot help but make reference to it. Beginning to unpack some of this auditory bias in our approach to language initiates a process of revealing what this bias has heretofore obscured.

For Davis, the deafened moment par excellence is that of reading. Since the advent of the printing press, the main way most people have experienced literary texts has been through a process of silent reading. Although we tend to emphasize the acoustic elements of language, words on a page are surrounded by silence. By forcing us to encounter language without sound, the act of reading itself becomes deafening. As Davis explains, "By the deafened moment, I am speaking (writing) of a contextual position, a dialectical moment in the reading/critical process, that is defined by the acknowledgement on the part of the reader/writer/critic that he or she is part of a process that does not involve speaking of hearing."[4] But as the phrasing itself points out, our language strains against the notion of this silence, infusing the ways we think about writing. To write something is still to "say" it. As the definition highlights, the process of deafening is not a neutral one. Deafening refers to "a silence with heavy significance; spec: a conspicuous failure to respond to or comment on a matter."[5] Our "conspicuous failure" to respond to the notion of deafening other than through recourse to lack and negativity ("to deprive" of a "power") has obscured the ways that approaching deafening as one incarnation of crip epistemic insight can expand our perspective on how languages function in literary contexts.[6] To deafen is also to bring into dialogue with the culture and history of the Deaf, a minority group still often not recognized as such. In focusing on the auditory elements of language, we miss the insights that Deaf history and language can provide into "issues about representation, communication, [and] ideology."[7]

Deafening modernism, then, involves both cultural and historical recovery—situating literary modernism in the context of the history of a frequently ignored minority—and the development of a critical lens, which I will variously term Deaf insight or Deaf epistemology.[8] This process will also help reveal some of the elements of modernist language to which we have been deafened by the incredibly powerful and institutionalized accounts of the period that have tended to exclude the deaf. Having reclaimed this context, *Deafening Modernism* engages studies of American Sign Language (ASL), a language that itself is distinguished by its inherent embodiment and visibility, to explore modernist literary experimentation.[9] The project's focus on modernism derives from that period's surprisingly pervasive interest in these experiments at the intersections of words, bodies, and images and the wealth of pragmatic and theoretical knowledge that Deaf culture can bring to their analysis. The process of deafening modernism, I suggest throughout, forces into silence our received readings of the period, providing us the opportunity to interrogate some of the assumptions about what language can and should look like that, in addition to being critical to literary developments at the time, continue to shape the ways we think about language and, through it, ourselves.

In this study, I have very deliberately chosen to concentrate on modernist works that are neither by nor about individuals who are deaf. While there remains a great deal of work to be done recovering and analyzing such works, my interest here is in examining the ways in which

Deaf studies illuminates texts with no obvious or literal connection to deafness.[10] In order to make the case for the relevance of Deaf insight to central issues within modernist literary studies, I have focused, with a few notable exceptions, on canonical texts. The Deaf-authored texts I do discuss—selections of contemporary ASL poetry—will serve as a basis for developing and illustrating a Deaf poetics, which I argue helpfully illuminates modernist literature. The decision not to address early twentieth-century texts by or about deaf people is both pragmatic and political. ASL was not recognized as a language until 1965, and ASL poetics did not really take off until the 1980s. As a result, deaf literature from the early twentieth century was by and large neither conceptualized nor performed in ASL. Moreover, the novelty and relative scarcity of film cameras at the time means that we have very few preserved examples of signing of any kind from the period. Beyond pragmatics, my selection of primary texts speaks to a gap within disability studies scholarship. While literary disability studies has repeatedly asserted the relevance of disability to all people, whether or not they identify as disabled, in practice the vast majority of disability and Deaf studies works focus on texts in which explicit references to disability or recognizably disabled bodies are present. This is an understandable strategy, but it unfortunately contributes to the mistaken belief that disability insight is only applicable in such contexts.

The problems with this logic become apparent when "Deaf" or "disabled" are substituted for other minority groups, particularly those for which there is a longer history of scholarship.[11] As Toni Morrison influentially argued three decades ago, a consideration of minority experience, specifically what she called an Africanist or black presence, is "central to any understanding of our national literature and should not be permitted to hover at the margins of the literary imagination."[12] This "minority" perspective is key not only because it adds to "majority" discourse but also because it fundamentally restructures it, an insight that has in many ways shaped the direction of literary scholarship over the past fifty years. It would seem rather absurd (one hopes) to argue that critical discussions of race should be limited to texts that prominently feature bodies of color or that queer theory provides valuable perspectives only when the characters or authors being considered belong to a sexual minority. But somehow the otherwise familiar notion that the margin constitutes the center loses its grip when it comes to discussions of disabled bodies. In writing a book about modernism and deafness that is not about deaf bodies in modernist texts, it is not at all my intention to suggest that deaf bodies be marginalized within the discourse; throughout the book, I argue for renewed analysis of the embodied nature of language. I am, however, interested in expanding the scope of literary disability studies by demonstrating the broad and nonidentitarian ways in which it might interact with other fields of study.

## Closeting Disability

The assumption of disability studies' limited relevance within the academy at large and the associated reflex to attempt to ghettoize disability derive from a series of deeply held but often-occluded cultural beliefs about normative embodiment, issues that critical analysis of disability brings to the surface. In addition to the deeply problematic desire to make invisible a group that, at 15 percent of the American population, represents the largest physical minority in the country, this impulse to marginalize both disabled individuals and discussions of disability represents a basic misunderstanding about the nature of disability itself.[13] While the pragmatics of negotiating daily experiences (often, more specifically, the legal structure established by the Americans with Disabilities Act) may require establishing a line between "disabled" and "nondisabled" bodies, in reality all bodies exist on a spectrum of ability and disability. Moreover, for most people, the status of the majority of these abilities remains in flux throughout their lives, and the meaning of a particular ability or disability can change dramatically based on context.[14] The experience of a visual impairment, for example, signifies something quite different when one is navigating a familiar route with a white cane as opposed to when one is in a new environment without a cane. While the idea that disability has no fixed meaning, or that everyone can in some way be thought of as disabled, problematically eschews the very real experiential differences between bodies that exist at different places on this spectrum, the deconstruction of the disabled/not-disabled binary usefully demonstrates the ways in which everyone has a very real and direct stake in discussions of and attitudes toward disability. While people do not wake up and find themselves a member of a different race or gender (without, at any rate, a great deal of expensive and informed consent on their part), many do wake up and find themselves disabled. Indeed, all bodies, if they live long enough, will become disabled.

Questions about normative embodiment raised by disability studies, therefore, apply to all of us. Not only, as Sharon Snyder and David Mitchell put it, does "the deficient body, by virtue of its insufficiency, serve[] as the baseline for the articulation of the normal body"; it raises the potentially unsettling notion that there is, in fact, no such normal body at all.[15] Disability reminds us of our mutability and, through it, our mortality. The fluidity of many kinds of disability also calls into question the presumed stasis of other forms of identification. As Lennard Davis argues in *Bending Over Backwards*, "inability spells the end of many identity groups; in fact it can create a dismodernist approach to disability as a nonidentity."[16] Disability provides a concrete example of the theoretical commonplace that identity is constantly in flux in ways we cannot always control.

This tension between how we like to think about our bodies and the ways our bodies actually experience the world has become a critical issue in the reevaluation of what we mean by the term "disabled." Somewhat ironically, given the emphasis on nonnormative embodiment apparently at the core of disability theory, the body itself has proven something of a sticking point. As Tobin Siebers explains, embodiment "appears as a bone of contention in disability studies because it seems caught between competing models of disability."[17] In line with the rise of diagnostic medicine and the surveillance of the body that Michel Foucault and others have chronicled, in the nineteenth and early twentieth centuries the disabled body was perceived primarily as a problem to be fixed.[18] According to this medical model, such corrective intervention was necessary either by modern medicine or (if that was not possible) the modern institution. In response to this demeaning of nonnormative bodies (which is to say all bodies), the disability rights movements of the 1960s and '70s argued that disability should instead be understood as a social problem; while an individual might be born with particular impairments, these only become disabilities when that person is put in a situation in which the social and/or physical environment is not accommodating. In this view, disability is largely a question of design. An individual with a mobility impairment, for example, only becomes disabled when confronted with a set of stairs. If we lived in a world that was designed to accommodate a wider range of physical and mental abilities rather than one that restricted access, the theory goes, disability would all but vanish.

As Siebers and others have pointed out, while the social model has been incredibly important, both in gaining political rights for the disabled and in reshaping the ways in which disabled individuals think of themselves, it also raises several problems of its own. Following the logic of the social model to its conclusion, one is left with the rather unsettling notion that there is no physical difference at all. If all bodies are disabled, then none are. While this might present a desirable ideal of human inclusiveness (a point that is itself debatable), it does not realistically represent the world that we currently inhabit, a world that is structured around differences that, while many may be exacerbated or produced by social inequality, do in fact include a range of bodily abilities. If an individual's vision is measured at 20/600, no amount of accommodation is going to make her able to read a book in standard print, and to deny this does violence to the lived reality of her body, suggesting that her experiences are not valid or significant. As Tom Shakespeare puts it, "the social model so strongly disowns individual and medical approaches, that it risks implying that impairment is not a problem."[19] Because "the social model defines disability as oppression," it also seems to foreclose on other, potentially more productive, ways of understanding disability.[20] The task ahead for disability studies, it would seem, is to develop understandings of disability that are able to take account of what Siebers refers to as "complex embodiment" while simultaneously recognizing (and seeking to ameliorate) the social factors that contribute to disablement.[21]

Where disability studies challenges our assumptions about bodily norms, Deaf studies puts pressure on those we make about linguistic practices. One of the reasons for the marginalization of Deaf studies (and people) has been ongoing misunderstandings about those practices. In addition to discomfort potentially raised by the fact that anyone can become deaf (and that nearly everyone will sooner or later experience some degree of hearing loss), the central premise of Deaf studies—that the Deaf are a cultural minority that possesses a distinct and complete language—shatters the myth of the universality of spoken language. It forces us to reevaluate our assumptions about what languages can look like and how they can function. As language is believed by many people to represent the dividing line between humans and other kinds of animals, any tinkering with these assumptions is met with icy resistance by those who feel their perceptions of themselves and their ways of defining their very humanity are being threatened.

Anxiety over definitions of language perhaps partly explains the incredible slowness with which the notion of ASL as a complete and natural language has spread beyond the Deaf community.[22] ASL was not recognized as a language until the 1965 publication of William Stokoe's *A Dictionary of American Sign Language on Linguistic Principles* and was not acknowledged by the Modern Language Association as a real language until 1997.²³ As Brenda Jo Brueggemann has noted, prior to that it had been listed as an "invented" language, immediately preceding Klingon.²⁴ It is still a widely held misconception, even among those who are highly educated, that ASL is not fully equivalent to other languages, that it is just a version of English on the hands or a system of gestural iconography. The pervasiveness of these beliefs can be measured in the fact that many doctors continue to counsel new parents against signing with their deaf infants because it will supposedly impede their acquisition of "real" language.²⁵

In addition to the discriminatory logic of this line of thinking, it is self-defeating in that it has prevented generations of linguists and other scholars from recognizing the ways ASL might illuminate their work. By virtue of the fact that signed languages operate in a visual modality, they offer exciting insights into the nature of language and human communication. This modality also makes them uniquely qualified to provide new perspectives on questions of the visual and embodiment within the context of literature. To begin to access these ideas, to deafen our discussions of modernist literature, involves an ironic undoing of the silence or "failure to respond" to issues surrounding Deaf culture and language that have caused us to overlook the ways these discourses can productively inform our understanding of English-language texts. While the political importance of recognizing this minority group and its contributions to wider culture are of great import and should not be overlooked, the matter is not merely one of inclusiveness. When we retrain ourselves to pay attention, to "listen" to things beyond the verbal, we find that Deaf culture and language have a great deal to say about concerns that are central to mainstream culture and, for the purposes of this study in particular, American literary modernism.

## Language Politics

My discussion of modernism focuses on four areas that dominated writing during the late nineteenth and early twentieth centuries, as well as later critical analysis of it: impersonality, primitivism, difficulty, and the image. Just as signed languages push us to reconsider the possibilities of language, modernist writers' desire to "make it new" through experimentation in these areas challenged preconceptions about the ways language could produce or destabilize meaning.²⁶ Part of the impetus for many of these experimental practices in the United States arose from contemporary cultural and political attitudes toward language, in particular, a push for standardization against which many writers situated themselves. The emphasis on linguistic conformity had dramatic consequences for the fledgling American Deaf community, as well as for other American linguistic minorities, and reintegrating Deaf studies into the narrative of American linguistic politics and practices necessitates examining Deaf history in conversation with these broader developments.

American English has always been a porous and shifting language. Even before European colonization of the Americas, the language was already being enriched through borrowings such as "guava," "hammock," "iguana," "canoe," and "manatee," all of which were taken from an English-language translation of Pietro Matire d'Anghiera's *De orbe novo* in 1555.[27] Linguistic contact between indigenous Americans and waves of multilingual European settlers, as well as the individuals arriving as slaves from various parts of Africa, resulted in a richly diverse idiom that predated the establishment of the nation. Many communities maintained their native language for both daily activities and publishing purposes. So much non-English-language material was produced during colonial times, in fact, that the British Parliament identified it as a means to generate revenue. The Stamp Act of 1765 included a specific tariff against non-English publications: "For every skin or piece of vellum or parchment, or sheet or piece of paper, on which any instrument, proceeding, or other matter or thing aforesaid, shall be ingrossed, written, or printed, within the said colonies and plantations, in any other than the English language, a stamp duty of double the amount of the respective duties being charged thereon."[28] As these examples demonstrate, later attempts at constructed nostalgia around a supposed "purer" usage of American English were entirely fictional; the universal usage of any form of English, much less a particular version of it, had never constituted an experiential reality in North America.

This linguistic diversity persisted through the founding of the nation. Indeed, as Alexis de Tocqueville posits in *Democracy in America*, its perpetuation can be thought of as a direct result of democratic government. By doing away with an aristocratic system that strictly separated people based on their socioeconomic station, linguistic borrowings and subsequent blurring were able to occur in all directions: "The constant restlessness at the center of a democracy leads ... to endless developments in the language.... Besides, democratic nations like change for its own sake, which is as obvious in language as politics. Even when they do not need to change words, they sometimes feel the desire to do so."[29]

For Tocqueville, such linguistic blending marked a productive shift away from aristocratic systems, in which both social station and linguistic behavior were more rigidly fixed. This tendency toward iconoclasm continued to be bolstered by America's status as a nation of immigrants. As Richard Bailey explains, from its founding through the beginning of the nineteenth century, "America was not demanding a rapid assimilations of other languages to English."[30] As had been the case in pre-Revolutionary America, immigrant communities within the country often maintained their native languages. Politicians took to recruiting new immigrants by publicizing the country in foreign languages. Citizenship status in early America, that is, was not dependent on the mastery, or even necessarily the usage, of English.

This productive tension of a national identity founded on the absence of a coherent identity came to be seen in a decidedly different light in the years surrounding the American Civil War.[31] In its aftermath, cultural diversity was perceived as contributing to the diverse political allegiances that threatened the existence of the nation. As part of that cultural diversity, linguistic difference was met with increasing skepticism. Anxieties over what it meant to call oneself "American," and the political stakes of there being no singular answer to the question, continued to trouble politicians and cultural commentators throughout the century following the war.

These tensions were exacerbated in the nineteenth and early twentieth centuries by an explosion in immigration. Between 1836 and 1914 alone, over 30 million Europeans migrated to the country.[32] By 1910, at a time when the country's entire population was just over 92 million, there were 13.5 million immigrants living in the United States. Congress responded by passing a series of laws restricting immigration: first the Page Act in 1875, which was followed in quick succession by the Chinese Exclusion Act of 1882, the Naturalization Act of 1906, the Immigration Act of 1921, the Emergency Quota Act of 1921, and the Immigration Act of 1924. Despite attempts to limit who was permitted into the country, the waves of newcomers had a profound impact on the nation, especially in light of the fact that, unlike the firm sense of national culture and identity that many brought with them, America was still in the process of attempting to identify itself as a unified country.

Further complicating matters, in 1898 the U.S. stepped onto the world stage as an imperial power.[33] Following its victory in the Spanish-American War, the United States gained control of Puerto Rico, Guam, the Philippines, and (temporarily) Cuba. That same year, it annexed Alaska, further extending the noncontiguous borders of the nation. At a time when many European powers were moving away from this variety of imperialism, the U.S. was just getting started. What this meant in terms of national identity was that the country now consisted of even more individuals who did not share a single history, culture, appearance, or language. The linguistic diversity that resulted is attested by a late nineteenth-century New York City guidebook, which described newspapers in "Russian, Swedish and Norwegian, Danish, Portuguese, Greek, Arabic, Chinese, Hebrew, and almost every language in the world."[34] In 1900 in Chicago, a city geographically removed from most other nations, it is estimated that two-thirds of the population spoke languages other than English; a staggering 500,000 spoke German, 125,000 spoke Polish, 100,000 spoke Swedish, 90,000 spoke Czech, and 50,000 spoke Norwegian.[35]

Unable to do much of anything about diversity in general, many Americans turned to language with an obsessive vigor that makes little sense when removed from this context. Unlike skin color or heritage, language, it was believed, could be modified. And nativists accordingly fixated on this process. As early American history demonstrates, there is no historical basis for the claim of a singular American English producing a unified body politic. Once the idea took hold, however, the construction of such a language rapidly became much more than just a matter of convenience. One of the clearest examples of the link made between communicative efficacy and larger questions of national identity is the Ford Language School, established by Henry Ford at his plant in 1914. In addition to providing language instruction, the school also regulated employees' hygiene and social interaction by appealing to the need for greater industrial efficiency. At the school, the notion of becoming more American, the stated goal for pupils, was a question of working in a manner that produced maximum financial profit, which would in turn contribute to the prosperity of the nation. Here and elsewhere, linguistic and cultural assimilation were explicitly linked to industrialized productivity.

In order to assimilate people into this hyperefficient language community, it was first necessary to determine precisely what American English was. An American Academy of Language (to be modeled on the French Academy) was proposed in 1894 with the goal of answering that question, and organizations such as the National Speech League, founded in 1916 by the National Council of Teachers of English (NCTE), and the Linguistic Society of America (1924) sprang up with a similar purpose. Part of the stated work of such groups was to separate American English from other varieties, a differentiation signaled by the promulgation of potential names for this national language: "American," "Amerenglish," "Statish," "Unitedstatish," "Inglish," or "Americanese."[36]

The notion of an "Amerenglish" quickly took on regulatory power. In 1907, Theodore Roosevelt declared, "We have room for but one language in this country, and that is the English language, for we intend to see that the crucible turns our people out as Americans, of American nationality, and not as dwellers in a polyglot boarding house."[37] Roosevelt believed that this linguistic preference should have specifically political consequences, and many people agreed. In the 1920s, individual states began issuing language legislation. The 1923 Illinois law, for example, declared that "the official language of the State of Illinois shall be known as the 'American' language," neatly separating America from both the foreign languages of immigrants and British English.[38] The implications on the social and political standing of individuals who did not speak English, or who did not speak it normatively, were far-reaching. As Roosevelt put it in "Americanism," "No man can be a good citizen if he is not at least in the process of learning to speak the language of his fellow citizens."[39] For many people, "American" came to signify "one who is fluent in American English," an idea put into law by the Naturalization Act of 1906, the first law to establish English-language literacy as a requirement for citizenship.

The force of this political argument was bolstered by the entry of the United States in the First World War, a conflict that introduced new waves of xenophobia, as well as a renewed desire for a recognizably American identity. In this context, as Joshua L. Miller explains, language "became understood as a surrogate for race and class differences. Those who could not or chose not to speak English or who spoke it in unfamiliar accents came to be viewed as unpatriotic and potentially subversive threats to national unity."[40] Where racial and religious discrimination might be frowned on, language remained (and, indeed, remains), by and large, an acceptable social prejudice.[41] Individuals who did not speak "standard" English were no longer "merely" different; that difference had a series of negative values attached. And, as the Ford schools demonstrated, this linguistic regulation often went hand in hand with other forms of enforced bodily conformity. Nowhere was this more clearly demonstrated than in the treatment of America's two indigenous non-English speaking populations: Native Americans and the deaf, whose socially vulnerable position enabled the government to remove them from their homes and place them in boarding schools where they could be forcibly restricted from using their languages.

## Boarding Schools

While there are obvious and very significant differences between the experiences of Native and deaf Americans, the similarities in the use of boarding schools to eradicate native language as a way to assimilate children into a perceived societal norm reveal the extent to which people in power were willing to go in order to perpetuate the illusion of America as a monolingual nation. Boarding schools had long been part of the indigenous experience, from mission schools to the indigenously run schools of the late eighteenth and early nineteenth centuries. In the late nineteenth century, however, mirroring the broader shift in attitudes toward American identity and language discussed earlier, these schools changed their pedagogical approach. After the Civil War, the government became more interested in establishing unified control over the schools. As Edward P. Smith, then commissioner of Indian Affairs, explained, the elimination of indigenous languages was key to that process. A boarding school, he argued, "takes the youth under constant care, has him always at hand, and surrounds him by an English-speaking community."[42] As the 1880 Board of Indian Commissioners annual report put it, "We no longer hear advocated among really civilized men the theory of extermination, a theory that would disgrace the wildest savage. As we must have him among us, self-interest, humanity and Christianity require that we should accept the situation and go resolutely to work to make him a safe and useful factor in our body politic."[43] Parallel to Roosevelt's speeches, the report links linguistic conformity to the health of the state.[44]

Similarly interested in linguistic assimilation was Captain Richard Henry Pratt, the man credited with developing the modern American Indian boarding school system. Pratt's experience working with American Indians came from working with prisoners of war in Florida, an important reminder of both the close temporal links between the Indian Wars of the nineteenth century and the establishment of boarding schools, as well as the strict regulatory nature of such institutions. Pratt felt that for a Native American child to achieve "absorption into our national life with all the rights and privileges guaranteed to every other individual," he would have to "lose[] all his Indian ways, even his language."[45] The impact of Pratt's philosophy was far reaching. By 1889, of the 36,000 American Indian children educated in boarding schools, 10,500 of them were in schools that followed Pratt's model.[46]

In the early twentieth century, the schools' pedagogy underwent another substantive shift. Whereas Pratt had believed in a fundamental equality between humans (that everyone was born a virtual blank slate and that differences were caused by inequalities in education), new policies that I discuss in more detail in chapter 2 came increasingly to be modeled on the logic that there were inherent and hierarchical differences between races. The perception of these differences contributed to the force with which language policies were implemented at the schools. Children were forbidden from using their native languages, and breaking this rule was met with the same punishment as if a child "used obscene language, fought, [or] stole property": teachers and principals "withheld food," "forced children to march, mop floors . . . or clean filthy bathrooms."[47] These punishments taught children to perceive speaking their native language as equivalent to committing acts of theft or violence. The penalties for the offenses varied but could include corporal punishment: "Teachers slapped the palms of hands, made students stand in the corner, lie on the floor in front of classmates, wear dunce caps, stand on one foot, and clean mortar between bricks with a toothbrush."[48] Older students were sometimes involved, "whipping the backs, buttocks, and thighs of boys and girls."[49] The use of non-English language, these penalties aimed to teach students, was a source of shame, something to be associated with embarrassment and pain.

The restricted environment of the boarding school—deliberately designed to separate children from their families and "Indian ways"—coupled with the youth of pupils made these schools a striking example of the reach of the government into the lives of its citizens and of the lengths to which it was willing to go to assimilate them into "our national life." In broader society, the government's options in terms of restricting language use were confined to passing "new laws, deportation threats, and other forms of social intimidation."[50] In the schools, however, there were few, if any, checks on what instructors could do. It was in this context in the nineteenth century that institutions for the deaf came to increasingly (and, ultimately, almost exclusively) center around linguistic assimilation, often employing similar tactics to indigenous schools to achieve their ends. To unpack these parallels, I begin with a brief history of attitudes toward signed language leading up to the late nineteenth century.

## History of Sign

Signed languages have been central to the development of modern Deaf pride and identity. "As long as we have deaf people on this earth," declared National Association of the Deaf (NAD) president George Veditz in 1913, "we will have signs."⁵¹ And, as passing references throughout Western literature demonstrate, as long as there have been communities of deaf people, this has indeed been the case. The earliest of these references comes in Plato's *Cratylus*, in which Socrates ponders the nature of names. "Answer me this," Socrates commands Hermogenes: "If we hadn't a voice or a tongue, and wanted to express things to one another, wouldn't we try to make signs by moving our hands, head, and the rest of our body, just as dumb people do at present?"⁵² Rather than being an aberration, as signed languages came to be viewed in certain circles in the twentieth century, Plato highlights the commonsense nature of their employment among the deaf. His ability to call to mind this image of signers as an example for his argument and his assumption that the reference will be familiar to Hermogenes suggest that deaf signers were not an infrequent sight in ancient Greece.

Plato was not alone among great Western thinkers in taking this view. Leonardo da Vinci similarly held that it was obvious and natural that the deaf would communicate manually, employing "movements of their hands and eyes and eyebrows and their whole person, in their desire to express that which is in their minds."⁵³ The association of the deaf with signs, the notion that they might be the "natural" mode of communication for individuals who could not process auditory language, in other words, has significant historical precedent. In both these accounts, signs are presented as effective means to communicate, a successful substitute for spoken language. There is no sense given that these gestures are inadequate to "express what is in their minds."

The perception of sign language as an effective, natural mode of communication for the deaf continued through the seventeenth and eighteenth centuries. Numerous philosophers were fascinated with what they called languages of gesture, and some became convinced that they were the forerunners of all language. While it was not the common view, René Descartes even held that "signs" employed by those "born def and dumb" represented a complete language.⁵⁴ The English doctor John Bulwer dedicated much of his working life to the idea that the language of gesture was the best means to educate the deaf. In *Chirologia, or, the Natural Language of the Hand,* he marveled at "that wonder of necessity which nature worketh in men that are both deafe and dumbe; who can argue and dispute rhetorically by signes, and with a kind of logistique eloquence overcome their amaz'd opponents; wherein some are so ready and excellent, they seem to want nothing to have their meanings perfectly understood."⁵⁵ The idea of a more "natural" language was a source of fascination because it seemed to suggest a link to the language used by man before the Fall, one, it was imagined, that had universal meaning and that was not artificially constructed.

Étienne Bonnot de Condillac was similarly convinced that a form of sign language, which he referred to as "the language of action," had predated spoken ones. What interested him most about such languages was their instantaneousness. While spoken language required that elements follow one another in a linear sequence, Condillac observed that in the language of action, one could communicate numerous pieces of information simultaneously. Accordingly, and anticipating the work of later scholars of ASL, he came to regard sign as the "language of simultaneous ideas," a point to which I return in chapter 3.⁵⁶ Although Jean-Jacques Rousseau believed that verbal speech was generally superior to sign, he also argued in *On the Origin of Language* that "visual forms are more varied than sounds, and more expressive, saying more in less time."⁵⁷ By moving beyond some of the inherent limitations of verbal communication, Condillac and Rousseau suggested, sign was not merely compensatory but might provide additional communicative possibilities that speech did not.

The two also reasoned that, because signs were directly connected with "natural" meaning and feeling, they represented a more honest form of communication. While these connections with nature later became problematic, what such attitudes offered at the time was a primarily nonpejorative (if still potentially condescending) way of thinking about signed languages. And after the once-dominant attitude that the deaf were not fully human, and therefore could not be taught, began to fade away, clergymen's initial attempts to share with them the word of the Christian god followed from this association. While teaching the deaf to speak (to "pass" to the greatest extent possible) was considered a goal, instruction at schools for the deaf was initially conducted in a combination of signs and speech. In 1755, Charles-Michel Abbé de l'Épée established the first free school for the deaf in Paris, France. This school, and others that followed, allowed deaf children, most of whom had never encountered other deaf people before, the opportunity to share the signs they had developed to communicate with their families and neighbors. Because these signs were thought of as a visible representation of speech, rather than a language with its own grammar (an idea that was nearly two centuries off), the home signs were standardized into an official French Sign Language that attempted to impose French grammar and word order onto the pupils' sign systems. Across the channel, in 1760, Thomas Braidwood established Braidwood's Academy for the Deaf and Dumb in Edinburgh, and in 1783, he moved it to London. The Braidwoodian method of education involved a combined method of a forerunner to British Sign Language and speech training.

Despite these developments in Europe, educational prospects for deaf American children remained quite limited. They were either placed in hearing schools, where they could not understand the instructor, or kept at home. Into this scene came Thomas Hopkins Gallaudet, a young preacher who fell into the world of education after meeting Alice Cogswell, the nine-year-old deaf daughter of his neighbor. In 1815, frustrated with the lack of available information on how to best educate Alice, Mason Cogswell asked Gallaudet to travel to Europe, in the hope that he would find a model in the deaf schools there that could be imported to the States. Arriving first in Great Britain, Gallaudet found himself rebuffed at the oral Braidwood school, which was hesitant to share its methods. Gallaudet did, however, meet Abbé Sicard, the head of the Institution Nationale des Sourds-Muets à Paris, and two of his students, Laurent Clerc and Jean Massieu, who invited Gallaudet to Paris to visit their school and to learn French Sign Language. Impressed by both the school and the highly educated Clerc, Gallaudet persuaded him to relocate to America, where the two founded the American School for the Deaf in 1817.

Following the French approach, American schools employed sign (or, more accurately, Simultaneous Communication) to educate students.[58] Before this time, deaf individuals had been spread out across the country, and the school provided one of the first opportunities for large groups of deaf people from diverse locations to congregate and share language, experiences, and culture. This situation, in which individuals find shared culture away from home rather than with their families, explains the central role that Deaf schools played within Deaf culture. Many of these early students hailed from Martha's Vineyard, an island off Cape Cod in New England that was home to the first Deaf community in the country. Because of a high rate of genetic deafness—in the late 1800s, one in 155 people was born deaf, nearly thirty times the national average—it was, for nearly two centuries, just as common to find islanders communicating with sign as with English. Both hearing and deaf islanders signed, creating an environment that was accessible for all.[59] Students arriving at Gallaudet's school brought this language with them, where it mixed with the French Sign Language of

Clerc and the home signs of other students to create the language that in the 1960s came to be called American Sign Language.

At the time, however, even educators who supported the use of sign language misunderstood its significance. Sign was believed to be a universal language, despite the empirical evidence demonstrating that sign languages of various nations were mutually unintelligible. While educators of the deaf who supported the use of signs (manualists) argued that sign was, in fact, a language, they described it as a language of pantomime or gesture. Helmer Myklebust summarized this view in *Psychology of Deafness*, arguing, "The Manual sign language used by the deaf is an Ideographic language.... It is more pictorial, less symbolic.... Ideographic language systems, in comparison with verbal symbol systems, lack precision, subtlety, and flexibility. It is likely that Man cannot achieve his ultimate potential through an Ideographic language.... The manual sign language must be viewed as inferior to the verbal as a language."[60] Such opinions were based on assumptions and impressions, as no full-scale examination by linguists of any sign language had yet occurred. They were widely accepted, however, even by deaf signers, who had been taught to think of their language as an inferior copy of English.

As subsequent studies have demonstrated, sign languages are not ideographic in the way Myklebust suggests. While ASL possesses some signs that seem to visually relate to their meaning (the sign for "tree," for example, consists of the dominant arm bent at a ninety-degree angle, with the palm wiggling like a tree in the wind), the vast majority of signs do not have this close correspondence. And those that do are equivalent to onomatopoetic words in English, such as "pop" or "boom," not an indication that the entire language is a grammarless system of pictures. As the linguist Ursula Bellugi explains, "When a gesture becomes a sign, its properties change, because as a sign it forms part of the linguistic structure of the signed language and thus becomes subject to grammatical rules operating in the signed language."[61] Even when signs appear similar to gestures, the former are not reducible to the latter. It was over a hundred years, however, before this misperception was corrected. At the end of the nineteenth century, the sign language used in schools was believed to be simply a more elevated degree of basic pantomime. Learning sign language was seen as an art, rather than being akin to learning German or French, and, accordingly, most educators of the deaf were not formally trained in it. Many picked it up from their pupils, a bottom-up approach to language that sharply contrasted with contemporary efforts to standardize and fix language and that contributed to a great deal of variation in the ways in which individuals signed.

Despite the mistaken views that these early deaf educators had of sign language, the program proved highly successful in teaching a population that had, until that point, remained largely beyond the reach of formal education, and this success led to the founding of additional schools for the deaf. In 1864, Gallaudet's son, Edward Miner, established the first college for the deaf, which in 1986 became Gallaudet University and which remains the world's only liberal arts university for the Deaf. By the end of the nineteenth century, there were eighty-seven schools for the deaf around the country.[62] Many of the teachers of these new schools were graduates of Gallaudet's, and they took with them the language and Deaf culture they had learned in his school. In this way, the language that eventually became known as American Sign Language was spread to deaf people throughout the country.

\* \* \*

It is at this point that we rejoin our broader story. As I described at the beginning of the chapter, by 1864 tolerance for linguistic diversity was dramatically decreasing. The push was to assimilate children into the majority culture, not to help them develop a language and cultural identity of their own. At the same time, advances in acoustic technology seemed to present new options for more closely aligning deaf education with this homogenizing zeitgeist. As Jonathan Sterne explains in *The Audible Past*, technological developments such as the telephone, the phonograph, and radio changed the ways people thought about sound: "As there was an Enlightenment, so too was there an 'Ensoniment.' A series of conjunctures among new ideas, institutions, and practices rendered the world audible in new ways and valorized new constructs of hearing and listening."[63] Part of these processes involved the ability to visually capture and record sound, to make it less ephemeral.

In 1874, Leon Scott invented a device, the phonautogram, that would enable the writing of sound. The machine was modeled like an ear and registered different vibrations that it could record with a stylus. Alexander Graham Bell and Clarence Blake produced a similar device that used an actual human ear.[64] Bell, building on his father's work developing a system of notation for speech, conceived of these machines as a way to approximate the experience of processing sound for deaf children so that they could learn to be more like the hearing.[65] He characterized the invention as "a machine to hear for them, a machine that would render visible to the eyes of the deaf the vibrations of the air that affect our ears as sound."[66] As Sterne explains, these efforts to create devices "to hear for them" were a major contributing factor in the development of sound reproduction. In addition to changing the ways that many modern writers conceptualized language, such inventions had a significant impact on deaf education in America. At precisely the time when Americans were becoming obsessed with establishing conformity, this technology represented a kind of miracle solution to the "cultural problem of deafness": the deaf could be trained "to pass as hearing people through their speech."[67]

Driven by excitement over this idea, Bell threw his full support behind what came to be known as an oral approach to deaf education. Oralism involved a focus on training pupils in speech and lipreading. More disturbing to some deaf people, it included at the time (and in some places even now) a simultaneous ban on the use of any kind of sign language, which it was (wrongly) believed would retard the student's progress with speech. Because this method of education fit so well with the broader cultural push for conformity, it very quickly achieved widespread popularity. The first purely oral school in the United States, the New York Institution for the Improved Instruction of Deaf Mutes, opened in 1867. Partially through the efforts of Bell, who believed that the deaf should be forbidden from intermingling (lest they reproduce and their children also be deaf) and using sign to communicate, schools across the nation began changing their method of instruction and adopting this new approach.[68] "People do not understand the mental condition of a person who cannot speak and who thinks in gestures," Bell insisted. "He is sometimes looked upon as a sort of monstrosity, to be stared at and avoided."[69] Mixing technology with eugenic philosophy, Bell sought to eradicate deafness by fully assimilating the deaf into mainstream society.[70] His approach won broader support when, in 1880, the Second International Congress on Education of the Deaf in Milan, Italy, issued a resolution outlawing the use of sign language in the education of deaf children.[71]

The results of the decision were dramatic. Nearly all deaf teachers were removed from their jobs, eliminating positive deaf role models for children who were isolated from other deaf people, as was almost always the case. As in American Indian education, in oral schools, children were physically punished if caught communicating with their native language. As one man recalled in a documentary on boarding school practices, "Whenever teachers and dorm counselors saw that I was signing, they would whack me on the hand with a ruler. I was 4½! Can you imagine smacking such a tiny hand?" Another man recounts a similar experience being caught signing at school: "[The principal] came up to me and mouthed the words 'you signed.' I had no idea what she was talking about. 'Give me your hand!' I put out my hand, and she smacked me several times. She repeated, 'You signed' and kept on whacking my hand."[72] The majority of students' time in class was spent repeating and memorizing sounds that would, proponents of the method argued, allow them to interact more easily with a hearing, nonsigning world. As a result, much less was available for studying the subjects their hearing counterparts were, which led to deaf children being characterized as intellectually inferior when they could not perform at the same level on tests. As James William Sowell, a product of the boarding school system, put it in his poem "The Oralist," "Minds they have as sound as yours but for hours you waste; / Spirits as impervious yearning for the light."[73] Such was the power to normalize that this kind of environment was seen as more desirable than having a minority culture within the United States communicating in a language other than standardized English.

## Writing Back

The legacy of Deaf boarding schools is mixed or, as Carol Padden and Tom Humphries put it, "powerful and conflicted."[74] While the schools removed children from their families and sought to normalize them through the acquisition of English in ways that were damaging to their self-esteem, they also provided a place for deaf people to come together and form community. Unlike indigenous children, it is entirely possible that students at deaf institutes had never met other deaf people before arriving.[75] It was at these schools that ASL developed, a fact that has heavily influenced the role that Deaf institutes continue to play in American Deaf culture. Despite these positive outcomes, the ways in which boarding schools played out national debates over language on the bodies of children remains deeply problematic, as do the ways that in the late nineteenth century the schools sought to systematically separate children from their minority cultural identities.

While progressives such as Bell and Pratt saw themselves as "saving" deaf and indigenous children by "restoring them to society," the damage done by forcibly restricting language use can be extreme. The act of separating an individual from his or her language is, as Toni Morrison reminds us, an act of deep structural violence above and beyond any physical violence experienced by the students in the schools. In her 1995 Nobel Prize acceptance speech, Morrison argued, "The systematic looting of language can be recognized by the tendency of its users to forgo its nuanced, complex, mid-wifery properties, replacing them with menace and subjugation. Oppressive language does more than represent violence; it is violence; does more than represent the limits of knowledge; it limits knowledge."[76] Boarding schools were designed to be locations where the "systematic looting of language" could most effectively be performed. The idea of limiting knowledge is particularly relevant to discussions of versions of oralist philosophy that disallowed the use of manual communication. Part of the oralist rhetoric was that children who learned to sign would never learn to speak. Terrified parents stopped using home signs with children and physically restricted them from doing so. No child, however, whether deaf or hearing, can learn to lipread as an infant. Even for children who would ultimately learn to speak and lipread English, this meant that during the first three years of life, years we know to be critical to brain development, children were denied access to any form of language, potentially interfering with intellectual development in ways that even later language acquisition could not ameliorate. So strong was the impulse to normalize, however, that linguistic "deviance" was perceived as more of a handicap than any potential developmental delays.

The use of boarding schools to force linguistic assimilation for both deaf and indigenous children created complex identity politics. On the one hand, the schools violently restricted students' development and access to their cultural language. On the other, they did provide access to the language of the majority, and perhaps more importantly, they provided the opportunity for the formation of unique cultural identities. No widespread Deaf identity existed before the boarding schools, and as Amelia V. Kantanski notes, such institutions also saw the development of a pan-Indian identity that could prove strategically useful for pupils.[77] The ways in which English was forced on students had a lasting effect not only on students but also on the English language itself, something that both Deaf and indigenous writers have capitalized on, challenging the boundaries of the English language that the schools worked so hard to enforce. As Kantanski argues in relation to the Native American schools, despite the systematic attempts of authorities to eliminate indigenous languages and cultures, "many American Indian writers were able to wrest control of both the content and the form of their self-representations and fictional literary productions out of the hands of the schools in acts of rhetorical sovereignty."[78]

Similar acts of "rhetorical sovereignty" play out in Deaf literature. Willy Conley's "Salt in the Basement: An American Sign Language

Reverie in English," for example, highlights the difficulty of the kinds of translation acts expected of students and reveals the limitations both of translation and of written English itself. The title of the poem offers insight into the contentious middle ground occupied by individuals whose national and linguistic identities were put into conflict by the assertion that only those who speak standard American English count as American citizens. It foregrounds the fact that the text to follow will involve a translation from ASL to English, that we should understand it in these terms, rather than as a performance of "imperfect" English. Whereas a hearing author might take for granted the fact that grammatical eccentricities would be understood in aesthetic terms, as formal experimentation, Conley's need to clarify this for readers highlights the perception of the deaf as a group whose English is flawed.

Further foregrounding questions of translation, the poem is presented in gloss, a transliteration in English of ASL signs that is specifically not a for-meaning translation. The beginning of the poem reads as follows:

me little, almost high wash-wash machine
down basement, me have blue car
drive drive round round
basement

happen summer time
me inside blue car
drive round round
basement

me drive every corner
drive drive drive
then BOOM! Me crash

there brown paper round tall
me get out of car
look inside brown round tall
many many small small
white rock rock
small white rock rock

for-for?[79]

Rather than attempting to conceal the difficulties of translation that standard English often masks, "Salt" places them front and center. The poem exists between languages, not comfortably inhabiting either, denaturalizing linguistic convention and forcing readers to consider how much is invisibly lost in the reverse transcription process, when a Deaf child like the one in the poem is forced to fill in the gaps through lipreading or Signed English, a popular communication system that uses select signs from ASL to produce a grammatical, syntactical copy of English on the hands.

The disconcerting sense of being between languages is amplified by the age of the speaker, a small child who reports what he sees, rather than translating or providing clarifying commentary. In distinctively ASL style, the poem begins by setting the scene, establishing the time and place of the events. The importance of the setting is emphasized through the repetition of "basement," three times within the first two stanzas. The poem's central object, the salt, is defamiliarized in this environment, suggesting the importance of context clues to determining meaning. This uncertainty about the salt is projected onto the reader through a presentation of the material in which it is not instantly recognizable: "many many small small / white rock rock / small white rock rock."

Through the process of determining what the substance is, the poem's speaker leads us through various linguistic ontologies, aligning each with a particular language. In English, the sign "for-for" translates to "why," suggesting that the child recognizes the substance but is puzzled at the unfamiliar context and asking for clarification. His father, however, responds to the English question—"What is it for?": "father told me for-for / outside road // me ask again for-for?"[80] In responding to the English, the father misses the point of the question, reinforced by the child's continued insistence that this answer is insufficient. Operating in separate linguistic modes, the two are communicating at cross-purposes. It is only when the boy sees the salt melt the ice for himself—"me look down white rock rock / burn burn hole many many / hole in ice / same-same ice in my lemon drink // me jaw-drop"—that he grasps the purpose of the substance he played with in the basement.[81] The child understands why the salt is in there not through a description but through a direct visual experience.

The ability to provide a version of such experiences is a unique feature of signed languages, one that I return to in more detail in chapter 4. In the gaps between the father's and the child's understanding, as well as between the child's and our own, "Salt" explores alternative epistemologies to those that emerge from languages in the aural mode. Moving beyond decades of research that sought to align ASL with spoken language in order to establish its status, the poem opts instead to focus on the differences engendered by their divergent modalities. The poem becomes about the diverse ways it is possible to perceive the salt, to understand and communicate its purpose. In ASL, for example, the signs for "brown paper round tall" would include more specific information about the bag's precise shape and size, as well as its location relative to other objects in the basement.[82] In English, we would get the specific noun "bag," which would clarify in a different way. Caught between, however, we are left in a state of confusion. By bending the English of the poem to illustrate the problems with translation, as well as the possibilities of alternative linguistic modes, "Salt" establishes a kind of rhetorical sovereignty. The poem suggests that something is lost in translation, that there are alternative ways to comprehend objects, and leaves us curious about what else they might reveal.

## Embodied Language

One of the fundamental components of these alternative ways of knowing, and one that I address throughout the book, is the fact of ASL's embodiment. As I explained earlier, spoken languages are also embodied. But both spoken and written language can be separated from the body, whereas there can be no disembodiment of ASL. This was particularly significant at the beginning of the twentieth century as new technologies made it easier than ever to divorce living from textual corpuses. As Juan A. Suarez explains, "The new media disassociated language from human corporeality. The typewriter, for example, interposed a mechanical contraption between hand and text and did away with the personal distinctiveness of handwriting. Other devices, in turn, detached oral language from the physical presence of the speakers and reattached it to inanimate objects. The voice was then disembodied and, therefore, dis-organ-ized."[83] It is out of this historical moment, which also saw the rise of first audio and then visual recording technology that allowed the separation of humans from their voices and images, that we get formalism, an approach to reading texts that detaches them from the external world.

The concept of explicitly focusing on language's embodiment was not new to American modernists. Walt Whitman, for example, had suggested such a blurring in "A Song of the Rolling Earth":

> Were you thinking that those were the words, those upright lines? those curves, angles, dots?
> No, those are not the words, the substantial words are in the ground and sea,

> They are in the air, they are in you.
>
> Were you thinking that those were the words, those delicious
>   sounds out of your friends' mouths?
> No, the real words are more delicious than they.
>
> Human bodies are words, myriads of words,
> (in the best poems re-appears the body, man's or woman's, well-
>   shaped, natural, gay,
> Every part able, active, receptive, without shame or the need of
>   shame.)[84]

For Whitman, the idea of language in bodies was a way to ground language in the personal rather than the abstract. What bodies as words offer, which "those delicious sounds out of your friends' mouths" do not, is communication that refuses the Cartesian split that would render the physical shameful (something Whitman challenged throughout his career). By contrast, if "human bodies are words" and the words "are in you," considerations of language become part of everyone's daily existence. Embodied language also offered a way of negotiating the general and the particular, as the abstract content of the language would be balanced by the literal presence of the human body that was either, according to varying formations, inscribed with words or composed of them.

If the ideas themselves were not novel, they were granted new urgency by the increased attempt to standardize both languages and bodies in the late nineteenth and early twentieth centuries. Modernist experimentations with the interaction of words and bodies on the printed page were also distinguished from earlier efforts by the concurrent rise in discourses surrounding bodily measurement, classification, and normatization. This merging of normative attitudes, as well as the development of the term "norm" itself, led to new crackdowns on individuals who either could not or would not conform.[85] As with fears over linguistic diversity, this deviance was perceived as not only undesirable but threatening to what was popularly described as a brave new world in which science could improve humanity.

If a large part of the impetus behind calls for the standardization of American English was synced to the standardization of American bodies—an intersection I refer to as *communicative norms* and describe in more detail in chapter 2—it makes sense that writers seeking to challenge both began investigating connections between the two, attempting to create a kind of textual-physical hybrid that in some way made present the body. Modernist writers responded to these communicative norms in several ways. One of them, outlined by Sarah Wilson, was to re-create the personal experience of hybridity of the modern individual in literary form. As she explains, "Formal experimentation . . . conceives of a text as individual, or logically parallel to the individual; in the context of melting-pot thinking, the text-as-individual produces a distinctive relation between reader and text."[86] The increasing diversity (and potential discomfort over that diversity) at the turn of the twentieth century was expressed through "polyglot formal effects akin to those found produced by immigration in the turn-of-the-century United States."[87] Texts came to parallel or represent bodies; textual form "broke" around bodies that proved difficult to assimilate into a homogenized norm.

A similar kind of breaking with the standard is traced in Michael North's *The Dialect of Modernism*, in which he investigates the use of racial dialect in modernist writing. "Dialect mimicry," he argues, "led to a breakdown of both the privilege that the standard enjoyed and the myth that there could be a 'natural' alternative."[88] By repeatedly referencing precisely the kind of language movements that standard English tried to repress, the use of dialect by writers such as Gertrude Stein, T. S. Eliot, Ezra Pound, and Hart Crane also called attention to the bodies that employed such language, bodies most likely to face discrimination in the push toward standardization.

The interest of most modernists in this kind of recognition was not to insert it into already existing forms of literature as a kind of inclusive practice but rather to employ it as a means to shatter form itself, to produce new hybrid forms including the two that I will be talking about in this book: embodied and visual language. In addition to the more obvious methods of including marginalized bodies and languages in texts (directly referencing such bodies), writers also began to experiment with less explicit possibilities. As I discuss in chapter 2, embodied language was most closely associated with earlier traditions of oral literature. This interest in reintroducing the body can also help explain the modernist obsession with "primitivism."

Not incidentally, within modernist literature, these issues are often raised in works that reference human hands. In Crane's "Episode of Hands," for example, a description of hands is used to establish a bond between a factory worker and the son of its owner and to signal a homosexual encounter between the two men. The owner's son's emotions are represented by the movement of his hands as he makes a physical and emotional connection with an injured worker: "As his taut, spare fingers wound the gauze / Around the thick bed of the wound, / His own hands seemed to him / Like wings of butterflies / Flickering in sunlight over summer fields."[89] Here, moving hands serve as code for something that cannot be spoken of in conventional verse; they call attention to the possibility of an unsanctioned erotic relationship between the worker and another man.[90] The hands are threatening because they shatter the myth of standardized communication's universality by foregrounding the bodies that do not fit comfortably within these paradigms, the bodies that it would be most convenient to marginalize and ignore.

This process becomes nearly impossible when such bodies insist on signifying in ways that cannot be separated from their physicality. As Helen Gilbert notes, what is deemed to be excessive movement is deeply problematic for structures of power invested in keeping bodies strictly under control, because such movement involves "resisting identities imposed by the dominant culture on individuals or groups and/or abrogating the privilege of their signifying systems."[91] Constraint of the natural movement of subjected bodies is achieved through the construction of strict social norms that can then be imposed from above as well as from within the community. Because of the subversive potential and focus on the individual of alternative means of signifying, they appear with surprising frequency in modernist literature as an ideal. It is such a language, written in the body, that Crane imagines to describe the responsibility of the future to the past in the "Cape Hatteras" section of *The Bridge*: "Thou hast there in thy wrist a Sanskrit charge / To conjugate infinity's dim marge- / Anew . . . !"[92] Significantly, this embodied message does not have a clear written equivalent; it must be transmitted through a distant and unfamiliar language rather than being translated into written English. Because it cannot be extracted from the body, it retains a kind of transience that the development of writing removed from the social dynamics of other languages, an ephemeral quality that appeared in numerous attempts to think through this intersection in modernist literature and one that analysis of ASL poetics and Deaf cultural dynamics will help us to flesh out.

## Visual Language

In addition to being embodied, signed languages are also, dramatically, visible. Indeed, a large part of what was being policed in these efforts to restrict bodies was precisely their visibility in public. As Michel Foucault and others have chronicled, modernity witnessed the rise of numerous technologies of vision that allowed bodies to be surveilled in increasingly intimate ways. Additionally, the invention of photography and the cinema during the nineteenth century meant that the world could be seen differently and that images of the world and of bodies within it could be preserved and more thoroughly analyzed. This increased visibility deeply influenced how modernist writers perceived their age. "I cannot repeat this too often," Gertrude Stein famously declared in "Portraits and Repetition," "any one is of one's period and this our period was undoubtedly the period of the cinema and series production. And each of us in our own way is bound to express what the world in which we are living is doing."[93] The cinema provided writers with new ways of thinking about images, as did advancements in modern art. "We are under the dominion of painting," Virginia Woolf commented in 1935, and as the sheer number of literary movements aligned with developments in painting or other engagements with the visual image—imagism, surrealism, cubism, vorticism, impressionism, dadaism—suggest, the question of how to merge these newly articulated ways of seeing with text remained a dominant concern throughout the period.[94]

If, as Rebecca Beasley has argued, "literary modernism is, paradoxically, a visual culture," however, it was not so in any straightforward manner.[95] The modernist period had a complex relationship to visual perception, engaging it in significant but not always consistent ways. On the one hand, new technological developments appeared to cement the realism of the visual image. Burgeoning disciplines such as anthropology similarly centered on the primacy of documentary visual observation and were constructed around a relationship between observer and observed. On the other, as I discuss in more detail in chapter 4, Martin Jay describes the modern period as marking a shift away from the scopic regime of Cartesian perspectivism, which he describes as being characterized by a "vigorous privileging of vision" that associated it with definitive truth.[96]

Part of this shift is attributed to the very elements of modernist culture that would have seemed to support the privileging of vision, a dynamic that P. Adams Sitney terms *"the antinomy of vision."*[97] "Modernist literary and cinematic works," he claims, "stress vision as a privileged mode of perception, even of revelation, while at the same time cultivating opacity and questioning the primacy of the visible world."[98] There is a similar tension between clarity and opacity in Crane's "Episode of Hands," which imagines direct communication through the body in ways that employ deliberately difficult diction and syntax. This paradox of communication that is at once more abstract and more concrete attended visual/textual as well as physical/textual hybrids.

As Michael North explains in *Reading 1922*, while the increasing availability of pictures from around the world might have been expected to provide clear and unbiased information, "photography's promise to end mediation simply made its audience all the more aware of it" and in so doing challenged the very notion of fixed truths.[99] The self-reflexivity that characterized modernity developed out of new visual technologies and practices—photography, cinema, the increasing ease of travel that allowed more people to see themselves through the eyes of others, and disciplines such as anthropology that involved looking at the cultures and practices of those others—all of which complicated any simple one-to-one translation between the truth and what one saw. Other emerging fields, such as public relations and psychology, also spread epistemological doubt about absolute truths. And the discourse of psychoanalysis similarly destabilized the idea that one could determine truth from what was visible, relying instead on hidden or repressed truths that could only be accessed through language and not images. These contradictory messages regarding images were not lost on writers. Stein believed that "the truth that the things seen with the eyes are the only real things, had lost its significance," though she continued to focus on the role of vision in her own work, including *Tender Buttons*, in which Stein borrows from Cubist philosophy and provides multiple angles (as well as emotional resonances) of an object simultaneously.[100] While more strictly in keeping with how vision works, this approach is so distinct from typical presentations of visual information in textual form that even today these portraits remain challenging.

## Overview

As with questions of embodiment, experiments into visual poetics repeatedly come up against a series of apparent contradictions that ASL, a visual and physical language without textual counterpart, is intriguingly positioned to mediate between.[101] Over the course of the next several chapters, I demonstrate how Deaf epistemology provides a vital and largely untapped resource for understanding the history of American language politics and the impact that history has had on modernist aesthetic production and the field of modernist studies by productively reframing questions that have been central to both: the tension between an emerging celebrity culture and theories of impersonality, the apparent paradox of an aesthetic simultaneously fascinated with primitivism and making it new, the juxtaposition and indeterminacy at the heart of modernist difficulty, and the apparent disjunction between imagism and epic in the careers of many prominent modernist writers. Throughout *Deafening Modernism*, I argue that Deaf and disability language, culture, and literary forms allow us to think these ideas together in ways that reveal relationships that are not simply contradictory. To support this claim, I draw on a range of methodological approaches, including literary analysis and history, linguistics, ethics, and queer, cultural, and film studies. In discussing Deaf studies in these unexpected contexts, it is my aim to highlight the contributions the field can make to broader discussions of the intersections between images, bodies, and text, as well as to contribute to the movement within both modernist and disability studies to enlarge the conventional boundaries of these disciplines. My goal is to tell the story of modernism from the perspective of Deaf and disability insight, to highlight the exciting new ways deafness as a critical modality invites us to think about topics we thought we knew. In so doing, I also hope to expand literary disability studies by demonstrating the importance of the field even and especially in places where no literal deafness or disability is located.

In chapter 1, I analyze the tension between modernist ideas of impersonality and the growing fascination with the celebrity poet. At the same moment that writers such as T. S. Eliot and Gertrude Stein were exploring ideas of impersonality in their writing, the circulation of their bodies within society as celebrities in newspapers, in journals, and at public lectures and readings was determining the ways their work was being read. To address the relationship of the authorial body and its personality or impersonality to literary work, I analyze ASL poetry by Debbie Rennie, Peter Cook, and Kenny Lerner, texts that by structural necessity are involved in an ongoing negotiation of that relationship. Drawing on these poetic texts in conversation with queer theory, I argue that sign literature enacts a model of embodied impersonality—a self-shattering that nevertheless refuses the disavowal of the embodied subject. Such a model of social interaction through literature allows us to reinterpret Sherwood Anderson's two volumes of critically ignored poetry: *A New Testament* and *Mid-American Chants*. Taken together, these texts suggest a model of poetic ethics based on interpenetration that paradoxically foregrounds the embodied subject even as it challenges its boundaries.

Building on the idea of alternative relationalities, chapter 2 examines how the use of embodied language and history in storytelling cultures enables a productive reading of modernism's interest in cultural memory that moves beyond accusations of primitivism to unpack both the ethics and pragmatics of this unexpected look to the past in the context of making it new. Drawing on the history of early twentieth-century Deaf boarding schools, I trace the development of communicative norms, which combine the growing interest in linguistic standardization with restrictive attitudes toward embodiment. The context of deaf educational practices reveals the force behind this push toward standardization and provides a model that illuminates the modernist discomfort over bodily signification that we witness in a variety of media, from the dance of Josephine Baker to the films of Charles Chaplin. In *Modern Times*, I argue, Chaplin draws on metacommentary related to his own aversion to the enforced speech of talking films to provide a nuanced portrait of the effects of enforcing communicative norms. These pernicious effects also underlie Sherwood Anderson's *Winesburg, Ohio*, in which the sheer number of townspeople who are either unable or unwilling to communicate through conventional speech demonstrates the extent to which the struggles of such individuals are symptomatic not of the problems of individuals but of a society whose prescribed modes of communication do not accommodate the diverse needs of its population. What these examples help to demonstrate is that the struggle against enforced linguistic and physical conformity at the beginning of the twentieth century was much more far reaching than is usually assumed. In conversation with the deployment of storytelling within Deaf culture as a response to such restrictions, the work of Chaplin and Anderson reveals the power of alternative artistic modes of signifying to shatter communicative norms.

This consideration of communicative norms establishes the impetus for the kinds of formal experimentation I address in chapter 3, in which I tackle the issue of modernist difficulty from the perspective of ASL linguistics. By approaching difficulty from the perspective of Deaf linguistic rights, I provide new ways for both enacting modernist difficulty and thinking through its implications. Focusing on juxtaposition (as demonstrated in collage poetics) and simultaneity (as seen in literary cubism), two of the most prominent ways in which modernist difficulty has been explained, I demonstrate how these dynamics emerge from manual languages as a result of their inherently visual and physical nature. Modernist poets themselves were intrigued by the political and aesthetic possibilities of such language. Hart Crane, for example, developed the idea of an "incarnate word," which represented an attempt to recall the physicality of language as a means to think through problems emerging from more standard written language that he perceived as dehumanizing in that it abstracted away from particular bodies and lived experiences. The consequence of this attempt to use the body to mediate between the general and the particular was an intense strangeness or difficulty in Crane's work that has led some critics to characterize his writing as failing and even to link this "failure" to his suicide. As studies of ASL reveal, however, dense linguistic figurations are actually effects of working at the intersection of bodies and words. I argue that one of the implications of this understanding of difficulty is that it allows us to rediscover the presence of bodies in modernist texts in which they appear to be absent. In the final section of the chapter, I take on this political project in the poetry of Gertrude Stein and William Carlos Williams and the art of the precisionist painter Charles Demuth.

Chapter 4 continues exploring what ASL might contribute to an ontology of the linguistic image by focusing on the qualities of movement and temporality and argues that the expanded description of the image suggested by such an ontology enables us to reconsider classifications of modernist works, specifically the apparent abandonment of imagism by H.D. and the supposed emphasis on sonority over vision in William Faulkner's *The Sound and the Fury*. I begin by tracing the history of the visual image's perceived relation to truth, as well as the ways modernist literature responds to these claims. I argue that the cinematic and visual techniques in the ASL poetry of Clayton Valli and Bernard Bragg demonstrate how the ability to manipulate temporality is not opposed to a present image but rather derives from the language's ability to produce material things in the world. These features—the indeterminism I discuss in chapter 3, the movement and engagement with temporality in Valli's "Dew on a Spiderweb" and Bragg's "Flowers and Moonlight"—reconcile the modernist fascination with the image as both inescapably tangible and present as well as multifaceted, shifting, and indeterminate. The negotiation of this impasse enables us to return to modernist classifications with a fresh eye, to challenge the traditional attribution of H.D.'s movement away from imagism and into epic poetry as a result of the limitations of the visual image, and to identify the ways in which the palimpsest functions as a visually structuring element of Faulkner's *The Sound and the Fury*. I conclude the book with an epilogue on the twenty-first-century textual body that considers both Deaf epistemology and modernist studies in the context of the Human Genome Project and genetic art.

Across these chapters, I demonstrate the extent to which ideas central to Deaf epistemology are embedded in debates that have surrounded modernism and modernist studies for over a century. But the project also has a broader goal. In *Narrative Prosthesis*, David Mitchell and Sharon Snyder argue, "While other identities such as race, sexuality, and ethnicity have pointed to the dearth of images produced about them in the dominant literature, disability has experienced a plethora of representations in visual and discursive works. Consequently, disabled people's marginalization has occurred in the midst of a perpetual circulation of their images."[102] In *Deafening Modernism*, I want to build on this argument. Through analysis of impersonality, primitivism, difficulty, and the image, I tease out how and why the marginalization of Deaf culture and bodies, as well as of Deaf studies as a field, has occurred parallel to (but too frequently not in conversation with) the ongoing fascination with issues of embodied and visual language within modernist studies. The difference is subtle but, to my mind, significant. I argue that part of the work of placing Deaf and disability studies into active dialogue with other fields involves moving beyond the assumption that such conversations can only occur at sites where disabled characters or authors are being represented or in which disability-related terminology is being used. Broadening the range of nonidentitarian possibilities for how we might think Deaf and disability studies together with other areas of literary and cultural analysis represents for me one of the more exciting directions in which literary disability studies might develop.

# 1 / Impersonality: Tradition and the Inescapable Body

> *A song, a spirit, a white star that moves across the heavens to mark the end of a world epoch or a presage to some coming glory. Yet she is embodied terribly a human being, a woman, a personality as the most impersonal become when they confront their fellow beings.*
>
> —H.D., *Notes on Thought and Vision*

In *Notes on Thought and Vision*, H.D. describes the Greek poet Sapho in terms that signal some of the preeminent tensions between impersonality, personality, and the embodied subject that emerge in both modernist writing and the scholarly tradition that has developed to analyze it. The writer here is specifically, terribly, embodied, but the boundaries of that body are porous, enabling her to be simultaneously "a song, a spirit, a white star"—an aesthetic creation, a source of inspiration, and an element of the environment. In the moment in which she encounters the other, however, impersonality transforms into personality, an embodied subjectivity, even as something of that impersonality lingers in the unexpected syntax of the description's final line and the pronoun's insistence on generality rather than specificity; "they" rather than "she." The poet is presented as impersonal—diffuse, porous, interpenetrated by the world around her—but simultaneously "a human being, a woman, a personality."[1]

The intriguingly ambiguous status of the body in H.D.'s description of poetic impersonality highlights the challenge that corporeality poses to the more canonical versions from which it is largely excluded and highlights the body's status as a potentially mediating force between the two, not merely a synonym of "personality" but an epistemic structure that illuminates both. Its frequent elision from the discourse represents a doubly missed opportunity, one that appears all the more striking given the hyperexposure of authorial bodies in the early twentieth century in the form of lecture tours, poetry readings, and an increasingly market-driven literary culture. Our narratives of modernism have been trapped between this highly personal celebrity and an apparently disembodied impersonality, the only resolution achieved by positing the latter as an elitist reaction against the former in a recapitulation of a high/low-brow binary that modernist scholarship has spent recent decades deconstructing.[2]

This is a critical impasse in which formulations of poetic relationality derived from ASL literature—where authorial personality and impersonality are structurally bound to the literal body of the artist—prove instructive. The model of embodied impersonality that I develop based on the work of the ASL poets Peter Cook, Kenny Lerner, and Debbie Rennie is also helpful in reevaluating heretofore marginalized modernist works that have been written off as out of step with the dominant models of poetic experimentation. By linking one such set of texts—Sherwood Anderson's *A New Testament* and *Mid-American Chants*—to elements of ASL literature, this chapter recovers their experimental value and engages them as a springboard for the production of alternative and embodied modes of poetic ethics.

## Depersonalization

From its most influential theorization in T. S. Eliot's 1921 essay "Tradition and the Individual Talent," the modernist doctrine of impersonality has proven something of a problem, both in the deconstructive, productively challenging sense and as a foundational ambiguity in need of clarification. Both impersonality and its doppelgänger personality attempt to communicate something about the interaction between writers and texts; as Eliot puts it, "this Impersonal theory of poetry is the relation of the poem to its author."[3] The essay's structure emphasizes the centrality of this relationship; the first half addresses Eliot's exploration of the ways that tradition should be incorporated into verse through an understanding "not of the pastness of the past but of its presence," while the second more specifically focuses on the status of the writer.[4]

According to Eliot, it is by recognizing this presentness of the past that the writer becomes capable of producing quality verse. The artist, that is, expresses not his or her own emotions of an event—the difference between art and the event is always absolute—nor Wordsworth's emotions "reflected in tranquility," but rather this complex interaction with tradition.[5] As Eliot explains, "impressions and experiences which are important for the man may take no place in the poetry, and those which become important in the poetry may play quite a negligible part in the man, the personality.... [The poet has] not a 'personality' to express but a particular medium, which is only a medium and not a personality."[6]

This sense of one's literary output deriving not from oneself but from external sources was far from novel. As Homer's invocation at the beginning of *The Odyssey*—"Sing to me of the man, Muse, the man of twists and turns driven time and again off course, once he had plundered the hallowed heights of Troy"—famously illustrates, the ancient Greeks believed in the power of entities external to writers who would speak through them in order to produce great works of art.[7] Similarly, ancient Romans approached genius as something one was temporarily inhabited by rather than as a stable category of identity.[8] In *The Poetics of Impersonality*, Maud Ellmann points out that this understanding of the poetic muse also characterized much of the romantic verse that Eliot specifically tried to distance himself from, especially as it reemerged in late nineteenth- and early twentieth-century discussions of automatic writing, in which spiritual guidance was said to assist writers who appeared to be unconscious.[9]

Despite these well-established precursors, impersonality was seized on as a distinctly modernist phenomenon, said to emerge from the alienating conditions of modern life. It is outlined in Eliot's "Tradition" in terms of the relation between writer and text; similar to the penetrative nature of the muses of geniuses, the impersonal writer became a medium, though one distinguished through the disembodied nature of the history that spoke through him or her. For Eliot, this set of relations allowed poetry to function as "an escape from emotion; it is not the expression of personality, but an escape from personality," an escape that necessitated "a continual self-sacrifice, a continual extinction of personality."[10] Of course, as Eliot cheekily notes in his conclusion, one must "have personality to want to escape from it."[11] In this apparently flippant remark, Eliot points up one of the most productive paradoxes in the essay. Personality must simultaneously be present and absent; a unified authorial conscious must exert control over the materials (to ensure that tradition is dealt with in the manner Eliot deems appropriate) at the same time that it is destroyed. The relation between text and author that Eliot defines as impersonal is itself predicated on personality even as, in the words of Sharon Cameron, "representations of impersonality suspend, eclipse, and even destroy the idea of the person as such, who is not treated as a social, political, or individual entity."[12] In ways that parallel H.D.'s description of Sapho more closely than may be initially apparent, within Eliot's argument is a foundational ambiguity about the relationship between the personal and the impersonal that is mirrored in his decision to publish a work calling for self-extinction in a magazine titled the *Egoist*.[13]

As a result of this ambiguity, the meaning of "impersonality" has never been as clear as might be expected given the significant role the concept played in the artistic output of the period. Ellmann questions whether impersonality "mean[s] decorum, reticence, and self-restraint? Does it imply concealment or extinction of the self? Or does it mean the poet should transcend his time and place, aspiring to universal vision?"[14] In addition to Eliot's own ambiguity, the notion of personality was further complicated through a series of diverse incarnations, including Ezra Pound's masks and personae, Gertrude Stein's impersonal autobiographies *The Autobiography of Alice B. Toklas* and *Everybody's Autobiography*, and W. B. Yeats's automatic script, all of which are often described under the same heading.[15] The slippage in definitions between these ideas and the fact that many of the questions Ellmann poses could be asked of Eliot's notion of impersonality or personality suggests a deconstruction that leads Ellmann to conclude, "the terms 'impersonal' and 'personal' have probably outlived their usefulness."[16]

And yet it is in part because of the complex interplay between personality and impersonality that the latter has remained a productive touchstone for interrogating the links between modernist authority and authorship. According to Rochelle Rives, Eliot

> allows us to see more clearly how impersonality might both decenter and build authority. On the one hand, ... modernist impersonality supports distanced and strange intimacies, wherein subjects and objects demonstrate their attachment to each other while preserving specific boundaries.... Authority, on the other hand, can be seen as an overt structure of invasion, a spatial situation that impersonality can also sustain, occurring precisely through the forms of interior "access" that enable impersonal connection.[17]

If personality and impersonality are not mutually exclusive, then neither are their implications for political engagement. Indeed, it is precisely because of the ways impersonality can be both mapped onto authoritarian notions of hermeneutic control and simultaneously open to radical fragmentation that it has remained a dominant part of the discourse, particularly in a post- (or post-post-) structuralist landscape that celebrates such problematics. Impersonality is at its most critically valuable precisely where it dismantles rather than "preserv[es] specific boundaries," boundaries between modes of discourse as well as corporeal subjects.

These tensions have also enabled impersonality to inform later twentieth-century theories, especially those positing the death of the author and the movement away from discussing individual authors and toward author functions. Both formulations push the corporeal subject even further from the aesthetic work in ways that have been critiqued as disregarding the significance of writers as subjects in the world.[18] In "The Death of the Author," Roland Barthes justifies this separation by arguing that authors exert tyrannical control over the meanings of their works. The death of the author, he writes, enables the dismantling of "the Author's empire": "Once the Author is gone, the claim to 'decipher' a text becomes quite useless. To give an Author to a text is to impose upon that text a stop clause, to furnish it with a final significance, to close the writing."[19] It is on the grounds of a similar relation between authors and authority that Michel Foucault describes the question of authorial identity or dis-identity as "one of the fundamental ethical principles of contemporary writing."[20] Authorial presence need not limit interpretive freedom in these ways. The status of the author's relationship to the text (and, through it, to the audience) does, however, have ethical implications that more explicit analysis of embodiment calls into focus.

## Celebrity Personality

One of the consequences of Eliotic impersonality and the tradition that followed in its wake was a turning away from associations between corporeal writing subjects and authors. Eliot's prominence within the academy and the significance of these formulations in particular to the development of New Criticism—an approach to literary analysis that privileged the text itself as arbiter of meaning, rather than authorial, historical, or cultural context—contributed to the ascendance of impersonality as a specifically anticorporeal project. As I indicated earlier, part of the narrative of impersonality's popularity situates it as a response against developments in early twentieth-century media culture that were more clearly aligned with bodily discourse.

For a long time, authorial personhood was separated off from accounts of impersonality, which was located firmly in the "high" modernist camp of the culture wars. As the high/low divide has receded, however, the widespread relevance of bodies—and, specifically, of writers as embodied subjects—has reemerged as a site of critical attention. This interest is evidenced in the recent explosion of scholarly works on modernist celebrity culture. Loren Glass's *Authors Inc.: Literary Celebrity in the United States, 1880–1980* (2004), Aaron Jaffe's *Modernism and the Culture of Celebrity* (2005), Faye Hammill's *Women, Celebrity, and Literary Culture between the Wars* (2010), Jonathan Goldman's *Modernism Is the Literature of Celebrity* (2011), Melissa Bradshaw's *Amy Lowell: Diva Poet* (2011), and Karen Leick's *Gertrude Stein and the Making of an American Celebrity* (2009) all attest to the difficulty of (and waning investment in) separating the bodies of early twentieth-century writers from their works.

As these studies demonstrate, fascination with the relation between bodies, texts, and culture was always a part of early twentieth-century discourse when the bodies of writers were, if anything, overexposed as developments in new media technology contributed to unprecedented levels of and possibilities for visibility. An explosion in print markets meant that writers had the ability to reach ever-expanding (and increasingly literate) audiences and that readers often came to books with prior knowledge of the individuals who wrote them. Standardized news stories, as well as the development of printing methods that enabled speed and the reproduction of visual images, increased newspaper and magazine sales, meaning that more and more Americans had access to the same stories. Both magazines and books also became less expensive to produce. Along with a rapid rise in national literacy rates, this increased production contributed to the emergence of a mass pulp-fiction market that engaged in an ongoing dialogue with the cultivated specialty markets of the supposed literary elites.

Despite resistance from some quarters, the rise of what Timothy Galow terms a "national celebrity culture" also impacted the ways writers interacted with readers.[21] One indicator of the extent to which audiences were increasingly fascinated with not only the works but the lives of authors can be found in the number of authorial autobiographies, which increased by 400 percent between 1880 and 1920.[22] The circulation of this information meant that the experience of reading literary texts was increasingly being shaped by what readers knew (or thought they knew) about authorial subjects. Both in response to and against this trend (as an attempt to keep the focus on their ideas), authors set off on lecture and reading tours that were hugely popular.[23] As Melissa Bradshaw explains, the early twentieth century was "a vibrant moment in American popular culture when poetry enjoyed mainstream popularity, audiences packed poetry readings, and readers avidly followed the honors, exploits and feuds of their favorite poets in the literary columns of daily newspapers."[24] Writers had become celebrities. Literary celebrity was not entirely new; Oscar Wilde and Charles Dickens, to go back two successive generations, had both been incredibly successful touring America and establishing themselves as well-known public figures as well as writers. But with the dawn of the twentieth century, the development of a vocabulary of international celebrity in the film industry, and the increased ease of travel and general economic prosperity that enabled individuals both to attend lectures and to purchase books for pleasure, such tours ceased to be charming oddities and rapidly turned into the status quo, what authors needed to do, either to sell their work in the first place or to attempt to retain some measure of control over the ways in which they and their work were discussed.

The reaction to Gertrude Stein's famous tour of America, undertaken after the successful publication of *The Autobiography of Alice B. Toklas*, illustrates the extent to which this circulation impacted the ways modernist writers were read. Galow describes the perception of Stein as a "bold and mysterious woman who had long been a topic of conversation in the American press, gaining such nicknames as the Mama of Dada, Mother Goose of Montparnasse, the high priestess of the Left Bank, the Mother of Modernism, and the queen bee of the expatriate hive, [who] had managed to generate a significant amount of interest in her persona without drawing audiences to her ideas."[25] As the passage emphasizes, Stein emerged from the tour a figure of fetishized interest, increasingly detached from the nominal source of her fame. Audiences who lined up in their hundreds and even thousands to watch Stein speak, to interact with her as an embodied subject, often had very little interest in her work. "Mother Goose of Montparnasse, the high priestess of the Left Bank" and "the queen bee of the expatriate hive" all reference details of Stein's personal life (where she lived) rather than how she wrote. And both "Mama of Dada" and "the Mother of Modernism" take more interest in gender (and in alliterative play) than in reflecting actual knowledge of Stein's art.

Far from extinguishing the personality of the work's creator, that is, public performances trafficked in the audience's desire to read a connection. The meaning of the works for those who were present became inexorably tied up in their ideas about the body present onstage. That audiences were only too willing to conflate poetic with authorial speakers is dramatically illustrated by the account of Amy Lowell's first public reading in 1915. Like Stein, Lowell eventually became incredibly popular as a reader and lecturer, but at this first reading, she was met with fierce audience hostility. As Bradshaw recounts in *Amy Lowell: Diva Poet*, Lowell began with the poem "Spring Day," the first section of which, "Bath," reads as follows:

> The day is fresh-washed and fair, and there is a smell of tulips and narcissus in the air.
> The sunshine pours in at the bath-room window and bores through the water in the bath-tub in lathes and planes of greenish-white. It cleaves the water into flaws like a jewel, and cracks it to bright light.
> Little spots of sunshine lie on the surface of the water and dance, dance, and their reflections wobble deliciously over the ceiling; a stir of my finger sets them whirring, reeling. I move a foot, and the planes of light in the water jar. I lie back and laugh, and let the green-white water, the sun-flawed beryl water, flow over me. The day is almost too bright to bear, the green water covers me from the too bright day. I will lie here awhile and play with the water and the sun spots.
> The sky is blue and high. A crow flaps by the window, and there is a whiff of tulips and narcissus in the air.[26]

Despite the sensual imagery—luxurious scents of narcissus and tulips, the fingers moving in the water, the playful suggestion of cleaving—the textual body in Lowell's poem is never actually placed on display. Covered by the water, its most suggestive qualities are displaced onto the inanimate: it is the day that is "fresh-washed and fair," the light's reflections that "wobble deliciously over the ceiling." Just as the water in the tub conceals the body in the text, so too do the poem's words, offering glimpses only of fingers and toes, rather than more intimate bodily parts.

The audience, however, could see nothing but the body, as though it were the poem and not the light "bor[ing] through the water," revealing what they felt should be kept hidden. They erupted, disconcerted not with the body of the woman in the poem but with the association they drew to Lowell's own. Listeners were unable to separate the poem's poetic voice from the woman they saw reading, to identify it as anything other than a confessional account of a sensual experience in which they apparently had no desire to fit the nonconformant body of Lowell, who was derided throughout her life for being overweight.[27] Reproducing this sentiment, the critic Margaret Widdemer later argued that Lowell "was going too far in her implicit demand that her personality be forgotten. It was inexcusable; it was rude."[28] Significantly in Widdemer's comments, personality becomes synonymous with the body; Lowell's reading is "rude" because it is perceived to be a description of the poet's own physical experience that violated proprietary norms. Despite taking place at the American Poetry Society, a venue in which one would have assumed audiences were accustomed to distinguishing between the poetic and personal "I," modes of engaging poetry had become so circumscribed by ideas of embodiment that they could not separate Lowell's poetic speaker from the physical presence of the woman speaking before them onstage.

However much the theory of poetic impersonality attempted to drive a wedge between authors and texts, that is, even during the years when this kind of poetry was most in vogue, the public's instinct was to do precisely the opposite. This was true even in the case of Eliot himself, the perception of whose work, especially his most famous poem *The Waste Land*, was very much shaped by ideas about the writer as a personality. As Lawrence Rainey explains in his history of the poem's publication, *The Waste Land* was publicized as a modernist masterpiece by the impresario Ezra Pound long before it appeared. Early reviews, however, suggest that not everyone was immediately won over. The poem was challenging, frustrating, fragmented. It often appeared difficult for the sake of being difficult, unnecessarily elitist. Assessing the poem, Conrad Aiken glumly noted, "there is a distinct weakness consequent on the use of allusions which may have both intellectual and emotional value for Mr. Eliot, but (even with the notes) none for us."[29] *Time* magazine wryly noted that the poem's "only obvious fault is that no one can understand it," and Charles Powell memorably referred to it as "so much waste paper."[30] Despite these unpromising readings, however, the poem went on to define a generation of writers. Even those such as Hart Crane who disliked it felt they could not ignore it.

One clue as to how *The Waste Land* could achieve this status despite the inability of many readers to make any sense of it can be gleaned in Malcolm Cowley's observation, in an article published in 1934, that "no other American poet had so many disciples as Eliot."[31] Eliot's authorial personality—cultivated in large part through the publicity machine that was Ezra Pound—as a difficult but brilliant and, moreover, *important* writer made both casual readers and critics engage with the work in ways they likely would not have bothered had the text been published anonymously. As Edmund Wilson, the future managing editor of *Vanity Fair* who came to be a supporter of the work, put it, "I found the poem disappointing on first reading but after a third shot I think it up to his usual."[32] The poem itself, that is, was not valued by everyone according to internal (or impersonal) merits. It was only through its relationship to Eliot, to "his usual," that readers such as Wilson came to view the work as significant. Had the poem not been by Eliot (the author, the personality, the embodied figure circulating in society), Wilson and others may well not have given it a second or third reading at all.

## Signed Personality

For better or worse, modernist texts were becoming increasingly entangled with ideas about the bodies of their authors. The difficulty of separating artist from text was so widespread a concern that it became the subject matter of many works, perhaps most famously the final stanza of W. B. Yeats's 1928 "Among School Children":

> Labour is blossoming or dancing where
> The body is not bruised to pleasure soul.
> Nor beauty born out of its own despair,
> Nor blear-eyed wisdom out of midnight oil.
> O chestnut-tree, great-rooted blossomer,
> Are you the leaf, the blossom or the bole?
> O body swayed to music, O brightening glance,
> How can we know the dancer from the dance?[33]

The poem is an extended meditation on ontology; visiting an elementary school, the speaker uses the disconnect between the pupils' perception of him as "a sixty-year old smiling public man" and his own thoughts on his love when she was a child to question which version of himself—if any—is authentic.[34]

Recognizing the multitude of identities emerging from perception, memory, and performance, the enactment of subjectivity itself must be performative, its own kind of art. And in a system in which there is no stable "dancer," in which the dancer only comes into being as such through the dance, the two can never be separated out. This question of artistic identity has been central to the development of Deaf theory and, more specifically, to the development of Deaf literary analysis. As ASL literature reveals, the human-body-as-art (and specifically literature) does indeed have critical consequences for how manual cultures think of both and how they create and preserve cultural memory.[35] It is precisely the inseparability of body from art that makes ASL texts useful sites of analysis for modernist theories of impersonality, particularly as they articulate themselves in relationship to personality and embodiment.

For manual literary traditions, the elision of the body that appears as a foundational principle of formalism is a structural impossibility. In sign language poems, the poet's "personality" is always already visible, is itself both the medium and a large part of the content of the work. Developing a better understanding of the relationship between authorship and bodies through recourse to ASL literature can aid our understanding of the relationship between celebrity and impersonality. In turn, the expansive body of criticism that has developed around these issues in literary studies over the past hundred years can help us recognize the implications and ethical possibilities of sign literature.

One of the most striking differences between signed and written texts is a literalization (and embodiment) of the problematic raised by Yeats. As Heidi M. Rose explains, in ASL, "the poem literally lives in the poet, and the poet gives the poem life through performance."[36] The metaphoric distance between bodies and words present in all written texts (even those that thematically foreground the body) collapses. In sign languages, the content of the message is inseparable from the body of the signer. To receive information, one must visually engage that body, a body that conveys grammatical information through the arms, torso, and eyes as well as the hands. It is a body that also cannot help but communicate certain extralinguistic information about the signer him- or herself, including (potentially) age, race, height, ability, and (depending on the fluency and style of his or her sign) educational background.

It should be noted that not all engagements with signed languages are visual. Signing DeafBlind individuals communicate using Tactile ASL, placing their hands over those of a signer in order to read tactilely what sighted deaf people would perceive visually (or hearing people aurally). Because of the ways it reroutes grammatical elements that sighted ASL users express through the face, Tactile ASL, though very similar, is not identical to visual ASL.[37] The majority of deaf people are only able to understand ASL when it is perceived visually, and they overwhelmingly tend to describe both their language and culture as visual.[38]

Despite the differences, like ASL, Tactile ASL insists on the recognition of a human signifying subject before semantic messages can be received; to perceive the message's content, one must be in physical contact with the other.[39] This basic reality of manual communication has interesting repercussions, one of which is its problematization of any concept of the death of the author or even the author as function. It also provides new insights into the later twentieth- and twenty-first-century impasse between identity politics and deconstruction, reflected in disability aesthetics in the tension between the political import of foregrounding "the actual bodies and mental conditions of . . . authors" and a postmodern sensibility that seeks to distance us from the perceived tyranny of biology (or biography).[40]

One particularly illustrative work in this regard is "Poetry" by the Flying Words Project, a poetic team comprising Peter Cook and Kenny Lerner that, like Conley's "Salt," works at the intersection of languages and cultures in order to demonstrate the unique significatory capabilities of ASL. "Poetry" begins with Cook repeatedly and rhythmically signing the word POETRY (or, more precisely, ASL POETRY which is distinct from the musically focused sign for nonmanual verse).[41] The sign ASL POETRY is etymologically linked to the signs for "expression" and "inspire" and moves outward from the chest—an offering up of the body, poetry as the expression of the self. The poem goes on to interrogate this link between the embodied production of the words and their semantic meaning through language play designed to highlight the way in which the words (like the sign ASL POETRY) emerge from and encircle Cook's body.

In the section most pertinent to our discussion, the poem's narrator paints a picture, the signs for both the canvas and the brush emerging organically from the repeated sign POETRY. Here the narrator—Cook—becomes both painter and painting. Role shifting, a key feature of ASL grammar, enables him both to spread the paint on the canvas and then to embody the image created by that spread paint, to become the work of art within the work of art.[42] Cook depicts the impact that the brush strokes have on the face being painted, and the interaction between the painting and the artist quickly becomes a struggle for control of the appearance of the art, for its meaning. There is a manic violence in the way the painter slaps and slashes the canvas, emphasized by the painting's grotesque expressions. These expressions allow the canvas to fight back against the painter's authorial control by comically rupturing both the painting and the poem.

Increasingly frustrated by his inability to gain control over his creation, the painter finally snatches the canvas and crunches it down into nothingness as the face struggles against compression before being destroyed and thrown away. In one way, the artist has asserted mastery; the troublesome painting is gone. In the process, however, he has had to destroy his art, thereby deconstructing his own identity as an artist. In this sense, the painting (which created poetic amusement for the audience) becomes more of an artist than the painter. The painter is also bested on the level of the poem. It is the painting with its irreverent comedy and surprisingly poignant struggle against oblivion that has the greatest impact. On multiple levels, the portrait the poem presents is that of the artist who is no longer an artist, the destruction of the division between artistic producer and object. The poem dramatizes the death of its author.

Even more instructive for our purposes is the way in which the thematic treatment of these ideas is mirrored in the structure of the poem. Cook, the author/artist, is the painter and the painting, as well as the poem's narrative voice. "Poetry" provides an ongoing metacommentary on Cook's relationship to his materials. And Cook-the-poet is anything but dead; at poem's end, he remains before us an undeniably living, breathing presence. "Poetry" is about nothing as much as the body, a demonstration of its ability to move through space, to make present various characters. In the absence of the body, there is no poem—and not just any body but Cook's in particular. Heidi M. Rose describes the significance of the artist's idiosyncrasies in the context of signed languages: "The performance nuances do far more than reveal an artist's individual style; they are integrally related to the *meanings* of the poem or narrative. It is these nuances, not the manual signs or non-manual grammatical markers alone, that give each poem its distinct identity because they are bound up in the *body* of the artist."[43] "Poetry" is what it is because of the fact that it is Cook's body performing it. In the hands of another poet, no matter how closely he or she attempted to mimic Cook's movements and expressions, it would be a different poem.

And yet Cook as omnipresent authorial figure does not exert tyrannical control over the text. "Poetry" has nothing to do with Cook as a biographical subject. Nor is it even necessarily an expression of Cook's poetic voice. Anything that we might identify as a poetic voice—Cook's perspective, his style of movement, his expressions—are taken over by the characters, by the poem itself. Here, the text speaks its author; it comes to life and takes control. The presence of Cook's body in the poem results not in his dictation of meaning but rather in the fracture of Cook himself as a coherent subject position. Part of what "Poetry" demonstrates is the fallacy of the assumption that authorial presence equates to authorial control.

To put that in terms resonant with our broader discussion, Cook's personality is extinguished; the impersonality of the text speaking through Cook is perhaps closer to Eliot's ideal than Eliot himself could have imagined. And yet we are never permitted to lose sight of the fact of Cook's presence, his humanity. "Poetry" presents a seemingly paradoxical embodied impersonality that suggests how we might rethink the relationship between texts and bodies in such a way so as to remain responsible to diverse lived experiences while still opening up to postmodern fluidity and eschewing a version of personality (or impersonality) that would align it with absolute authorial control.

While the idea of poetic impersonality and authorial presence may seem fundamental contradictions, ASL poetry illustrates the ways in which embodied impersonality is not only a theoretical but an actual solution to the impasse. What is more, this embodied impersonality is ethically suggestive in ways that prove instructive in our rereadings of both canonical and marginalized modernist texts. ASL literature fundamentally problematizes the separation between authorial body and text (one cannot point to "Poetry" as an aesthetic object distinct from Cook's body).[44] "Poetry" offers an alternative variety of impersonality, one based on a literal interpenetration of authorial and textual bodies.

As analysis of public poetry readings reveals, the relationship between bodies and texts was a critical question for readers and authors at the beginning of the twentieth century. As I demonstrate in the next section, the implications of such blurring usefully illuminate the engagement with these issues within written modernist texts. The emphasis on an Eliotic conception of impersonality—one that, as I have shown, the reception of his own work complicates—has prevented us from fully exploring some of the other models of impersonality developed at the same time, particularly those that, like the embodied impersonality of the Flying Words Project, highlight the significance of corporality.

## Interdependency

In the poetry of Sherwood Anderson, we can observe an attempt to think through such embodiment in the context of print culture's steady movement away from the embodied roots of literature. Unlike Eliot, whose interpretation of "tradition" primarily emphasized a written literary tradition, Anderson remained much more interested in models of literature developed in more ancient storytelling cultures. In these societies, cultural knowledge was preserved and transmitted through living bodies, and literature served a decidedly social function. Drawing on this history enabled Anderson to incorporate ideas about embodiment into his own conceptions of authorship and texts in his two volumes of poetry, *Mid-American Chants* (1918) and *A New Testament* (1927), to refasten bodies back onto texts from which print culture had removed them.[45] Because of his sustained engagement with the social function of literature and his attempt to produce written literature that remained responsible to people's lived experiences, Anderson's poetry provides an intriguing example of how the ideas of embodied impersonality and interpenetration present in ASL literature might look when translated onto the page.

One way that Anderson envisions the alternative relational space opened by storytelling is as a series of interpenetrations. His poetry repeatedly returns to the image of bodies entering and merging with one another. A model of interpenetration destabilizes the concepts of self and other by problematizing any easy dividing line between them as the boundaries of the body become literally porous. Disabled bodies provide one of the most visible illustrations of these kinds of interactions, as they are the most likely to find themselves merging both metaphorically and literally with objects and other subjects through complex series of relationships with assistive aids such as prostheses, implants, catheters, and other devices, as well as through caretaking relationships in which one or more individuals provide functions for others (seeing, moving, using the bathroom, for example) that are conventionally thought of as actions only performed by the self (as in some ways constitutive of the self).

As dependency theorists have argued, within a society that firmly establishes independence as the marker of personhood, interdependence or interpenetration can serve a powerfully subversive role by reminding us of the fiction of that independence. All humans exist in webs of relationships in which they assist and are assisted by others. Ignoring this reality means ignoring the ways we actually interact in the world. In *Love's Labor: Essays on Women*, Eva Kittay explains that, "by excluding ... dependency from social and political concerns, we have been able to fashion the pretense that we are independent—that the cooperation between persons that some insist is *inter*dependence is simply the mutual (often voluntary) cooperation between essentially independent persons."[46] This process, she continues, not only marginalizes those among us who are most visibly dependent but also mischaracterizes the ways in which all people interact. In addition to physical or mental needs or preferences related to age, illness, or disability, these also include the political, social, cultural, and racial realities that bind us all together.

From an ethical standpoint, the fiction of this independence establishes firm lines between ourselves and the people we encounter, which in turn permits us to behave disrespectfully or callously toward them. By recognizing these interconnected relationships, dependency theorists have argued, we might also begin to engage in more responsible ways toward other subjects. As Kelly Oliver states, "Our dependence ... brings with it ethical obligations. Insofar as we *are* by virtue of our environment and by virtue of relationships with other people, we have ethical obligations rooted in the very possibility of subjectivity itself. We are obligated to respond to our environment and other people in ways that open up, rather than close off, the possibility of response."[47] A greater appreciation of these intimate interconnections, this ethics of care postulates, would lead people to treat others better, even if only out of self-interest.[48] While this might strike some people as naïve (or at least premature), immediate changes in behavior are not necessary for the concept of such an ethics to be useful.

Adopting alternative ways of conceptualizing our relations with others has the potential to change the ways in which we behave toward them. Anderson's writing engages the idea of interdependence and pushes it one step further into a conversation about interpenetration. One limitation of dependency theory is its a priori assumption of the presence of two (or more) discrete subjects. As disabled bodies themselves demonstrate, however, this discreteness is not necessarily the given we imagine it to be. By suggesting relationships in which the participants may no longer be fully distinguishable from one another, Anderson's model offers an even more radical notion of the links between ourselves and others.

Like "dependency," the term "penetration" carries with it a great deal of negative baggage. The idea of being penetrated implies a vulnerability that has been linked to misogynist constructions of female sexuality and has therefore come to be seen as demeaning. "Penetration" is also haunted by the specter of violence against the self, both in the practical terms of rape or other forms of physical violence such as stabbing and more metaphysically, because during even consensual penetration, the entrance of something external into the body requires a sacrifice of the fiction of the self as a discrete entity essentially separate from other subjects and from the world around it. For Anderson, however, it is precisely the sacrifice of this fiction that becomes the starting point for ethical behavior.

Within queer studies, theorists have similarly postulated this site as a location for a radical reconsideration of the relationship between self and other. As Leo Bersani explains, "The self is a practical convenience; promoted to the status of an ethical ideal, it is a sanction for violence."[49]

Doing away with this fictional self has the potential to lessen the violence, enacted against disabled bodies that are excluded from personhood through reference to fictional autonomy. However jolting the notion of the discrete self as fiction might be, the porous nature of the body is a scientific reality as well as a social ideal; the skin that appears to separate us from the world around us is made up mostly of empty space. It is only because our senses are not precise enough to register this reality that we maintain the belief that our bodies are closed off. In abandoning this fiction by "shattering . . . the psychic structures themselves," we open a space to consider alternative relationalities not based on this mythical construction of the self.[50]

As Michel Foucault argues in a now famous description of social interactions, the development of "new relational possibilities" or "way[s] of life . . . can yield intense relations, . . . a culture and an ethics."[51] Thinking about the potential for interaction, in other words, is not merely an academic exercise. Pondering this possibility, Bersani registers both the potential of the idea and, like Anderson decades earlier, the dangers of linking these new relations to static notions of coherent and discrete subjects. As he notes, "Our thinking about new ways of being together has been predominantly reactive, against established relational modes," and has not "led to a questioning of the prioritizing of difference itself as a foundational relational structure."[52] Both Bersani and Foucault are thinking specifically of homosexual relationality, but their ideas have implications for how we think about the ways any two (or more) individuals interact, particularly the ways these interactions can occur through language and literature. The stakes of such interactions are potentially quite high. As Luce Irigaray suggests, developing new ways of being with others is the necessary next step in contemporary ethics: "A culture of being with the other is still to be worked out. This is a task for our time, not only an intellectual luxury or an apolitical stake, not even a moral or religious duty. To learn how to be with the other is a new stage, and perhaps the most important step, toward our becoming humans."[53] By situating these issues within the context of literature, ASL poetics respond to the push that Irigaray identifies to move them away from religion and morality and toward cultural and aesthetic practices.

What is so intriguing about the ways Anderson depicts relationality is that he forces a reconsideration of Bersani's difference in precisely these spheres. The bodily relationship that Anderson aligns with the kind of poetics he perceives as more socially responsible involves a willingness to be radically open, to do away with the boundaries of one's body in order to connect both with other people and with the environment. In "A Poet," Anderson explicitly lays out the links between such relationality and his poetic practice:

> If I could be brave enough and
> live long enough I could crawl inside
> the life of every man, woman and child
> in America. After I had gone within them
> I could be born out of them. I could
> become something the like of which has
> never been seen before. We would see
> then what America is like.[54]

Achieving artistic instinct, seeing "what America is like," is here dependent on a distinctly interpenetrative act, with the speaker crawling inside the subjects of his work, being "born out of them" in a process that emphasizes physical difficulty and the need for bravery. The poetic ideal posited involves abandoning the boundaries of his body and merging with those of his poetic subjects, coming to know them by becoming them.

In line with theories of an ethics of care, Anderson postulates that once individuals recognize their interdependence, they will have a greater sense of responsibility for and to the others around them. This responsibility is evidenced in his descriptions of encountering potential poetic subjects on the streets of Manhattan in his poem of the same name and feeling intensely guilty that he is unable to tell all of their stories. No longer just random people on a street, the people whom the speaker encounters are transformed into individuals to whom he has specific responsibilities: "To me there came men whose hands were withered. My / soldiers were small and their eyes were sunken. In them / was the pain that sobs, the great pain that sobs."[55] The storytelling process becomes a space where these soldiers can ameliorate their pain by entering into a relationship with the storyteller. The characters in the poem become him; the poem describes the poetic process as one in which "the men / who are old have entered into me."[56] In contrast to the Cartesian split of intellectual and physical matters, "Manhattan" suggests that it is precisely through this embodied interpenetration that "understanding came in to me."[57]

Interpenetration is also a central theme in "Song of Theodore," a name that derives from the Greek for "gift of god," which resonates in the Christian tradition with the notion of the sacrifice of one's physical body for one's people. Here, the poet enters the presence of his subject as a "lover":

> I would touch you with the fingers of my hands. In my
> eyes a fire burns. The strength of my imaginings is beyond
> words to record. I see the loveliness in you that is hidden
> away. I take something from you. See, I embrace you I take
> you in my arms and I run away.[58]

It is through this intense physicality that the speaker (touching, embracing, eyes burning) is able to access what has been hidden away and to transfer it to himself. The poet enters the body of the other but is simultaneously penetrated by the stories he then takes away to record.

Afraid of the intimacy of this process, of proving inadequate, the poet imagines withdrawing from the world, going into nature and solitude and making his body powerful. These musings last only two short stanzas, however, before he finds himself back in the city possessed by the presence of the people. Challenging the idea of his work as old-fashioned, Anderson's conception of poetry here is not of romantic escape to nature but is located in the bustle of the modern city. It is only there, and not when secluded from the masses, that the words come, that the poet gains a sense of purity and gender identity: "Here in these words / I am become a man."[59] The physicality of masculinity and sex, of intense embodiment, is not contrasted with aesthetic or intellectual pursuits but aligned with them. The poem's final stanza ties the process specifically to hands:

> What cunning fingers I have. They make intricate designs.
> On the white paper. My cunning fingers are of the flesh.
> They are like me and I would make love always—to all
> People—men and women—here—in Chicago—in America
> —everywhere—always—forever—while my life lasts[60]

It is the fingers "of the flesh" that will both partake of the bodily exchange and then engage in a mediated version of that exchange through the paper on which they record the knowledge they have obtained.

Similar language is employed in "The Healer," in which the speaker asserts,

> My body does not belong to me.
> My body belongs to tired women
> who have found no lovers.
> It belongs to half men and half women

My body belongs to those who lust and those who shrink from lusting.⁶¹

These links are also extended to the natural world, to "the roots of trees" and "a cunning wind," a connection Anderson elaborates on in "Song for Lonely Roads," in which this already multiply penetrated speaker further opens himself to the environment.⁶² In contrast to Ezra Pound's command that modernist verse should "make it new," the poem is infused with a sense of the circularity of artistic production—"The tale is old, / It has been told / By many men in many lands"—that ends with the poet including the natural world in this process of artistic creation:

The singer dies,
The singer lives,
The gods wait in the corn,
The soul of song is in the land.⁶³

Like Whitman's *Leaves of Grass*, reminding the reader of the fiction of the body as fixed and stable, Anderson finds poetic inspiration in the interdependencies of bodies, words and world.⁶⁴ In both "Song of Theodore" and "The Healer," he describes a process of reconnecting literature with the organic in an ecological ethics that extends the link between writer and text outward as a way of redressing the damage that modern technology has done to words, language, and culture.

The absorption of the body of the poet in the voices of the poem in "Poetry" is presented as a simultaneously violent and ecstatic annihilation of the individual artist, who is both entirely necessary and peripheral to the art. As in "Song for Lonely Roads," the kind of radical openness that Anderson envisions renders the discrete artist almost beside the point; the song continues whether or not he lives or dies. In Anderson's poems, the figure of the poet appears as a being that sacrifices itself by offering up its body as a conduit for cultural transmission. Rather than abandoning the individual self in a move toward complete impersonality, however, Anderson repeatedly returns to the consequences for the body of such a process, presenting it as physically painful and degrading. In "The Cornfields," for example, the speaker/poet explains, "On my knees I crawled before my people. I debased myself. // The excretions of their bodies I took for my food. Into the / ground I went and my body died."⁶⁵ Similarly, in "Manhattan," the speaker describes the agony and then the vitality taken from "the men / who are old [and] have entered into me."⁶⁶ What emerges is an ethic of poetic impersonality, in which to be a poet is to extinguish personality as Eliot suggested but also to foreground the imagined consequences for particular bodies.

In "Word Factories," Anderson explores the implications of reversing his association between words and bodies. In "The Healer," people become words as they enter the poet. Here, by contrast, the act of interpenetration renders the words as people. Like "Lonely Roads," the poem begins by invoking ancient storytelling traditions: "Long ago an old man sat on a log."[67] The conceit of the poem is that "words are / living, breathing things" that need care because they have been damaged by the industrialization of the printing process: "They are the children of men that have been put to / work in a factory. Their little bodies / have become bent and stooped and twisted"—not only embodied, that is, but embodied in decidedly nonnormative ways.[68]

To care for the words—to preserve the stories—the speaker (having been taught by the old man at the beginning of the poem) implores the reader, "Will you give a word nourishing food, carry him for a day in the warm / body of yourself, as a maid carries with due modesty a babe in her belly."[69] The emphasis throughout the poem is on the visceral discomfort of this process: "There is a tough gnarled new word / that has lived for a long time in a corner / of my brain. He has set up an insanity / there. Sometimes for days I do not dare / go near the corner of myself where the / word sits crouched, ready to strike, to / spring."[70] With the speaker's head inhabited by words that are neither wholly external nor internal to him, he forfeits his existence as a discrete being.

Across these poems, the artistic process is presented in terms of interpenetration; the words do not exist separately from the poet, nor the poet from the words. For Anderson, this dynamic was key to the way in which storytelling societies had transferred information through the generations and was something he was keen to approximate (and revive) in written work. In emphasizing the artist as embodied personality, however, Anderson was far from reinscribing him as a domineering presence. As he demonstrates again in "The Healer," and like Cook in "Poetry," Anderson's poetic speaker is repeatedly fractured by the creative process:

> My body does not belong to me.
> My body belongs to tired women who have found no lovers.
> It belongs to half men and half women.
> My body belongs to those who lust and those who shrink from
>     lusting.

> It shall be consumed with fire on a far horizon.
> The smoke that arises form my burning body shall make the western skies golden.[71]

Again, the writer is imagined to exist in interpenetrative relationships. Not only does he enter these specifically marginalized subjects ("tired women who have found no lovers," "half men and half women," "those who lust and those who shrink from lusting"); they consume him, taking over his body. This porous site of relationality is similarly able to be open to the environment, extending the interrelations surrounding the artwork outward so that the smoke of the writer's body consumed by nature reemerges as aesthetic creation, rendering the "western skies golden." In Anderson's poems, this is the end point of the ethical responsibility that Emmanuel Levinas locates in the face of the other, the call to an extinction that manages to remain all about the body, interpenetration that results in embodied impersonality.

## Impersonal Ethics

For Anderson, bound by the written page, this new mode of literary ethical relationality remains metaphorical. ASL, as I have argued, possesses a capacity to literalize it. In addition to blurring boundaries between text and writer, and in line with Anderson's gesture outward toward the environment, this also includes reconceptualizing the relationship between audience and artist. The fact that ASL poetry is so foundationally about the body, about the relationship between bodies—the poet, the text's characters, the audience—means that ASL poems are unique nexus of social interaction. And because they are about particular bodies in particular moments in space and time, because (as ASL does not have a widely used written form) they utterly refuse mechanical reproduction, they have an immediacy that is entirely linked to and constitutive of the meanings of these works.

Indeed, this immanence is so central to the meaning of an ASL poem that some critics have raised the question of whether a signed text, performed by an author in isolation (and not recorded) can be properly called ASL literature. It is often the interplay between audiences, authors, and texts that enables meaning. Ben Bahan, a celebrated ASL storyteller, describes how these interpersonal dynamics impact textual production: "There has to be a shared mind-set between the audience/culture and the teller to make the tale work. This reiterates the interwoven nature of the triad [artist/audience/text]. The way tellers conduct their work reflects their perception of the culture, and the desired outcome of their work depends on the culture's perception of the way they conduct it."[72] The complexity of this interplay is heightened by the fact that audiences often approach ASL literature from vastly different educational, linguistic, and cultural backgrounds.

This overlap between audiences and authors is ethically suggestive. It means that, in addition to being aesthetic objects, works of ASL literature are also (and foundationally) sites where humans encounter other humans, where they recognize one another as human and interact through language. The social element of poetry derives from our origins as oral or storytelling peoples, and it is temporarily re-created in modernist poetry readings and lectures. There is a long philosophical tradition of attaching ethical significance to the moment of looking into the face of the other, something necessitated in ASL by the fact that several of its grammatical features are communicated specifically through the eyes.[73] As I alluded to earlier, Levinas has defined "the face of the other man as being the original locus of the meaningful," the place where humans recognize that "no one can stay in himself; the humanity of man, subjectivity, is a responsibility for others, an extreme vulnerability."[74] To view an ASL poem is always already to engage in this ethical exchange with a subject that identifies itself as human through its use of language, to take on this responsibility for the other.[75]

The implications of this interrelatedness have served a very specific role in Deaf history. Until recently, the deaf were perceived as languageless and, therefore, as subhuman. In order to counter this misperception (and to gain financial support), during the nineteenth century American educators of the deaf held public exhibitions in which deaf pupils would be put on stage to perform poetry before a hearing audience. Poetry was seen as one of the most effective ways for children to make the case for their humanity, to establish connections with potential patrons by emphasizing similarity where the audience had previously perceived only difference. As Jennifer Esmail explains, such events demonstrated "signed languages' positive attributes, as well as the deaf students' intellectual capacities, including their understanding of abstract concepts and ability to write in English and other languages."[76] The spectacle of the children's bodies proved powerful precisely because the moment of their recognition occurred through language. Thus, poetry was deliberately staged as the site for the encounter between audience members

58 / IMPERSONALITY

and pupils in which viewers were forced (sometimes for the first time) to acknowledge the full humanity of the signing subjects on stage.

> Of Being Numerous
>
> Obsessed, bewildered
>
> By the shipwreck
> Of the singular
>
> We have chosen the meaning
> Of being numerous.[77]

Poetry exhibitions created an opportunity for members of the audience to rethink their understanding of the ways they related to the people surrounding them. As George Oppen suggests in his epic poem "Of Being Numerous," this negotiation between group and individual, which we might also read in relation to authors and audiences, was central to the development of twentieth-century experience. In different ways, Anderson, Cook, and Lerner all explore how poetry opens a space in which individuals can recognize and reflect on their own interpenetrated natures and the responsibilities to others that arise from this foregrounding of shared humanity. Debbie Rennie's "Missing Children" similarly capitalizes on the erasure of boundaries between self and other, as well as between self and text, in ASL poetry to interrogate some of the meanings we have chosen, or might choose, for being numerous.[78] The poem tells the stories of a series of children—from Nicaragua, South Africa, and Ireland—who are lost to violence. The children are linked through the central image of missing-children leaflets, which both connect them to one another and function structurally to return the viewer from the locational specificity of each section to the present neutral space of the poem's frame. The poem begins with a child handing the speaker one such picture. Rennie then shifts to occupy the perspective of the face on the leaflet, asking in the wide-eyed and innocent expression of a child, "Have you seen me?" The narrator sadly shakes her head no, and the flyer is picked up by the wind, tumbling before landing on the ground, in a movement that becomes the sign for DEAD.

The role shifting of the opening section allows Rennie to portray something of the physicality of each of the characters (their styles of movement, eye lines, and expressions), rather than simply describing them. In doing so, Rennie highlights the distance between herself—as an adult occupying a different national and at times ethnic and racial subject position—and the endangered children, while simultaneously connecting to them through the profoundly intimate act of giving them voice through her body. Similar to the characters in "Poetry," whose voices write their author, Rennie's poetic voice is punctured by—is inseparable from—the bodies and voices of the children she seeks to represent.

The poem begins with a child handing the speaker one such picture. Using role shifting to portray all of the characters in the scene, Rennie moves between the child, the narrator, and finally the picture on the leaflet. Literature's ethical potential has often been associated with the ways it appears to permit readers to see the world through the perspective of a distinct subjectivity (the writer's, if not fully the characters'). Through role shifting in ASL, that perspective shift is embodied as the speaker becomes different characters through nonmanual signifiers including eye line, body language, posture, and facial expression. Rennie's poetic voice emerges at the intersection of these perspectives as they are all conveyed through the same body.

This technique drives the first section of the poem, "Nicaragua," which tells the story of a young boy working in a coffee field with his father. In a pattern that is repeated throughout the piece, the section opens with the specific, the picture on the leaflet, before drawing back to provide broader context. Rennie begins with close-ups of the poem's central characters planting and then zooms out to show the entire field, full of people at work. Suddenly, the trees open to reveal lines of soldiers, their frenetic movements sharply contrasting the gentle rhythms of the field workers. As the soldiers shoot their way through the field, bodies fall in their wake, conveyed with a distance shot, the bent two classifier representing upturned legs. Rennie cuts between the terrified face of the little boy and the cocky arrogance of the soldier emptying his gun into the bodies of the workers.[79] In slow motion, the boy reaches up to make a peace offering, and the soldier, still smirking, discharges his weapon into the boy's body, the section ending in an explosion of grief.

The poem builds on this thematic consideration of the nature of violence, which becomes increasingly complicated and enriched by the structural interpenetration inherent in its language. In a poem so explicitly about violence, this blurring of boundaries is pointed and at times uncomfortable. In the poem's final section, "Ireland," Rennie uses this discomfort to thematically address the cyclical nature of violence, as well as to highlight our own participation in it. The section begins with the image of a child comically imitating the actions of his father, first mimicking his walking style and later the way he constructs and throws a grenade. Unlike the father's more assured movements, the boy is clumsy, repeatedly glancing up toward his father seeking approval.[80] The scene then cuts to a giggly girl picking flowers in a field with her father just before the grenades appear in the sky above them. The section concludes with an explosion so violent that it punctures through to the poem's frame, sending the missing-children leaflets flying and the narrator scrambling to recollect them.

Unlike in the poem's first two sections, in which violence is perpetrated by more clearly delineated malefactors (sharp-moving soldiers with guns who laugh maniacally while decimating the villagers), this final section provides a more complex meditation on the nature of violence. No longer is it so easy to distinguish transgressors from victims, especially when, at the end of the poem, Rennie includes the grenade-throwing boy in her list of lost children.

The interpenetrative structure of ASL enables Rennie to enact the idea of our shared vulnerability and culpability in acts of violence as well as to make the same point on a thematic level. Through her body, these marginalized characters gain voice. They take over Rennie's body, speaking her, so that the images we are left with are not Rennie's features but somehow the eyes and expressions of the children. The narrator's—and Rennie's—participation is itself also problematized. While Rennie's engagement is beneficial in that it gives voice to these marginalized, forgotten children (part of whose tragedy is that they tend to die unknown, to never appear on the kinds of leaflets that frame the poem), the structure of ASL characterization means that in the boy's copying his father's actions, he in the final sections is actually copying Rennie. The distance collapses; there is no "father," no comfortable separation between the different characters in the poem, between the characters and Rennie, between ourselves and the poet. We are all, the poem both suggests and demonstrates, all of them.

"Missing Children" interrogates the ethics of blurring the line between author and text and, by implication, that between audience and author. More than simply describing these overlaps, the poem enacts them, *is* them. As in "Poetry" and in Anderson's work, the body of the author is simultaneously foregrounded and exploded. Whatever we might describe as Rennie's poetic voice is shattered by the expressions and movements of the poem's characters. This shattering provides one answer to Foucault's call for new relational modes by deconstructing the subject as a discrete entity and emphasizing interpenetration. "Missing Children" enacts a means of poetic self-shattering that refuses the removal of the body (thus avoiding the violence of ignoring authors' human subjectivity) but also plays with the pleasure of losing the self in others. Put another way, and to return to the terminology from the beginning of the chapter, it demonstrates how embodied literature enables the simultaneous performance of both personality and impersonality.

When ASL poetics is placed in the context of the fraught relationship between modernist impersonality and corporeal subjectivity, what emerges is not only a resolution of the tension through the development of an embodied impersonality (or impersonal embodiment) that accounts for both. We also gain a rich context in which to situate neglected modernist works that were ahead of their time in experimenting with these intersections. Together, these texts suggest a poetic ethics of interpenetration that, when brought to bear on ASL literature, opens the possibilities for how we conceptualize the relationship between writers, texts, and environments. Reading such works together, that is, is beneficial in multiple directions. In the next chapter, I move away from discussions of poetics and ethics to experiment with another way of thinking deafness and modernism together, this time by focusing on Deaf history.

# 2 / Primitivism: Communicative Norms and the Ethics of the Story

> *Such a body might be out of step with the modern, technologically advanced world: diagnoses like hysteria, neurasthenia, even constipation and eye strain, registered the stress placed on the body by civilization, and suggested that compensatory action was necessary. Even those who wished to offer the body as the site of authenticity were forced to posit a return to an atavistic substratum which created a temporal discontinuity in their idealizations, a fantasy of primitivism.*
> —TIM ARMSTRONG, *Modernism, Technology and the Body*

In *Modernism, Technology and the Body*, Tim Armstrong argues that modernity placed complex demands on individuals by requiring them to navigate a range of new environments and ideas, the pressures of which were frequently registered in physical and psychological ailments—neurasthenia, hysteria, eye strain. In this context, fantasies of a premodern, primitivist world in which neither these new stressors nor their bodily implications needed to be addressed operated as welcome escapes from the technologically driven present. The psychological explanation that Armstrong suggests attempts to reconcile one of the persistent tensions running through aesthetic modernism: a pervasive interest in all things new—the mechanized, technologized, automatized steel and speed of, on the industrial front, Henry Ford and, on the aesthetic, movements such as futurism and vorticism—and the growing obsession with forms of art and consumer goods associated with the past; the primitivist turn first in the visual arts and then in dance and literature. As in my analysis of the gap between celebrity culture and impersonal aesthetics in chapter 1, I want to return to this tension from the perspective of Deaf epistemology in order to unpack the ways we might understand these competing narratives as more than simply contradictory.

For a long time, as the scholar Sieglinde Lemke explains, "modernist aesthetics and the assembly line were conflated in the popular imagination."[1] The speed and steel of modern life were understood to have direct impact on declarations of aesthetic principles such as those we find in the futurist manifesto, which famously "affirm[ed] that the world's magnificence has been enriched by a new beauty: the beauty of speed. A racing car whose hood is adorned with great pipes explosive breath—a roaring car that seems to ride on grapeshot is more beautiful than the *Victory of Samothrace*."[2] Despite the weight this version of modernism has held in our narratives of the period, however, the drive to innovate through an embrace of the technological and a rejection of a particular idea of the past describes only one version of modernist aesthetics.[3] Its notion of temporality in particular always sat uncomfortably with the simultaneous fascination that modernist writers and artists had with a variety of imagined others who were made to represent an aesthetic that explicitly challenged that model.

Perhaps no one better exemplifies this multidirectional thrust than Josephine Baker. Born in St. Louis in 1906, Baker traveled to Paris in 1925 as part of *La Revue Nègre*, an all-black musical show organized by Caroline Dudley Reagan. The show's finale was the now infamous *dans sauvage*, set against a backdrop of a jungle intended to evoke an Africa to which Baker herself had never been. According to Phyllis Rose, Baker "play[ed] up the image of herself as a natural," performing in what seemed to be only feathers and jewelry and dancing alongside her partner, Joe Alex, in a manner apparently spontaneous and animalistic, allowing the audience to interpolate her as the ultimate other.[4]

Baker's performance as Fatou in *La Folie du Jour* at the Folies-Bergère in 1926 continued this conflation of primitivist fantasies. Baker appeared in a g-string adorned with silk bananas. As Carole Sweeney has noted, in these performances Baker embodies the dialectical pull of modernism toward both past and future: "Baker was equally held to be a personification of the modern spirit that turned its gaze to the future as much as to the past. She was the figure who symbolized excesses of both the already imagined primitive past and the yet to be imagined modern future: the living symbol of a modern primitivist aesthetic."[5] The angles of her body visually echoing those of a cubist painting, her body contorting and gyrating to modern music, all while enabling audiences to project onto her ideas about the past as an escape from modern social and bodily norms, Baker appeared to present the best of all worlds. The supposedly non-Western Other was constructed as being separated not only by space but by time, a remnant of what for modern audiences appeared both a simpler and more desirable epoch. The appeal of this distancing drove interest in primitivism across art forms. As Robert Goldwater explained in his landmark 1967 *Primitivism in Modern Art*, "The champions of primitive art saw in it unique characteristics which could be opposed with advantage to any subsequent evolution of style. It was an ideal from which most other art was a falling-away, and to which all other art was to be compared. They did not defend, they eulogized."[6] By evoking an Africa meant to signify as both geographically and temporally distant, Baker positioned herself as a living embodiment of a fetishized vision of the past.

Much of this fantasy was specifically linked to corporeality; commentary on Baker frequently described her body as signifying in ways that went beyond the limitations of specific linguistic messages. Indeed, for the interpolation process to function successfully, she could not be seen to fully answer back in language even when she was speaking onstage. Despite singing as well as dancing in the shows, it was nonverbal communication that most intrigued both audiences and critics. As Sweeney summarizes,

> The primitive subject is transparent and readable to its audience, who might know the truth of the black subject without the need for articulation at any linguistic level, . . . the words unimportant in themselves as they are a sensual, aural antidote to moribund intellectualism. . . . It is the sensation, the almost physicality of the words, rather than any inherent meaning, that offers her audience suggestions of a dream island-scape, articulating the secret desires of the modern subject and allowing the listener access to the uncorrupted prelapsarian paradise of the primitive subject.[7]

The appeal of an "uncorrupted prelapsarian paradise" is formulated as a mute sensuality through which modern voyeurs can engage in "secret desires" but to which they are not responsible, an evocation of a mythical past to which they need not answer. The movement to displace the geographic onto the temporal is at least in part an attempt to render it less threatening; if it belongs to the past, it does not constitute a danger in or to the present. Primitivist spectacle created spaces where people could appear to be rebelling against contemporary mores without actually challenging the systems of power embedded in them. The semantic content of the language Baker used in performance was superseded by the other forms of communication of her body.

In both these performances, and the critical reaction to them, we can trace a conflation of what are two significant and linked, though rarely discussed as such, aspects of modernist primitivism: the mapping of space (geographically distanced "others") onto time (the popular belief that such "others" belonged to earlier stages of history) and the association of embodied communication with this earlier, mythical stage of development. In both these ideas, primitivism becomes the dialectical opposite of modernity. As Elazar Barkan and Ronald Bush explain in their introduction to *Prehistories of the Future*, however, the inclusion of geographically othered peoples and cultures into the category of the primitive was a specifically modern development: "Previously, when art historians spoke of the 'primitive,' they usually had in mind the 'naïve' style of Pre-Raphaelite and Colonial American painting—that is, artifacts of the West's own childhood. In the late nineteenth century, however, primitive painting came increasingly to connote the geographically exotic 'savage'—the violence and energy of the barbaric—even as violence was beginning to receive its 'positive' modern spin."[8] Primitivism, that is, takes a geographic or racial distinction (the cultures of non-Western countries or of people of color within Western countries) and turns it into a temporal one (something from the past, a simplicity to which, given the craze of modernity, it might be desirable to return).

It should perhaps come as no surprise that turn-of-the-century writers and thinkers were confusing time and space. As Stephen Kern persuasively argues in *The Culture of Time and Space, 1880–1918*, this kind of overlay developed out of contemporary ideas in physics. One of the consequences of Albert Einstein's 1905 theory of special relativity, which suggested the relativistic nature of both space and time as a result of time dilation—the slowing of time based on frames of reference—was the realization that time and space were not separate entities. As Hermann Minkowski, who first explicitly explored the ramifications of this in a 1908 essay, proclaimed, "henceforth space by itself, and time by itself, are doomed to fade away into mere shadows, and only a kind of union of the two will preserve an independent reality."[9]

Numerous art forms experimented with the implications of this conflation from an experiential perspective. As had been the case with the borrowing of Darwinist evolutionary science into the realm of the social, anthropological, and artistic, however, many of those imagined implications were decidedly racist, enabling those who were predisposed to do so to label non-Western cultures and peoples (or people of color generally) as primitive. The hugely successful 1933 film *King Kong* famously dramatized this logic by representing the exotically othered inhabitants of Skull Island as displaced not only in space but in time, sharing their island with dinosaurs and other Jurassic creatures.

Expanding the modernist canon to more appropriately take account of this problematic move requires a consideration of the ways space and time are yoked together. The geographic expansion of the New Modernist Studies—evidenced by such important anthologies as Douglas Mao and Rebecca L. Walkowitz's *Bad Modernisms* (2006) and Laura Doyle and Laura Winkiel's *Geomodernisms: Race, Modernism, Modernity* (2005)— powerfully argues for the inclusion of non-Anglo American or western European modernisms in the cannon. And Susan Stanford Friedman's "Periodizing Modernism: Postcolonial Modernities and the Space/Time Borders of Modernist Studies" convincingly suggests that this project of inclusion impacts our understanding of the temporal boundaries surrounding "modernism" as well, requiring an acknowledgment of the different historical moments in which cultures encountered and reacted artistically to modernity.

Deaf studies contributes to this discourse by making visible the extent to which much of what drove the interest in primitivism—particularly the nonverbal communication—was very much a part of cultures that existed in modernity's present tense. Largely missing from the discussion of the role that ideas about primitive embodiment played in early twentieth-century fascination with so-called primitive art forms has been analysis of the relationship between embodiment and language. Conversely, the explosion of interest in modernity's language politics— demonstrated by recent studies in multilingual modernisms, including Joshua Miller's *Accented America* (2011) and Sarah Wilson's *Melting-Pot Modernism* (2010)—have not addressed the interrelation of bodies, disability, and language practices. Through an exploration of the assumptions about language and bodies that came together in the regulatory practices surrounding deaf bodies in the early twentieth century—a set of practices I term *communicative norms*—this chapter explores how perceptions of language played into modernist primitivism and how adding language to our discussion of the ways modern bodies explored alternatives to this regulation enhances our understanding of them.

## Regulating Bodies

The standard reading of modernist primitivism, as Armstrong outlines, is that it constitutes a kind of release valve for the period's ever-increasing regulatory pressures. The hyperrepresentation of the bodies of othered individuals, particularly in the arts, was interpreted as one such escape from the systematic repression of embodiment in most other areas of life. Reflecting on the early twentieth century, Theodor Adorno observed that "anything that is not reified, cannot be counted and measured, ceases to exist."[10] In many ways, this process of classifying and evaluating became the guiding philosophy of the age. The rise of industrialism and statistics provided people in the late nineteenth and early twentieth centuries with new ways of measuring and regulating not only products but practices and bodies, a process that the history of sign language use in the United States can helpfully illuminate. Tellingly, the word to describe these standards, "norm"—indicating "a standard or pattern of behavior that is accepted in or of a group"—is dated by the *Oxford English Dictionary* to 1900.[11] Whereas earlier cultural moments had discussed ideal practices and bodies as unachievable goals, the new notion of the norm was meant for more pragmatic applications.

Bodies that did not conform were subject to new regulatory intensity, a process that had dramatic consequences for individuals who were now seen as not just different but disabled. People who in previous generations would have largely lived anonymously within their communities found themselves being probed, diagnosed, and institutionalized. As Lennard J. Davis puts it, "when we think of bodies, in a society where the concept of the norm is operative, then people with disabilities are thought of as deviants."[12] In what had rapidly become a fiercely normalizing society, such deviance was viewed as not only undesirable but threatening to what was perceived as a brave new world in which science could improve humanity.

Given the pervasiveness of this mind-set, it is unsurprising that the drive to standardize also spilled over into the realm of the linguistic. In the United States, a country that lacked the equivalent of a regulatory body like the French Academy, concerns arose that American English had become too inclusive and was lacking in precision. Questions of language became intimately bound with those of national identity, an issue that was particularly fraught during the late nineteenth and early twentieth centuries as a result of the aftershocks of the U.S. Civil War as well as massive waves of immigration. As I discussed in the introduction, one's abilities in English came to be viewed as a means of drawing a clearer line around who counted as American.

This logic, intended to exclude from the American body politic anyone who did not speak standard American English, proved deeply offensive and injurious to members of communities for which English was not the sole or primary mode of communication.[13] In addition to indigenous Americans and immigrants, this also included the deaf.[14] Explaining deaf education in a 1913 letter, Alexander Graham Bell summarized a widely held belief that "in an English speaking country like the United

States, the English language, *and the English language alone*, should be used as the means of communication and instruction."[15] The idea was that to be an American, one had to speak "like an American," in an increasingly standardized American English.

As regulation of both language use and bodies intensified, a new kind of norm developed in the space where the two intersected, which I refer to as a *communicative norm*. This set of norms regulated not only the kinds of language people used but also the ways their bodies looked, moved through space, and interacted with other subjects while engaging in linguistic activities. In the century that has passed between that time and our own, scholars have become adept at analyzing texts and situations for their relationships to norms connected with gender roles, race and ethnicity, class, sexuality, and, increasingly, ability. But despite the prevalence of communicative norms, the regulation of this aspect of our lives remains underanalyzed.

The oversight is significant because it speaks to our tendency to, as David Appelbaum puts it, "devitalize[] voice," as well as language more broadly.[16] Identifying and thinking through communicative norms forces us to confront the physicality of our linguistic practices, something with which centuries of Cartesian dualism in general, as well as a particular distaste for bodies in some branches of modernist writing and criticism, has left us uncomfortable. It also reminds us of the ways that commentary on performances such as Baker's very specifically sets them outside contemporary discussions about language in more explicitly political spheres. To celebrate the nonverbal communication of Baker's body over her more standardized verbal speech is to fly directly in the fact of prevalent attitudes toward and policies surrounding language use at the time.

The mapping of concerns about embodiment (as well as racist and nationalist attitudes) onto particular linguistic communities is not, as I demonstrated in the introduction, restricted to those that employ manual languages. But sign languages, precisely because of their inescapable physicality, provide a uniquely rich site from which to analyze the intersection of cultural tensions over linguistic and embodied norms. Like other kinds of nonverbal bodily communication, manual languages serve as a litmus test, revealing attitudes toward nonnormative bodies and identities. As Lennard Davis argues, "when sign language is repressed as a signifying practice, what is repressed is a connection with the body."[17] Since ASL is a language that cannot be separated from the body and the corporeal produced anxiety, it is often perceived as threatening. It makes defiantly visible the fact that the normative mode of expressive communication—verbal articulation—is not the only way in which linguistic information can be transmitted.

Late nineteenth- and early twentieth-century attitudes toward manual languages (which were, at that time, not recognized as languages at all) demonstrate the extent to which the vast majority of American society was uncomfortable with having its assumptions about language denaturalized. Paralleling the move in modernist primitivist discourse to associate particular bodies and practices that called attention to the body with prior states of human development, signing deaf individuals, along with people of color and non-Westerners, increasingly found themselves being classified as subhuman.

## Deaf Bodies Signifying

Derogatory attitudes toward embodied communication resulted from modern ideas about the "appropriateness" of certain bodies visibly signifying in nonstandardized ways. While reactions to Baker's performances illustrate the extent to which it was societally acceptable (and even encouraged) for individuals to be interested in attractive women of color using their bodies nonnormatively to communicate, the same was not the case for bodies perceived as disabled. These bodies, the developing field of eugenics insisted, needed to be hidden from view wherever possible, if not altogether eliminated. Sign languages, which very visibly call attention to the same bodies that conformist logic would seek to render invisible, was seen to be in direct conflict with this normativizing impulse. This had not, however, always been the case. In the early nineteenth century in America, sign language flourished, particularly after the 1817 creation of the first school for the deaf by Thomas H. Gallaudet and Laurent Clerc, the American Asylum for the Deaf at Hartford, Connecticut, which encouraged manual communication as a means of instruction.

Despite this interest, by the late nineteenth and early twentieth centuries, there was a radical change of direction in terms of attitudes toward deaf education, and fierce debates sprung up over the role sign language should play in it. The long-standing belief that manual communication represented an earlier stage in human development was linked with scientific theories to create an argument against it. As the noted anthropologist and early filmmaker Felix-Louis Regnault, a proponent of such arguments, explained, "All savage peoples make recourse to gesture to express themselves; their language is so poor it does not suffice to make them understood: plunged in darkness, two savages, as travelers who often witness this fact affirm, can communicate their thoughts, coarse and limited though they are. With primitive man, gesture precedes speech."[18] Such ideas firmly situated manual communication as a relic of the past. And unlike primitivist fantasies that identified the past as a site to be mined for ways to evade modern stagnation, detractors of nonverbal expression argued very strongly it should stay there.

Oralists declared that signing would prevent deaf children from learning to speak, the movement's primary goal. Connections between manualism and inferiority were made explicit by educators such as Emma Garrett, who declared, "if speech is better for hearing people than barbaric signs, it is better for the deaf."[19] Attitudes toward the deaf were intertwined with popular theories about "degenerate" or "inferior" races; as S. G. Davidson wrote in 1898, sign language was "immeasurably inferior to English," and any "culture dependent upon it must by proportionally inferior."[20]

Such arguments also received support from pseudoscientific theories that proposed racial hierarchies and that capitalized on the fierce nationalism and xenophobia of the time. Oralists in particular were quick to characterize those who signed as animalistic. Leis Dudley, one of the founders of the Clarke Institution, described signing deaf students as "young creatures human in shape but only half human in attribute."[21] And Susan E. Hull was only one of many oralists who explicitly linked signed languages of the deaf to those used by American Indians, her point being that neither represented full human development. Signing with deaf children, she declared, would "push them back in the world's history to the infancy of our race, . . . [Because it was the language of] American Indians and other savage tribes," she insisted that "sons and daughters of this nineteenth century [should not] be content with this"[22]—at least, that is, when it came to Anglo deaf children.[23]

While there was a brief moment when some Deaf schools did not segregate based on race (Kendall School for the Deaf at Gallaudet University, for example, did not become segregated until 1906), between 1869 (when the North Carolina School for Colored Deaf and Blind was founded) until 1978 (when the last segregated deaf school closed in Louisiana), southern schools for the deaf established either separate buildings or campuses for deaf children of color. While white deaf schools across the country switched to either fully oral or combined methods, schools for children of color continued to instruct their pupils in sign. When asked at an 1882 convention of the American Instructors of the Deaf whether his school had made any effort to "teach colored children" using the new oral methods, he replied that "in a separate building, one mile from the main institution, there are thirty colored children ... with a separate teacher in charge. No instruction has been given in articulation, and none will be given at present."[24] As Douglas Baynton summarizes, while schools "throughout the south joined northern schools in pushing deaf people to rise, as they saw it, to become fully human by abjuring sign language, this was apparently not considered as significant a need for deaf people of African descent."[25]

While the history of American language politics and attitudes toward individuals perceived to have nonnormative bodies are generally read as separate, what these accounts reveal are the complex ways in which cultural ideals of language and embodiment combined to create communicative norms whose implementation was inconsistent but that had significant consequences for the ways that language was conceptualized. While the regulation of bodies has been much discussed, the relationship of language to that regulation remains undertheorized. This is a significant absence because, as demonstrated by the case of Josephine Baker, ideas about language, bodies, modernity, and primitivism cannot be neatly separated out. Despite this general trend, there were modernist writers and filmmakers who recognized the significance of linguistic regulation on bodies. In the next sections of the chapter, I consider how an understanding of communicative norms can contribute to our readings of Charlie Chaplin's *Modern Times* and Sherwood Anderson's *Winesburg, Ohio*.

## Gesturing Back

Just as the rise of oralism challenged embodied forms of communication, the switch from silent films to "talkies" displaced the nonverbal body as the sole or primary means of communicative exchange in cinema. The impact of this switch is perhaps most famously dramatized (and satirized) in Charlie Chaplin's 1936 *Modern Times*. From the first exhibited film in 1894 to the release of *The Jazz Singer* in 1927, the only sounds associated with motion pictures were nonnarrative musical accompaniments. Outside of intertitles, which were used to varying degrees, it was the actors' responsibility to communicate plot and dialogue through body language. Indeed, it was precisely their ability to effectively transmit information through gesture and facial expression that made them famous.

The move to talkies saw the effective end of the careers of many early silent-film stars, while others struggled to adapt. The longest holdout against this shift was Charlie Chaplin, whose fame, wealth, and unprecedented creative control over his projects enabled him to resist until *The Great Dictator*, released in 1940, more than a decade after spoken-dialogue films became the industry standard. Chaplin initially had no interest in talking pictures. He complained to the periodical *Motion Pictures* that talkies were "spoiling the oldest art in the world—the art of pantomime. They are ruining forever the great beauty of silence.... It is beauty that matters in pictures—nothing else. The screen is pictorial."[26] *The Great Dictator* thematically addresses the distasteful power of the voice in cinema through its parody of Adolf Hitler and his manipulation of mass media through what many people described as the hypnotic power of his voice.

In *Modern Times*, the final (quasi-) silent film Chaplin made, he addresses the move to spoken-dialogue pictures and the assumptions undergirding the notion that spoken language is an inherently superior mode of communication both thematically and structurally. The film follows the story of a factory worker who finds himself subject to intense regulation in a series of specifically modern ways. After suffering a mental breakdown caused by the stresses of industrial labor, he is forcibly taken to a psychiatric hospital. Upon his release, he is mistaken for a communist labor leader and imprisoned. Throughout the film, the worker is on the run from authority figures that seek to normativize his deviant body. Along the way, he meets up with a young women attempting to evade a version of child protective services, which wants to send her to an orphanage after the death of her father. Together, the pair devises schemes for finding food and earning money. Ultimately incapable of conforming, they end the film walking off into the sunset of a dusty mountainous landscape, in what has been read as either a liberating escape from the confines of modern city life or a kind of death.

One of the most notable things about the film is its treatment of language, specifically its attention to embodied communication. The film's first sequence, which audiences in 1936 might reasonably have expected to include spoken dialogue, takes place in the factory. We are introduced to the worker on the assembly line, mechanically twisting rivets. Unlike his peers, the protagonist struggles to keep up with the speed of the line as his bodily urges—scratching, swatting an insect, sneezing—cause him to fall behind at the same time they call attention to the body qua body. His interactions with other workers occur in silence, but in each exchange it is entirely clear what is being communicated: displeasure at Chaplin's character's inability to keep up, the trading of insults, the protagonist blaming another worker when the boss comes to chastise him for having to halt the production line. *Modern Times*, that is, opens with Chaplin demonstrating the ability of the body to effectively communicate in the absence of spoken language.

Despite the film's emphasis on silent communication, it is not entirely devoid of human speech. To make his point about its limitations, Chaplin allows the human voice to appear only when mediated through technology. The boss of the factory speaks to workers through a giant CCTV-style screen. The inventor describes his automated eating machine through a gramophone. Significantly, none of the characters that employ verbal speech in the film are particularly sympathetic, and none of the information they convey in this manner is of any great significance. Rather, the mediation serves to demonstrate the inhumanity of such communication. When the protagonist finally does vocalize—the first time Chaplin's voice had been heard in a film—it is to sing a song constructed of nonsense, bits of various languages along with a great deal of gibberish.

This climactic final scene, in which the song appears, is structured around a rejection of specific verbal utterances. The gamin, having become a popular dancer at a local café, has secured a job for the worker, provided he can sing in the evening's show. In order to remember the words of his song, the worker has the gamin write them out on his cuffs. As he dances, however, the cuffs fly off, and he is left wordless before an increasingly restless audience and looking helplessly at the gamin. "Sing!!" Her response is presented on intertitles as she points to her mouth and face. "Never mind the words." The gamin's gestures contribute to the idea that what is important is still the body, the face of the worker in the performance, rather than the lyrics themselves. The worker follows her advice, giving the café patrons their dinner performance, and Chaplin demonstrates his ability both to sing and to use the new technology of sound to his audience; but rather than illustrating the superiority of speech, the performance provides an example of the power of voice detached from semantic content. What makes it successful within the film as well as on a meta level is not the words (which make no sense) but the nonlinguistic ways in which Chaplin's body signifies, the fact of the voice as part of that physicality.

*Modern Times* has been critiqued for its rather blunt commentary on capitalism, but the analysis it provides of the danger of communicative norms is incredibly sophisticated. At a time when very few people were drawing connections between linguistic standardization and norms of embodiment, Chaplin's worker dramatically demonstrates the dangerous consequences, both for the individual and for society, of forcing bodies to express themselves in standardized ways. The mediated speech of the factory boss and the inventor are pointedly dehumanizing. It is not just that the assembly lines turned people into cogs in machines—an argument that was being made elsewhere, most famously by Karl Marx—but that this process was intimately linked to language. Despite the assumptions being made in other contexts about the significance of standardized verbal communication, here speech functions as the butt of the joke, serving to draw our attention to a character's ignorance rather than his or her skill or intelligence.

One of the more comical presentations of this idea comes in the bathroom scene, in which the tramp's cigarette break is cut short by the appearance of his boss's face on a giant screen. This is one of the few places in the film where verbal and nonverbal communication are directly juxtaposed. Having just lit his cigarette by striking the match on his butt in a gesture that draws attention to his body, the worker is interrupted by the boss, who barks, "Hey! Quit stalling. Get back to work. Go on!" The worker replies with arm movements—shrugging his shoulders, gesturing to the sink to suggest that he was just washing up—that are less powerful than the language of the boss (which the worker is compelled to obey) but that enable the worker to clearly communicate what he means and that, significantly, are depicted as more human (and humane) than the technologically mediated speech.

This pattern—the automated machines, or humans in positions of power functioning as and through machines, quashing individuality represented by nonconformist embodiment—is repeated throughout the film, with consequences that teeter on the edge between comedy and tragedy. When Chaplin's worker returns to work after his bathroom break and gets into the rhythm of the assembly line, he finds himself unable to stop and experiences physical tics even when he has left the line to go on his next break. Henri Bergson famously defined the comic as a situation in which a human behaves in such a way as to appear machine-like, and these sequences have often been cited as illustrative of precisely this dynamic.[27] But funny as they are, the threat underlying them is clear. Chaplin's worker becomes so mindlessly caught up in the production line that when he falls behind, he dives head first into the machine in order to continue twisting his rivets. The magic of cinema enables this to produce one of the film's best-known images: that of Chaplin winding his way through the gears of the machine before it is reversed and he is brought back up. But there is a discomfort in the humor, emphasized by the reaction of his fellow worker, who desperately tries to prevent Chaplin from jumping into the machine, recognizing that, in the logic of the noncinematic world, such an act constitutes suicide.

And while the worker emerges from the machine physically unharmed, he does suffer a mental breakdown. Obsessed with the notion of twisting, he chases two women whose dresses have large buttons (one on the butt and the other on the breasts) that he mistakes for rivets, attempting to assault them. Again, the threat (here of a specifically sexual nature) lurks barely beneath the surface of the comedy. The regulation of bodies and language, *Modern Times* demonstrates, can have catastrophic consequences on individuals, as well as on society more broadly. The solution provided in the film—the series of punitive institutions that the character is thrown in when he cannot perform normatively—masks the structural nature of the problem by assigning it to the individual in an enactment of the medical model. Just as he was put in a police van after wandering into a protest earlier in the film, at the end of this scene the worker is tossed into an ambulance. The institutions are barely distinguished and, as we might expect given that the worker's difficulties arise from problems inherent to the structure of society rather than individual deviance, prove equally ineffectual.

For Chaplin, far from being a throwback to a primitivist fantasy of the past, embodied communication functioned as an effective contemporary means to challenge these regulatory pressures as well as to call attention to their dangers. Within the film, spoken language is presented as yet another way in which individual bodies become mechanized and standardized. Its status is not accepted as an inherent truth, as was the case in most early twentieth-century contexts, but rather is something in the process of being negotiated in an ongoing and decidedly political struggle. The intertwining of linguistic and other kinds of regulatory standards provides one of the film's most nuanced critiques of modern times, one that has been surprisingly overlooked by generations of critics who have largely assented to the belief that physical communication does indeed belong to a moment in the past and that Chaplin's engagement of it, even when successfully executed, can only signify a kind of primitivist nostalgia.

One of the few Chaplin critics to recognize the flaw with this argument was, somewhat unexpectedly, Winston Churchill, who had met

Chaplin when the actor was visiting London. In an article for *Collier's* in 1935, the future prime minister describes how Chaplin developed his pantomime skills while touring the Channel Islands and performing for an audience who spoke a Norman French patois and could therefore not understand the spoken language of the company. Intrigued by the power of embodied communication to bridge such gaps, Churchill argues that "pantomime, of which [Chaplin] is a master, is capable of expressing every emotion, of communicating the subtlest shades of meaning. A man who can act with his whole body has no need of words whatever part he plays."[28]

Rather than suggesting that the voice serves as a pale imitation of spoken language that traffics only in crude approximations or fetishizing it as did so many of his contemporaries, Churchill recognizes the ability of nonverbal bodily communication to transmit subtle shades of meaning, equal to the nuance of oral language. Crucially for our purposes, he also rejects the popular logic that linked such physical communication to the past and aligned verbal speech with the future. Churchill notes,

> It is a favorite cliché of film critics, in discussing talking pictures to say that we cannot go back. In effect, they suggest that because technical progress has given us sound, all films must be talkies and will continue to be so forever. Such statements reveal a radical misconception of the nature of progress and the nature of art. As well say that, because there is painting in oils, there must be no etchings; or that because speech is an integral part of a stage play, dialogue must be added to ballet. To explore the possibilities of the non-talking film, to make of it a new and individual art form, would not be a retrograde step, but an advance.[29]

Here, Churchill demonstrates remarkable insight into the notion of verbal speech as just one in a series of modes of effective expression. Unfortunately, his vision of a future in which film could maintain a wide range of communicative options that need not include standardized verbal communication proved short-lived; Chaplin did not go on to make the serious silent films that Churchill imagined. Just three years after Churchill's article, Chaplin had begun filming on what was to be his first spoken-language feature film. But the article intriguingly explores some of the potential for nonverbal expression at a time just before speech monopolized the cinema.

For Churchill, part of the draw of embodied communication, rather succinctly expressed in the title of one of the sections of his article— "Gesture

More Effective than the Voice"—is its presumed universality. He imagines the importance of new silent films primarily for individuals from countries that do not have the financial resources to produce films in their own languages or even to rewire existing cinemas for sound. Moreover, as he puts it, "the primitive mind thinks more easily in pictures than in words.... They [silent films] will promote, or destroy, the prestige by which the white man maintains his precarious supremacy amid the teeming multitudes of black and brown and yellow."[30]

Here, Churchill reenacts the same tension between ideas of embodiment that were rehearsed in discussions of Josephine Baker, as well as in the rationale for instructing deaf children of color in sign while converting schools for white deaf children to oral methods: even as early twentieth-century thinkers seemed enormously desirous of celebrating the body as a kind of modernist ideal for breaking with standards, they remained incapable of entirely excising from their ideas about it the primitivist association between embodiment and othered peoples and cultures. Through a kind of cultural cognitive discourse, the embrace of the body functioned simultaneously as celebrated marker of a new age determined to shed the hang-ups of the past and as evidence of an ongoing commitment to those same hang-ups.

## Modernism and Gesture

This conflicted attitude about bodies and communication—on the one hand celebrating their productive potential, on the other engaging in primitivist logic about their functionality—was shared by many literary critics who attempted to locate in physical communication a useful alternative to dominant modes of spoken language but who were unable entirely to escape from problematic perceptions of embodiment. At the same time that avant-garde poetics were pushing for a technologized, dehumanized aesthetic, the increasing visibility of bodies on screens, in magazines and newspapers, and in rapidly urbanizing metropolises around the world was difficult to ignore.

The influential New Critic R. P. Blackmur's 1952 *Language as Gesture* offers a take on the subject from the perspective of literary criticism, celebrating gesture while simultaneously complicating its relationship to the body. For Blackmur, gesture functions primarily as nonsemantic meaning behind and around words. "Gesture, in language," he explains, "is the outward and dramatic play of inward and imaged meaning. It is that play of meaningfulness among words which cannot be defined in the formula in the dictionary."[31] It both comes before language and is the cherry on top of linguistic communication, in either case, not necessarily tied to the physical body.

Blackmur emphasizes this point by drawing examples of gesture from various fine and plastic arts. "It is gesture," for example, "that makes a stone figure a sphinx, and it is gesture that makes the great Sphinx a smile."[32] In this formulation, gesture is imagined as specifically disembodied; it signifies something like a spirit that resides in the process of artistic creation or in the art object but not in the embodied human subject. This is perhaps most clear when Blackmur cites a passage from *Hamlet*, which he identifies as illustrative of the way gesture reinvigorates language. "Do not these words rise from what is past and fall toward what is coming, and both rise and fall as a gesture, almost his last, out of Hamlet himself?" he inquires. "We see how order and cadence and the ear of the poet give the actor all that he has to do except that most arduous thing, put the gesture in the words into the gesture of his mere voice and body."[33] By situating gesture in the act of artistic creation that produces the language (or in the language itself), the creator as embodied subject is specifically elided from this account.

At other points, however, Blackmur it very much interested in the vitality of bodies. Discussing gesture as the necessary solution to his friend's writer's block, he provides the following advice:

> What he has to do is to forget the whole theory of stenography or reporting and make the words of his pen do not only what the words of his mouth did, but also, and most of all, what they failed to do at those crucial moments when he went off into physical gesture with face and hands and vocal gesture in shifting inflections.... Since what is being played with is meanings and congeries of meanings, what is wanted cannot be articulated in a formula, but on the other hand it cannot be articulated at all except when delivered within a form.[34]

Here, it is specifically the physical face, hands, and throat that enable gesture, even if the body is somewhat unceremoniously transmuted into form. However much as Blackmur may try to sublimate the physical into such bland descriptors, it is physicality that enables words to "go beyond their normal meanings" and "become gesture."[35]

The way in which gesture becomes a sliding signified between the embodied and the disembodied for Blackmur is indicative of the fraught relationship that many modernists had with the idea of corporeality and that high modernist literature had with forms of art and entertainment such as jazz music or dance that specifically foregrounded the (othered) body. There is a repeated attempt in Blackmur's account to turn gesture into something abstract, but as his inability to entirely detach it from its embodied roots demonstrates, it is precisely this foundation that give gesture the subversive force that he is seeking. This attempt to separate the idea of gesture from the body gesturing is yet another reminder of both the widespread discomfort with physicality that governed communicative regulation at the beginning of the twentieth century and the problematic ways our analysis of literary experimentation tends to gloss over the social and physical ramifications of it. This elision also represents a missed opportunity in terms of imagining experimental linguistic alternatives. As *Modern Times* demonstrates, if bodies and language are inextricably intertwined in the policies that seek to enforce communicative norms, so too are they linked in the subversive practices that undermine them. Sherwood Anderson's *Winesburg, Ohio* takes up this idea, illustrating the wide-reaching social effects of such regulation and specifically positing a return to ancient storytelling practices as a means to reestablish the link between language and embodied community.

## Communicative Freak Show

Like Chaplin's film, a silent anomaly in a world of sound, *Winesburg, Ohio*'s engagement with small-town life over the bustle of the metropolis functions for many people as a kind of anachronism. While sharing with so-called high modernism (and with Chaplin) a commitment to both technical innovation and resisting standardization, Anderson's book blends this formal experimentation with a more explicit thematic interest in the body. By highlighting the constructedness of communicative norms as well as their damaging effects, Anderson denaturalizes language practices that were widely assumed to be inherent. He employs the figure of the storyteller to suggest a means of challenging standardization that involves blending elements of modern literary practice with those of oral traditions in order to subvert norms by emphasizing individual bodies and their idiosyncratic ways of using language.

*Winesburg, Ohio* consists of a series of interconnecting stories of characters that Anderson refers to as "grotesques." Grotesques have a long history in literature of representing the common or folk elements of human life. As Mikhail Bakhtin has argued, the representation of the everyday often serves a transgressive function because "the grotesque . . . discloses the potentiality of an entirely different world, of another order, another way of life."[36] While modern thought had begun to redefine individuals who deviated from the standard in this way as abnormal and in need of regulation, Anderson reconstitutes the grotesque according to its earlier meaning as representative not of a fringe minority but, because no one entirely matches the standard, of the shared human condition.

To further emphasize the point, Anderson's grotesques are defined not only by idiosyncratic (and potentially essential) physicality but also through a kind of logical fallacy. As he explains in the text's introductory story, "The Book of the Grotesques," grotesques are people who become twisted through their obsession with definitive truths: "the moment one of the people took one of the truths to himself, called it his truth, and tried to live his life by it, he became a grotesque and the truth he embraced became a falsehood."[37] The book is thus framed by the idea that a preoccupation with such truths, the belief that one has discovered the one and only "right" answer or way to deal with a situation (what we might call a standard), is destructive. Here, Anderson turns accepted thinking on its head; what is grotesque is not the "aberrant" physical body but rather the conformist thinking that would seek to standardize it. Rather than constituting a deviant minority, for Anderson, the grotesque is a category that can, that indeed does, include everyone.

In "Godliness," the narrator links the development of such grotesque thinking to the proliferation of print media and the linguistic standardization that accompanied it. "Books, badly imagined and written though they may be in the hurry of our times, are in every household, magazines circulate by the millions of copies, newspapers are everywhere," he complains. "Much of the old brutal ignorance that had in it also a kind of beautiful childlike innocence," a sense of individuality, "is gone forever."[38] *Winesburg* celebrates individuality by presenting the stories of people out of step with this drive toward what was defined as progress. Through character studies that explore people's diverse imperfections, Anderson demonstrates the folly of assuming that there is a singular way of being or that this is a goal we should strive to achieve.

The sheer number of characters in *Winesburg* who do not fit easily into the confines of these standards serves to denaturalize them. Significantly, much of the distinctness of the townspeople is related to their style of communication. Joe Welling, for example, stands out because he speaks more than is considered normal. These overwhelming outbursts are presented as uncomfortable and are repeatedly associated in the story with physical distinctness. Welling is described as being "small of body and in his character unlike anyone else in town."[39] His manner of speech frustrates even the descriptive efforts of the narrator, who does not know precisely what to say about him. Welling is first characterized as "a tiny little volcano that lies silent for days and then suddenly spouts fire," before the narrator decides that he is actually more "like a man who is subject to fits."[40] Significantly, this latter description translates the power of Joe's nonnormative speech into the rhetoric of disability.

The reader is left in a similar position of not knowing quite what to do with Joe's speech. As the narrator explains, Joe "was beset by ideas and in the throes of one of his ideas was uncontrollable. Words rolled and tumbled from his mouth."[41] Structurally, these words repeatedly threaten to take over the story, running on and on, bouncing from one idea to the next with only the slimmest pretense of connection. In reading these passages, in which Joe philosophizes about Wine Creek or decay, the reader is put in the position of the other characters, wishing that Joe would be quiet, that he would more closely approximate the norm.

Ultimately, however, Anderson reveals that this communicative oddity proves to be an asset. It makes Joe a highly successful baseball coach by confusing the opposing team, and it allows him to overcome the hostility of Tom and Edward King when Joe attempts to woo Sarah King. Because Joe does not engage with or recognize normative conversational modes, he remains oblivious to the hostility of the two men, who arrive angry and armed to insist that he stop seeing Sarah. By speaking to them in his idiosyncratic and highly excitable way, Joe is able to diffuse the tension and win them over without ever recognizing (or at least acknowledging) the danger. The story ends with the three walking back to see Sarah, with Tom and Edward struggling to keep up with Joe's quick pace.

Characters' unique speech habits do not always function in *Winesburg* to resolve conflict. Elmer Cowley's inability to express his frustration at being perceived as queer, for example, frequently translates into bursts of violence. In response to a traveling salesman, whose goods, Elmer believes, will contribute to his family's financial decline, Elmer can only communicate his ideas by brandishing a rifle and shrieking. "Everyone stands around and laughs and they talk but they say nothing to me," he later complains. "Then I feel so queer that I can't talk either. I go away. I don't say anything. I can't."[42] When he finally does manage to confront George Willard, whom he sees as representing the condescending townspeople, he is able to speak but only by simultaneously moving his body. When he tried to talk, "his arms began to pump up and down. His face worked spasmodically."[43] Attempting to force his ideas (and body) into normative postures is so difficult for Elmer that the strain manifests itself in physical tics.

Seth Richardson also fails to behave and speak according to convention. His mother is both frustrated and awed by this deviance: "She expected from all people certain conventional reactions to life. A boy was your son, you scolded him and he trembled and looked at the floor. When you had scolded enough he wept and all was forgiven.... Virginia Richmond could not understand why her son did not do these things."[44] It is not Seth's specific behavior, that is, but rather his refusal (or inability) to conform to the convention that befuddles his mother. It also complicates her own actions by making it impossible for her to react according to societal scripts, which causes her no end of difficulties as a parent. When Seth returns after disappearing for a week with some friends, for example, Virginia's planned reprimands unravel in the face of his direct and unashamed explanations. As these characters' interactions reveal, deviation from the norm impacts not only the individual but all those around him as well. Once a person fails to buy in, the whole system is put in danger of collapse. The outreaching effects of Seth's deviance shine light on some of the motivations behind the effort put into regulating the use of signed and other minority languages.

This policing applied not only to what one said but also to what one did not say. Much of Seth's distinctiveness in particular is expressed by his silence. While his mother wants to read this silence as indicative of deep thought or grand plans, Seth insists that he merely has no desire to engage in the idle chatter he observes around him. "'Everyone talks and talks,' he tells Helen White. 'I'm sick of it. I'll do something, get into some kind of work where talk don't count.'"[45] For Seth, idle chatter, people "perpetually talking of nothing," is what is wrong with the town. It drives a wedge between him and George Willard, who Seth asserts "belongs to this town," as well as between him and Helen White.[46]

Seth is initially drawn to Helen by her own communicative distinctness. When the two are children, Helen writes Seth copious quantities of notes, tucking them into his possessions at school or sending them through the post. That Seth never replies to these notes does not deter Helen, and it is her acceptance of this alternative mode of communication (or lack of overt communication) that Seth finds appealing. He even allows himself to imagine staying in the town in order to be with her, walking together in silence. Ultimately, however, he decides that she is part of the town in a way he feels he is not. He imagines that Helen will end up with someone like George Willard, "who talks a lot," and will therefore start to become "embarrassed and feel strange" when he is around.[47]

Like Seth, Enoch Robinson's communicative distinctiveness leaves him isolated from the people around him. As the narrator explains at the beginning of his story, for Enoch "nothing ever turned out" because "he couldn't understand people and he couldn't make people understand him."[48] For a time, Enoch appears to be very successful. He moves to New York City, where he marries, has children, and hosts an artists' salon. He becomes overwhelmed, however, by the conversations of the people he has surrounded himself with. "Leaning back in their chairs, they talked and talked with their heads rocking from side to side," he observes. "Words were said about line and values and composition, lots of words, such as are always being said."[49] Enoch initially tries to participate in these conversations but "didn't know how. He was too excited to talk coherently. When he tried he sputtered and stammered and his voice sounded strange and squeaky to him. That made him stop talking."[50] Enoch has ideas to contribute to these discussions, but his perception that his own style of speech is nonnormative keeps him from fully engaging.

As an alternative, Enoch "began to invent his own people to whom he could really talk and to whom he explained the things he had been unable to explain to living people."[51] After a while, he decides that he prefers the company of these imaginary friends, with whom he can be "self-confident and bold," to the people in his life, and he retreats from society and leaves his wife.[52] He attempts to connect with a young woman by explaining the significance of his fantasy friends, but his emotion frightens her away. The imaginary people leave with her, and Enoch dejectedly returns to Winesburg. While he had once longed to go home, the desertion of his friends makes the return bitter. Once in Winesburg, he finds himself unable to communicate with anyone other than George Willard, the town reporter, whose job and experiences serve as a link between many of the stories.

Like Enoch, Louise Bentley also does not know how to express herself in ways that make sense to others, and her failure similarly drives her into isolation. Described as "neurotic" and "oversensitive," Louise is born into a house notably devoid of emotional connection, a cycle she repeats with her son, David.[53] As a young girl, Louise was singled out as odd because of her intelligence, and she never works her way back from that outsider status. As the narrator explains, "It seemed to her that between herself and all the other people in the world, a wall had been built up and that she was living just on the edge of some warm inner circle of life that must be quite open and understandable to others."⁵⁴ She tries to form a connection with her husband by explaining herself honestly, but her efforts are "always without success. Filled with his own notions of love between men and women," John Hardy is unable to understand or appropriately respond to Louise's unconventional ideas.⁵⁵ Ultimately, she stops trying to bridge the gap and retreats into eccentricity.

Ironically, it is this inability to communicate with one another that most strongly links the characters in *Winesburg*; rather than representing individual deviance, it is what they share. The fact that so few in Winesburg are able to achieve the kinds of connections with others that Louise strives for using conventional speech demonstrates that the walls that frustrate her are symptomatic not of the problems of individuals but of a society whose prescribed modes of communication do not accommodate the diverse needs of its population. Despite rising pressures at the time for bodies to conform lest they be classified as deviant (or, to use Enoch's word, "queer"), Anderson's descriptions of these characters are remarkably lacking in pathology. By emphasizing the proliferation of communicative differences within the town, and by occasionally even exploring the productive aspects of these differences, he shifts the focus away from the idea of "flawed" individuals and onto the problematic expectation that individuals should all communicate in a singular way.⁵⁶

## Telling Stories

Having thus denaturalized communicative standards, Anderson sets about imagining potential solutions. For him, key to resisting communicative norms was the development of the figure of the storyteller, which functions as a subversive presence within his work. Anderson was not the only early twentieth-century writer who experimented with the role of storytelling; Edgar Lee Masters's 1915 *Spoon River Anthology*, for example, follows a similar structure to *Winesburg* in order to give a glimpse into the gritty, unidealized lives of people from a fictional town.

What makes Anderson's take on storytelling unique is that it presents this storytelling as a response to the very modern problem of communicative norms. It is this element that keeps Anderson's interest in the storyteller from devolving into mere primitivism or "nostalgic impulse[]."⁵⁷ His perspective on storytelling was not one shared by many of his contemporaries. For many people, the dawn of the twentieth century was perceived as an opportunity to violently break with the past. This included previously popular literary techniques, which were now seen as not only dated but regressive. E. M. Forster summarized the presumed connection between storytelling and primitive thinking in *Aspects of the Novel*:

> The more we look at the story . . . the less shall we find to admire. It runs like a backbone—or may I say a tape-worm, for its beginning and end are arbitrary. It is immensely old—goes back to Neolithic times, perhaps to Paleolithic. Neanderthal man listened to stories, if one may judge by the shape of his skull. The primitive audience was an audience of shock-heads, gaping round the campfire, fatigued with contending against the mammoth or the woolly rhinoceros, and only kept awake by suspense. What would happen next? The novelist droned on, and as soon as the audience guessed what happened next, they either fell asleep or killed him.[58]

Forster's description demonstrates not only a contemporary distaste for storytelling but an outright disdain for it. As the passage suggests, this was primarily because of its intimate connection to the physical body, to the ways narrative was once shaped by the desires of an audience, desires that were physical as well as intellectual (the need to overcome audience fatigue with excitement). This kind of communal storytelling, with its insistent present-ing of the body, is something from which at least one strand of modernist writing was committed to distancing itself.

Anderson, however, remained fixated on the figure of the storyteller throughout his career. "I am in my nature a teller of tales," he explains in "The Modern Writer," and tales, storytelling, chants, and songs constitute the single most prominent theme in his body of work.[59] While also embracing formal experimentation, for Anderson the act of storytelling represented not a submissiveness to standard forms but rather a powerful tool of resistance against the standardization that paralyzes so many of the characters in *Winesburg*. Rather than rejecting (or celebrating) the figure as an ancient relic, Anderson emphasizes its modern relevance. Far from representing a "no longer feasible, decidedly obsolete sociocultural ideal," storytelling is presented as a means to showcase the value of diverse individuality, to connect what had been valuable about older traditions with new models of literature and the new political situation in which modernist writers found themselves.[60] Karl Kroeber expresses a similar interpretation of the social function of storytelling in *Retelling/Rereading*: "Genuine storytelling is inherently antiauthoritarian, . . . for stories are told only by individuals, not groups. Inherent to all such individuation is the potentiality for subversion, especially because a story is 'received' by individuals, no matter how large and homogeneous the audience of a telling, each of whom simply by interpreting for himself or herself may introduce unauthorized understanding—all the more dangerous if unintended."[61] By drawing our attention to the disastrous consequences of conformity for individual characters, Anderson's stories similarly function to highlight individuality and, more specifically, individual bodies. Storytelling produces spaces in which those bodies can interact with one another in and around language. Intriguingly, contemporary storytelling societies bear out the idea that this mode of interaction, rather than representing a throwback, continues to serve a valuable subversive function.[62]

## A Story of Hands

Anderson discusses the potentially transformative power of storytelling experiences throughout *Winesburg, Ohio*, but nowhere are the social implications of these strategies explored more thoroughly than in "Hands," the story that begins the cycle and that first introduces readers to George Willard. "Hands" tells the story of Adolph Myers, a "fat little old man" who has relocated to Winesburg and been renamed Wing Biddlebaum after being run out of his Pennsylvania town following accusations of inappropriate conduct toward his male students.[63] The details of these encounters are left vague; the only things the reader is told explicitly are that Biddlebaum does not understand the anger of his pupils' parents and that he often uses his hands to express himself: "Wing Biddlebaum talked much with his hands. The slender expressive fingers, forever active, forever striving to conceal themselves in his pockets or behind his back, came forth and became the piston rods of his machinery of expression."[64]

"Hands" has been read by recent critics as a parable about the stifling power of sexual norms and the fierce reaction against perceived homosexuality in small-town America. As Thomas Yingling argues in his influential article "The End of Collective Experience," "Hands" depicts "homosexual panic and... the privilege of self-assured heterosexual men to mark and brutalize those who differ from them in appearance, speech, and behavior."[65] The text's most obvious insinuation for contemporary readers is, indeed, that Biddlebaum's difference can be understood in terms of his sexuality, which is deemed so deviant that he is forced first to flee and then to live the rest of his life strictly regulating his behavior. This reading provides valuable insight into the devastating effects of enforced norms on noncompliant individuals and fits well with the theme of sexual and gender policing that runs throughout the text.

The story does not, however, make clear whether Biddlebaum is in fact sexually interested in men (his students or any others). Biddlebaum himself gives no sign that he recognizes such desires. Yingling interprets this lack of recognition as "further evidence . . . of how successfully repressed are these desires," but it is also possible that it is simply evidence of the lack of such desires, that Biddlebaum's uniqueness can be located not (or not only) in his sexuality but in the nonnormative linguistic practices that are the only definitive evidence of his difference within the book.[66] That one difference might be confused with the other is unsurprising. Ideas about what bodies should and should not be doing, after all, govern both sexual and communicative norms.[67]

While assumptions about Biddlebaum's abilities and linguistic practices are linked to ideas about his sexuality, however, the two are not synonymous. Given our lack of vocabulary for discussing communicative norms even today, it makes sense that we, like the Pennsylvania townspeople in the story, map our reading of Biddlebaum's difference onto a concept more readily at hand: that of apparently transgressive sexuality. But the text very significantly never clarifies the nature of Biddlebaum's touching of his students. Indeed, it emphasizes that the specific allegations of fondling are the inventions of an intellectually disabled young man who, having developed a crush on the teacher, confuses fantasy with reality: "In his bed at night he imagined unspeakable things and in the morning went forth to tell his dreams as facts."[68]

The testimony of the other students suggests that Biddlebaum did touch them—"He put his arms around me. . . . His fingers were always playing in my hair"—but does not explain whether either the boys or Biddlebaum understood these interactions as sexual in nature, much less whether Biddlebaum's habit of speaking with his hands is indicative of his sexuality.[69] The only definitive deviance that Biddlebaum demonstrates in the text is the perceived excessive physicality of his language, which sexuality is not the only (or necessarily the best) framework for interrogating. Given that more than a century after the events depicted in *Winesburg* it is still widely assumed that standardized verbal speech is the only legitimate mode of communication, it is critical to interrogate these ideas to gain a fuller understanding of not only Anderson's text but also the political and social realities of individuals who, like Biddlebaum, communicate in ways deemed unacceptable.

In addressing these issues, Anderson is not only ahead of his time but in some ways ahead of our own. Demonstrating surprising insight into the value of diverse communicative strategies, Anderson emphasizes how it is Biddlebaum's attempt to restrain his hands, to communicate "normally," rather than some inherent quality, that reduces him to a shell of a man, "forever frightened and beset by a ghostly band of doubts" and isolated from the others in Winesburg.[70] Biddlebaum's shattered character provides one of the text's most poignant explorations of the long-term effects of enforced communicative conformity. This figure is sharply contrasted with the powerful speaker Biddlebaum becomes when permitted to express himself in the way he finds most natural. Under his tutelage, his pupils "began also to dream," and his comments to George about the dangers of conformity and the need to "shut your ears to the roaring of the voices" of the townspeople are piercingly perceptive.[71] The story's poignancy is rooted in the fact that Biddlebaum is unable to apply these ideas to himself.

Biddlebaum's hands, like Joe Welling's explosive speech, are also portrayed as prodigious in other ways. They enable Biddlebaum to pick fruit at a rate that far exceeds anyone else. Because of this, "they became his distinguishing feature, the source of his fame.... Winesburg was proud of the hands of Wing Biddlebaum."[72] Due to his earlier trauma, however, Biddlebaum cannot interpret his difference, particularly difference related to his hands, as anything other than terrifying: "The hands alarmed their owner. He wanted to keep them hidden away."[73] By leaving vague the nature of Biddlebaum's interaction with his students, and by stressing Biddlebaum's physical and intellectual capabilities, Anderson perceptively locates the handicap not in Biddlebaum himself but rather in the complex act of self-policing necessitated by the mob violence he encounters. Like Chaplin's worker, Biddlebaum finds himself out of place in a world that insists on expressive standardization.

In addition to poignantly illustrating this problem, "Hands" is also the story in which Anderson most directly suggests a solution. Throughout the book, a number of characters are only capable of expressing themselves to George Willard. I described this dynamic earlier in relation to Enoch Robinson, but it is also a sentiment expressed by Wash Williams and Doctor Parcival, among others. For Biddlebaum, the effect of Willard's presence is physically, as well as psychologically, restorative:

> In the presence of George Willard, Wing Biddlebaum, who for twenty years had been the town mystery, lost something of his

timidity, and his shadowy personality, submerged in a sea of doubts, came forth to look at the world, ... The voice that had been trembling became shrill and loud. The bent figure straightened. With a kind of wriggle, like a fish returned to the brook by a fisherman, Biddlebaum the silent began to talk, striving to put into words the ideas that had been accumulated by his mind during long years of silence.[74]

The one distinguishing feature about Willard to which we might attribute this power to enable others to open up is that he is the town reporter. One way of understanding the situation is that, as the storyteller figure in the text, Willard represents a connection to a tradition of embodied communication that Biddlebaum craves, having been denied by a fiercely normalizing society the kind of physical language with which he feels most comfortable.

Throughout the book, Willard functions as the modern personification of the storyteller, even if it is in a somewhat fallen form. Seth explicitly links Willard to the behavior and idle chatter of the townspeople, and Elmer Cowley believes that "George Willard ... belonged to the town, typified the town, represented in his person the spirit of the town."[75] Willard is not set apart from the normativizing behavior of those around him. These apparent flaws are actually very much in keeping with Anderson's theory of the storyteller, whom he perceived as fundamentally intertwined with (and, as I discussed in chapter 1, penetrated by) the people whose stories he told. By serving even in this diluted capacity to share the stories of the people from the town, Willard creates enough of a link to enable various characters, most notably Biddlebaum, to connect to an older and embodied tradition that was more celebratory of diverse forms of expression. In this, Anderson provides a glimmer of hope for his otherwise isolated and largely miserable cast of characters. Reconnecting with this more ancient model of interaction that foregrounded physicality, physicality that by its very nature could never be uniform, suggests a way of reclaiming and celebrating the distinctiveness that, under a regime of standardization, can only function to isolate and disable.

Reading Anderson within the context of historical attempts to standardize deaf people's language use through a devaluation of its physicality reveals how striking Anderson's "story of hands" and its sensitivity to people's needs to communicate in the form they find most natural was.[76] Like Biddlebaum, many deaf children who were forbidden to use manual communication (and were therefore denied access to language during the crucial first years of life) suffered long-term cognitive, psychological, and social impairments. These efforts also had a detrimental effect on the children's education; forced to spend their days practicing speech and lip-reading skills that would, it was argued, allow them to more closely approximate an arbitrary norm meant that there was little time left for education in content areas that would prepare them for successful careers and futures.

By imagining a very similar scenario, Anderson was able to posit a solution that involved not enforcing standards but rather permitting individual difference, encouraging rather than stigmatizing those who did not conform. For him, storytelling cultures represented a model that would allow for the celebration of these differences by using literature as a site of social interaction that could foreground diverse bodies. In fact, this is precisely what has happened with the development of Deaf culture, which is centered around face-to-face interactions and has a strong tradition of storytelling. Recognizing Anderson's insightful discussion of these complicated issues provides us a way of reevaluating his work as forward thinking, rather than as a naïve project overly invested in the past. Exploring the idea of communicative norms also provides a new (and highly political) context for understanding modernist linguistic experimentation more broadly.

What the language politics surrounding early twentieth-century deaf Americans reminds us is that the communicative norms challenged by *Modern Times* and *Winesburg, Ohio* were not nostalgic attempts to reclaim aspects of a primitivist fantasy of the past but rather a matter of pressing contemporary concern. A great deal of critical work, like so much of modernist fascination with the so-called primitive, has problematically identified these discussions of embodiment as anachronistic. As we continue to work through the meanings of the ways modernist writers and critics have negotiated their shifting relationships to space, time, and modernity, it is vital to remain aware of the specific political agenda that seeks to associate particular ideas or practices with the past in an effort to discredit them.

# 3 / Difficulty: Juxtaposition, Indeterminacy, and the Linguistics of Simultaneity

*Modern Times* and *Winesburg, Ohio* demonstrate that there was a broader awareness of the politics surrounding communicative norms during the modernist period than is generally recognized. Both texts dramatize the kinds of regulatory pressure and even corporal punishment inflicted through both official and unofficial channels on individuals who failed to conform. This policing of communicative difference in social situations sits in sharp contrast to the reactions toward linguistic experimentation in the work of many of Anderson's and Chaplin's contemporaries who deliberately broke with convention in the pursuit of an aesthetic of difficulty. It is only fairly recently that such "high" modernist techniques have been registered as socially engaged, and when these discussions have occurred, they have almost always been perceived as unrelated to accounts of language use in individuals and communities deemed "disabled."[1] Recognizing the privileged position required to engage in aesthetic experiments without fear of corporeal reprisals (receiving a negative critical review is, after all, a very different experience than being institutionalized and physically forced to use language normatively) is key to recovering the context in which both aesthetic and pragmatic practices of nonstandard language emerged in the early twentieth century.[2]

In broad terms, modernist linguistic experimentation needs to be understood as part of a larger quilt of related (though often cognitively dissonant) developments in language politics. The visual and physical languages of the Deaf also contribute more specific insight into how we analyze two of the most frequently discussed elements of modernist difficulty:

juxtaposition and indeterminacy. This context helpfully brings to the fore the (often suppressed or unrecognized) resonances that written experiments have with embodiment. In making these links through manual languages back to the body, it is my aim to present a complex picture of the ways we might think through the relationship between modernist artistic practices and corporeality that push beyond the common narrative of linguistic fragmentation responding to a combination of the literal breaking of bodies in the trenches of the First World War and the alienated modern psychology that developed out of that shared trauma.

As the dominant narrative goes, in combination with rapid developments in technology—particularly those in medical technology that grew out of a need to treat wounded veterans—this fragmentation led to an interest in the "broken" body. In *Modernism, Technology and the Body*, Tim Armstrong argues, "modernist texts have a particular fascination with the limits of the body, either in terms of its mechanical functioning, its energy levels, or its abilities as a perceptual system."[3] While these texts were inspired by actual bodies and literal limits, however, the ways in which wounded soldiers and civilians were appropriated into modern philosophy and aesthetics quickly moved to the kind of narrative prostheses that David T. Mitchell and Sharon L. Snyder have demonstrated deploy the disabled body as cipher. In the context of an aesthetic of fragmentation, these (often newly) disabled bodies became the cultural symbol of the alienated, fragmented state that many artists associated with modernity itself.[4]

In other words, both modernism and modernist criticism have frequently made use of the disabled body in the service of aesthetics but have failed either to account for the lived realities of such bodies or to capitalize on the disability insight of individuals whose bodily abilities were impacted by the war but who may well not have understood their new embodiments in the terms dictated by the criticism. The problem of colonizing the disabled body as symbol is that it provides a set of expectations (of brokenness, lack, deprivation, limit) that make it difficult to recognize the more creative conversations opened up by a crip epistemology. In this chapter, I want to move away from the standard representation of the modern disabled body as fragmented by pushing the conversation onto this more productive cripistemic ground and exploring what the linguistics of American Sign Language reveal about that most culturally valued of modernist traits: difficulty. Specifically, ASL linguistics gives us new ways of thinking about two of the key components of modernist difficulty—juxtaposition and indeterminacy—and of recognizing the links between these qualities and the body. In some cases, this context helps explain heretofore undervalued and misunderstood references to embodiment in difficult modernism, and in others, it makes us sensitive to the meaningful absences of bodies within difficult texts.

## What Is Difficult about Modernist Difficulty?

The idea of difficult art works is, of course, not a uniquely modern one. What distinguished early twentieth-century texts was the way writers turned difficulty itself into an aesthetically valued category, as opposed to a byproduct of their work. In "The Metaphysical Poets," T. S. Eliot claimed difficulty as a defining characteristic of modern art that emerged directly from encounters with modernity: "It appears likely that poets in our civilization, as it exists at present, must be *difficult*. Our civilization comprehends great variety and complexity, and this variety and complexity, playing upon a refined sensibility, must produce various and complex results. The poet must become more and more comprehensive, more allusive, more indirect, in order to force, to dislocate if necessary, language into his meaning."[5] To do this, Eliot imagined that the process through which words signified needed to be reconsidered, dislocated through techniques such as juxtaposition and collage not only into new meanings but into new ways of meaning.

This fascination with deliberate difficulty was not restricted to Eliot or even just his poetic circle. As Leonard Diepeveen notes in *The Difficulties of Modernism*, around 1915 there was a shift in the application of "difficulty" as a descriptor. Whereas before it had primarily functioned as a critique of individual authors, now it was seen as characteristic of an entire cultural and artistic movement, a necessarily widespread response to the "variety and complexity" of "our civilization."[6] The details of how this difficulty was enacted varied from text to text, but across these different flavors, juxtaposition and indeterminacy emerged as common threads that seemed to present specifically modernist interpretations of what it meant for works to be challenging. Perhaps no example illustrates this quite as neatly as the epigraphs from Eliot's *The Waste Land*. As I discussed in chapter 1, almost immediately upon its publication in 1922, *The Waste Land* came to serve as a representation of (and, therefore, often a straw man in arguments about) difficult modernism. In the space of just a few lines, and before the poem formally begins, the epigraphs enact both of these modes of difficulty, as well as demonstrating how the two could interact.

In contradistinction to the explosion of mass-market popular works that were perceived to be accessible, texts associated with high modernism frequently incorporated archaic knowledge that harked back to a classical education that the majority of people did not possess. *The Waste Land* plays on this dynamic by opening in untranslated Latin and Greek from the *Satyricon*: "Nam Sibyllam quidem Cumis ego ipse oculis meis vidi in ampulla pendere, et cum illi pueri dicerent: Σίβυλλα τί θέλεις; respondebat illa: ἀποθανεῖν θέλω."⁷ While it has become a critical commonplace to challenge the rigid separation between popular and elitist culture—what Andreas Huyssen terms "the Great Divide"—barriers to general accessibility were a significant part of high modernist aesthetics, even when they were treated with a certain degree of sarcasm by their writers.⁸ The unattributed lines present the reader with an immediate challenge, a barrier of multiple classical languages suggesting a particular level of erudition necessary to work through the poem. Layered on top of this is the difficulty of negotiating the unexpected juxtaposition of the ancient with the modern. Even before its publication, *The Waste Land* was marketed as the quintessential modernist poem, a uniquely modernist view of a uniquely modern world. To get to the portrayal of that hypermodernity, however, these lines force the reader to first negotiate the ancient.

The poem's second epigraph—"For Ezra Pound *il miglior fabbro*"—introduces another aspect of modernist juxtaposition: the movement between public and private references and knowledge. Understanding the line demands translation—"the better craftsman"—as well as a recognition of the allusion to canto 26 of Dante's *Purgatorio*, in which the poet Guido Guinizelli (the first to write in *Dolce Stil Novo*, the "sweet new style" of which Dante was a disciple) praises Arnaut Daniel, a twelfth-century troubadour whose excellence Pound had described at length in his 1910 *The Spirit of Romance*.⁹ For the reference to make sense, we need not only to know our Dante but also to have personal information about Pound, his relationship to Eliot, and his role in editing *The Waste Land*.¹⁰

The epigraphs build on this juxtaposition of personal and scholarly references to create webs of interlocking meanings. Juxtaposition itself, described as deriving from both the fragmentary nature of modern life and experiments with montage in the cinema, contributes to the challenge of reading the poem by continually destabilizing the frame of reference. Like the movement between scholarly and personal registers, the shift between "high" and "low" culture—the incorporation of scenes from music halls, the use of dialect, the movement between classical Latin referents and contemporary scenes of bad sex, to list just some of the examples present in the body of the poem—contributes to the instability, the difficulty for the reader of working out what is significant.

That question of what (if anything) is to be taken seriously in the process of reading the text leads to the second mode of difficulty I want to discuss: indeterminacy. In *The Poetics of Indeterminacy* (1981), Marjorie Perloff memorably describes allusive chains of the possibly meaningful that we see in poems such as *The Waste Land* as "reverberating echo chamber[s] of meaning," in which "the symbolic evocations generated by words on the page are no longer grounded in a coherent discourse, so that it becomes impossible to decide which of these associations are relevant and which are not."[11] In addition to the destabilization of juxtaposition, readers are faced with the unsettling notion that even if they work out possible relationships between the register-jumping "pearls that were his eyes" and "that Shakespeherian rag" in "A Game of Chess," for example, there is no guarantee that the resonances that appear for them are "correct," that there is a "correct" reading of this particular poem, or that there are "correct" readings of anything at all. Eliot's contemporary Hart Crane provided an explicit defense of this kind of apparent obscurity in a letter to Harriet Monroe, in which he argued, "as a poet I may very possibly be more interested in the so-called illogical impingements of the connotations of words on the consciousness (and their combinations and interplay in metaphor on this basis) than I am interested in the preservation of their logically rigid significations."[12] Preserving "logically rigid significations," making conventional sense, both Crane's and Eliot's work suggests, was decidedly not the goal of modernist poetics.

While interpretive dead ends are, again, not unique to this historical moment, the level to which their creative process self-reflexively called into question the very reading practices that had traditionally been employed to provide meaning was something new. This nihilism of interpretation has often been linked to the nihilism that many readers take away from the poem's vision of the modern world as they scramble furiously and sometimes futilely with fragments that refuse to cohere. That Eliot seems to be engaged in a kind of game—particularly in his use of a scholarly apparatus that refuses definitive resolution to an even greater degree than the text itself—has not undermined the general consensus that the poem's meaning is that there is no meaning, that it is the condition of the modern world to refuse truth or understanding.[13] The poem both thematically points toward and structurally enacts this fundamental indeterminacy.

Despite the ways that New Criticism—with its emphasis on close readings of the text alone, divorced from authorial and readerly bodies—developed out of critical work by Eliot, who also helped establish the institutional hold of the approach, such difficulty actually did promote an unexpected engagement with embodied subjects: specifically, those of readers. In line with the appearance of bodies in unexpected places, which I discuss toward the end of the chapter, the ways in which readers (and critics) have responded to juxtaposition and indeterminacy are often described in decidedly visceral ways. Through surprising juxtapositions and a withholding of explanation, readers committed to making meaning out of difficult modernist texts must fill in the gaps in whatever ways their own knowledge or backgrounds allow. One of the pragmatic consequences of such difficulty, that is, is the development of an intensely personal, and even physical, relationship between reader and text.[14] As Diepeveen argues, "Difficulty is an odd aesthetic experience; using their whole bodies, people react viscerally to difficulty, often with anxiety, anger, and ridicule. The public debate about difficulty and its scandalousness, then, was much more than a story of elitism and middle-class anti-intellectualism. It was also a story of anger, of pleasure, and of the body."[15] By demanding new kinds of reading practices, difficult modernist texts engaged the bodies of readers in new and often uncomfortable ways. Through their relation to readers, even those texts considered the most indeterminate linked up with (and were dependent for their meanings on) concretely embodied subjects. As I will demonstrate, ASL linguistics reveals even more unexpected ways in which difficulty leads us back to the body.

## Linguistic Simultaneity

One of the reasons both juxtaposition and indeterminacy are uncomfortable for many readers is that they challenge the linear progression either from one idea logically to the next or via a deductive reasoning process that involves collecting pieces of evidence as one moves forward through a text toward an interpretation. This sense of linear progress is deeply connected to the structure of language itself in ways that became an explicit part of linguistic discourse at precisely the same time that modernist writers began challenging the coherence of the poetic line.

Conventional spoken and written languages, those that difficult modernist writing aimed to complicate, are necessarily linear. Indeed, as Ferdinand de Saussure argues in his *Course on General Linguistics*, a text that came to shape much of twentieth-century literary criticism's attitudes toward language through its role in the development of structural linguistics, linearity (along with arbitrariness) is an essential quality of language.¹⁶ As Saussure put it, "the signifier, being auditory, is unfolded solely in time from which it gets the following characteristics: (a) it represents a span, and (b) the span is measurable in a single dimension; it is a line."¹⁷ While the apparent simplicity of the assertion had caused many people to overlook it, Saussure argues that this linearity "is fundamental, and its consequences are incalculable. Its importance equals that of Principle I [the arbitrary nature of the sign]; the whole mechanism of language depends on it.... In contrast to visual signifiers (nautical signals, etc.) which can offer simultaneous groupings in several dimensions, auditory signifiers have at their command only the dimension of time. Their elements are presented in succession; they form a chain."¹⁸ Although Saussure mistakenly dismisses the possibility of languages in the visual mode, his analysis significantly identifies "visual signifiers" as possessing "simultaneous groupings in several dimensions," which he contrasts with the linear unfolding of auditory language (as well as systems of written language based on them).¹⁹

The linearity that Saussure identifies with spoken and written language occurs at both phonetic and syntactic levels; letters and sounds must proceed one after another in order for an utterance to make sense within words, and words in sentences must likewise appear in a fairly rigid order for sentences to have meaning. To either verbally articulate or write the word "dog," for example, the letters or sounds for each phoneme must appear in a particular, sequential order. Any change to this sequence (odg, ogd, gdo, god, dgo) results in either nonsense or a separate signifier. Alteration to that temporal unfolding (attempting to produce the letters or phonemes simultaneously) also fails to produce semantic meaning.

Similarly, words within a sentence, while they can sometimes be placed in different orders, must nevertheless unfold in a single dimension. The reasons for this linearity derive from the channels through which such languages are both produced and received. While signed languages deploy a variety of articulators—hands, arms, torso, face, mouth, eyebrows—which can signify independently of one another, the production of spoken language involves the interdependent apparatus of the throat.²⁰ It is not physiologically possible to express multiple linguistic messages simultaneously through the same apparatus. Similar structural limitations impact the receptive abilities of listeners processing language aurally; strenuous effort is required to attempt to decode overlapping linguistic messages, and such efforts usually result in failure.

Just as linearity is an essential feature of meaning production in spoken and written language, simultaneity is central to the way that signed languages function. The human visual system—that is, the system through which signed languages are most typically processed—is decidedly more adept at decoding multiple messages simultaneously.[21] As the linguists Howard Poizner, Edward Klima, and Ursula Bellugi note, "Rather than relying primarily on the order of items and fine temporal processing, sign language is organized in co-occurring layers and requires the processing of spatial relations." This "multilayering of linguistic elements is a pervasive structural principle."[22] As Saussure suggested, that is, visual languages are indeed multilayered and able to function in multiple dimensions. And these qualities have a significant impact on the ways signed languages function, particularly in the options they have for encoding information in words.

What is perhaps most significant about this analysis is the relationship it establishes between the spatial capabilities of signed languages ("multilayering," "spatial relations") and their implications for temporality, a relationship I explore in more detail in chapter 4. Where other forms of language progress horizontally, the (vertical) layering of information onto individual signs enables a rich use of simultaneity. Rather than strings of information unfolding on the horizontal axis, signs can encode linguistic information in "multilayered" bundles that are stacked vertically.

As Margalit Fox suggests in *Talking Hands*, this simultaneity results from both the ability of signers to produce multiple linguistic messages at the same time and the ability of viewers to decode them: "Because the human visual system is better than the auditory system at processing simultaneous information, a language in the visual mode can exploit this potential and encode its signals *simultaneously*. This is exactly what all signed languages do. Whereas words are linear strings, signs are compact bundles of data, in which multiple units of code—handshape, location, and movement—are conveyed in virtually the same moment."[23] This simultaneity results in part from the way morphology functions in signed languages. To change the root sign "look at" to "watch," "stare," or "look at for a long time," for example, the modifications are stacked on top of the original sign, and they take place in the same temporal moment. As opposed to unfolding over time, "complex signs are formed from simple ones by altering the spatial signal *while the simple sign is being made*.... ASL can... expand simple words... into elaborate matrixes of related meanings."[24] One example of such layering in ASL is the group of signs that the ASL linguist Carol Padden refers to as "agreeing" or directional signs. Included in this group are words such as "give," "help," "ask," and "hate." Encoded within these signs is information regarding subject and object; the signs move through space from the former to the latter.[25] Some signs—"send," for example—can also be encoded with information regarding the nature of the sending, its exhaustive distributional aspect (send to each) and its iterative aspect (send repeatedly); the sign can be altered to mean to send to one person, to send to all people in a group, to send many times to one person, to send many times to each person in a group, and so on.[26] Unlike English, which appends information with additional words, prefixes, or suffixes in a horizontal chain ("house" becomes "houses," "done" becomes "undone," "send" becomes "send to me," etc.), ASL often layers this data onto the original sign. So with a single sign, one can indicate the concept "I sent repeatedly to each person," a phrase that is cumbersome and awkward (as well as horizontally extended) in English. Or, as figure 3.1 illustrates, information regarding a word's temporal aspect can be layered onto an original sign, so that the messages "study continually," "study regularly," "study for prolonged period," "study over and over again," and "study in a hurry" can all be expressed with vertical alterations to a single sign.

Some of the other places we see this vertical layering most dramatically in ASL are adverbs and negation. American Sign Language does not have adverbs that occur as separate signs. Rather, the information that would be provided through the addition of an adverb to a verbal string of words is stacked on top of the sign for the verb itself. In ASL, there are eleven kinds of adverbials communicated through the face.[27] For example,

Face: /mm/_____
Hands: HER HUSBAND COOK-[dur] DINNER
"Her husband has been cooking the dinner with pleasure."[28]

Here, the "mm" represents a facial expression (nonmanual signifier) that expresses the adverbial phrase "with pleasure." As this rendering of the translation indicates, the information is stacked on top of the signs, rather than unfolding horizontally, and grammatical information is communicated through various parts of the body.

Negation in ASL functions similarly. The phrase "Mary is not buying a car," for example, would be signed as follows:

Face: /neg/_____
Hands: MARY BUY CAR
"Mary is not buying a car."

Here, the negation (communicated through a head shake) continues throughout the entire verb phrase. Again, the information is expressed simultaneously rather than sequentially.

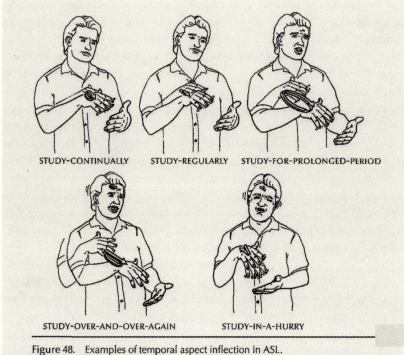

Figure 48. Examples of temporal aspect inflection in ASL.

FIGURE 3.1. Line drawings of men signing "study continually," "study regularly," "study for prolonged period," "study over and over again," and "study in a hurry." In addition to depicting the positions of the hands and arms in each sign, the images also include body position and facial expression. (Clayton Valli, Ceil Lucas, and Kristin J. Mulrooney, *Linguistics of American Sign Language: An Introduction*, 4th ed. (Washington, DC: Gallaudet UP, 2005), 106)

In the next section, I tease out some of the ways we might think about this vertical stacking in relation to indeterminacy in the work of Hart Crane. Before doing so, however, I want to address the way in which another form of simultaneity in signed languages might contribute to discussions of juxtaposition. In addition to possessing this inherent layering potential, signed languages also have the ability to transmit multiple messages simultaneously through separate articulators. This is most apparent in the deployment of the two hands to express distinct messages. One hand might reinforce the message expressed by the other, contradict it, or complicate it. The Deaf American poet and linguist Clayton Valli's "Tears of Life" is structured around precisely this relationship. In it, the poet creates a rhythm by alternating between one and two signs.[29] The right hand tells the narrative of a life, as an individual grows up, marries, has a child, and dies. The other hand repeats the sign "tear" by moving downward across the cheek and then back up in a loop that recalls Gertrude Stein's claim that there is no such thing as repetition: "a rose is a rose is a rose."[30] Each time the cycle is repeated, the meaning of the sign changes as it interacts with the various events being recounted (tears of sorrow at death, joy at births, etc.). Each hand articulates separate linguistic content that is given new meaning when the two are read together.

Through this juxtaposition of meanings, "Tears of Life" enacts the speculation of W. J. T. Mitchell, put forward in the introduction to the first book-length collection of essays on ASL literature, that "one could imagine a bilingual performance in which speech and gesture had a contrapuntal or even contradictory, ironic relationship."[31] Among other things, this relationship can signal the discomfort of moving between cultures, languages, or worldviews that I suggested was behind the experimental language use in "Salt in the Basement." Even more significantly, however, is the way the text links this sliding signifier (produced through juxtaposition) to the vertical axis—the tear moving upward and downward on the signer's cheek, in contrast to the horizontally, temporally unfolding life events taking place on the right hand. Despite the apparent simplicity of "Tears of Life," the poem provides metacommentary on the function of both indeterminacy (vertical layering) and juxtaposition (through its use of the two hands to express distinct linguistic messages). Moreover, it situates this commentary in explicit relation to its thematic consideration of human subjects.

## New Thresholds, New Anatomies

The poet Hart Crane was similarly intrigued by the notion that bodies possess extrasignificatory potential to stack additional information onto words.[32] As I highlighted in responses to Sherwood Anderson, as well as in R. P. Blackmur's contradictory engagements with the body, such explicit treatment of embodied subjectivity within modernist works was often viewed as regressive, as unproductively out of step with modernity. And this perception has also shaped the reception of Crane's experiments at the conceptual intersection of words, images, and bodies. Though he worked during the same period, publishing collections of poetry in 1926 and 1930, Crane's writing never fit comfortably with the high modernism of his generation. Unlike (and in response to) the sparse language and cynicism of many of his contemporaries, Crane's lyrics are decadent and romantic, overflowing with emotion. Crane unabashedly viewed himself as inheritor of an ecstatic tradition of prophesy to which he hoped his poems could contribute. As Eliza New described, "Hart Crane is the American poet of Awe."[33] While his verse shared with writers such as Eliot and Pound an intense difficulty, it was a difficulty not arising primarily from webs of erudite and encyclopedic references but rather growing out of Crane's attempts to imagine alternative modes of communication that might bring about new ways of knowing.[34]

Given how different Crane's fervent belief in the metaphysical potential of poetic language was from most of his peers, it is unsurprising that his work was often met with a great deal of skepticism. While Crane was praised, both during his short career and since, as immensely talented—Harold Bloom described his poetic gifts as surpassing "those even of Whitman, Dickinson, Eliot, Frost, Stevens"—it is almost always with a caveat.[35] The most abiding ideas in criticism of Crane for a very long time were that his poetic ambitions were ultimately a "splendid failure," as the title of Edward Brunner's 1985 book puts it, that he was, in R. P. Blackmur's words, a "distraught but exciting splendor of a great failure," and that this "poetics of failure" was directly linked with the poet's 1932 death at sea, presumed a suicide.[36] Joseph Riddel, writing of one of Crane's last published poems, "The Broken Tower," exemplifies this strand of argument, describing the work as dramatizing "once and for all in our time, the pathetic gesture of a man dying into his work. In other words, it seems to do just what Crane's life was dedicated to—it turns the self into a poem."[37]

While critical appraisals have moved somewhat away from describing Crane as a failure, the idea that some sections of Crane's poems are much more successful than others, and that this incomplete success directly contributed to Crane's personal difficulties, remains a commonplace. Part of the impetus to collapse Crane's marginalized—depressed, alcoholic, and gay—body with his poetry, despite decades of critical training schooling us to be cautious of these kinds of moves, stems, as I suggested earlier, from the writer's own approach to the relationship between bodies and language. Some of the aspects of Crane's work that have been read as failing resulted precisely from his experimentation with the boundaries between the physical and the written, features that more recent linguistic analysis of actual embodied (signed) languages reveal as necessary components of physical language.

In "General Aims and Theories," an essay in which Crane lays out his poetic method, he describes his attempt to create "a new *word*, never before spoken and impossible to actually enunciate."³⁸ For Crane, such words were impossible to enunciate because they were not verbally articulated but rather expressed in other ways. His description of this language as "genetic" and "organic" and his insistence that "new conditions of life germinate new forms of spiritual articulation" highlight the connection Crane identified between the kind of poetry he sought to write and the physical.³⁹ Crane references the link between language and bodies throughout his work, including the two figures from my section title: the "new thresholds, new anatomies!" he imagines in "The Wine Menagerie" and the "signature of the incarnate word" that appears in "Voyages."⁴⁰ The second of these, like the "livid hieroglyph" from "At Melville's Tomb," connects Crane's ideas about living language to writing and signal his desire to in some way represent ideas he associated with such language on the page.⁴¹

Crane linked physical language with what he describes as "the organic principle of a 'logic of metaphor'" that served as the basis of his writing and that required readers to become involved in the production of meaning by deriving "the implicit emotional dynamics of the materials used," which were "selected . . . for their associational meanings."⁴² As opposed to what Crane calls "ordinary logic" in the apology for his work sent to Harriet Monroe, this "genetic basis of all speech" involves a layering of meanings on top of one another.⁴³ While Crane (in a fabulous example of understatement) fully admits that readers often find "certain initial difficulties in understanding" his poems, he maintains that this kind of overlapping (and nonlogical) web of associations allows him to go "through" language and access a deeper meaning, the "crystal Word" he describes in "The Broken Tower" or the "Imaged word" at the end of "Voyages."⁴⁴

In "Voyages," a six-part poem composed between 1921 and 1926, Crane explores the significance of these embodied words. Drawing on the influence of Walt Whitman, the work is an extended meditation on the intersection of languages, bodies, and love. Parts of the poem were inspired by his relationship with the merchant seaman Emil Opffer. In a letter to Waldo Frank describing his love, Crane declares, "I have seen the Word made Flesh. I mean nothing less, and I know now that there is such a thing as indestructibility."⁴⁵ This idea of what it might mean to have a written word made flesh (or flesh made written word) provides an insight into one way of interpreting the poem.

The first section of "Voyages" establishes the problem of meaningful communication. Standing on a beach, the speaker observes children playing and ponders how to express to them the sense of profound danger he feels at the edge of the sea.

> Bright striped urchins flay each other with sand.
> .....................................
> And could they hear me I would tell them:
> O brilliant kids, frisk with your dog,
> Fondle your shells and sticks, bleached
> By time and the elements; but there is a line
> You must not cross nor ever trust beyond it
> Spry cordage of your bodies to caresses
> Too lichen-faithful from too wide a breast.
> The bottom of the sea is cruel.[46]

As readers of Crane's poetry might immediately notice, this poem provides us with some uncharacteristic anchors; we have a recognizable setting (the beach), characters (the speaker, the children, and their dog), several end-stopped lines, and even sentences that contain easily identifiable subjects and verbs (none of which are features Crane is known for). This perception of readability, however, is part of the point made by situating this section (which was originally written as a separate poem several years earlier) within the context of the rest of the piece. The speaker here is stymied, unable to express his concerns. As Evelyn J. Hintz notes, "The child's mode of communication is alogical and nonsyntactical.... To tell them one would have to speak their language."[47] In the first section of the poem, the speaker is unable to do this, unable to get beyond linear speech, and it is this frustrated communication that creates the need for the remaining five sections.

The opening stanza of "Voyages II" directly responds to the final line of the first (the bottom of the sea is cruel), firmly linking them, but the shift in style is immediately apparent.

> —And yet this great wink of eternity,
> Of rimless floods, unfettered leewardings,
> Samite sheeted and processioned where
> Her undinal vast belly moonward bends
> Laughing the wrapt inflections of our love;[48]

In the contemporary world, some measure of a poem's shift into linguistic experimentation is marked by the place at which the spell-check function on one's word processor goes into overdrive. For "Voyages," this is that place. Both the diction and the syntax become more convoluted—Harold Bloom describes it as "even more elliptical... than Crane's usual *praxis*"—as the poet experiments with an alternative kind of language that might overcome the difficulties of the previous section and access a transcendent meaning, the "paradise" the speaker refers to in the section's final line: "The seal's wide spindrift gaze toward paradise."[49]

As Crane suggests in his critical writing, the logic of his poems is associative; its orgiastic overflow of associations recalls Perloff's description of indeterminate poems as "reverberating echo chamber[s] of meaning."[50] The opening image of the sea as a "wink of eternity" both provides one of Crane's characteristic counterintuitive word pairings (the sea as simultaneously bounded in time and infinite) and links this paradoxical language to the body (wink). The next two lines play with the contradiction; in the second, we have images of the infinite, the "rimless floods" and unconstrained or unshackled movements leeward, away from the wind. In the third, by contrast, the sea is described as bounded, samite sheeted, wrapped in rich silk fabric, associated with death (a theme that will be played on throughout the poem), and processing in a confined, orderly fashion. "Sheeted" also refers to sails, linking up with the nautical reference in "leewardings."

It is at the location where the sea is constrained that the speaker comes into contact with it. Here, the sea's vast belly bends toward the moon, laughing the wrapt inflections of the love between the speaker and another who is introduced simply by the pronoun "our," a kind of absent presence. In the stanza's last two lines, we again have a tension between constraint and release. The belly curving toward the sky seems at first an image of freedom, but hidden within "bends" is an association with confinement, with forcing an object from a straight form to a curved one, as in the bending of bow strings.

"Laughing the wrapt inflections of our love" allows for the sea laughing at the lovers or somehow bringing their relationship into existence through the laughter. The laughing also resonates aurally with the lapping of the waves. "Wrapt inflections" overlays "rapt"—affected with rapture or transported to a state of bliss—with the force of being wrapped up, concealed, or hidden (a particularly loaded set of associations for those who want to read Crane's work biographically). Individual words here function as entire stories, entire poems in themselves. Inflections brings us back to the idea of bending, as well as to verbal inflections (inflections in tone), once again signaling the body. This play on inflections returns in the section's fourth stanza, where the "gliding shoulders" of a previous draft was changed to "turning shoulders" so that the line in the final version reads, "mark how her turning shoulders wind the hours."[51] Turning ties us through bending back to inflections and the link between embodiment and communication between the sea and the speaker. It is, significantly, the sea's belly that is the subject to which the verb "laughs" is attached.

This conceptual pairing occurs again in the stanza when the lover is encouraged to "hasten while her penniless rich palms / Pass superscription of bent foam and wave."[52] "Pass" here suggests both "pass along" (communicate) as well as "move beyond," and it is her palms that do the passing. The content of that communication, the knowledge of "bent foam and wave," again recalls inflections (bent) and binds the speaker and the sea in a communicative exchange. The deeper, secret knowledge that the speaker seeks to access is directly associated with embodiment in the third stanza, when the speaker exhorts his lover, "O my Prodigal," to "Complete the dark confessions her veins spell."[53]

Throughout the rest of the poem, Crane continues to associate embodied language both with access to a kind of understanding not possible with conventional communication and with a proliferation of meaning. In "Voyages IV," the speaker describes the sea's "Portending eyes and lips... making told / The chancel port and portion of our June," body parts again communicating information about the intense love affair (the experience of "our June") through a series of interlocking and overlapping religious and nautical images.[54] Later, the speaker explains that "In signature of the incarnate word / The harbor shoulders to resign in mingling / Mutual blood, transpiring as foreknown," linking this new kind of communication with writing (and, by extension, with Crane's own project).[55] In the final section of the poem, Crane associates "dialogue with eyes"— an image that already suggests at least two speakers or perspectives—with "Creation's blithe and petalled [or multifaceted] word."[56]

As these swirls of ideas suggest, Crane's method is one of accruement; he accumulates images rather than sorting them, allowing them to dance around the reader's mind forming these connections. A reading of the poem begins to emerge based on these webs of associations alone, before one starts logically mapping out the lines, questioning how precisely the sea, the speaker, and the lover are related or how it makes sense for inflections to describe the quality or condition of an emotional relationship. As Thomas Yingling explains, "meaning such as it occurs in Crane, is a process of indeterminacy, is constituted precisely in the abrupt disfigurements and dislocations, in the sudden clarities and semantic possibilities."⁵⁷ Yingling links this proliferation of meaning to what he calls "homo*textual* promiscuity," but what I find interesting is the way these "semantic possibilities" are presented alongside images of embodied communication.⁵⁸ Throughout the poem, information is expressed directly through unexpected parts of the body: the belly, the veins, the palms.

Despite critiques of Crane's logic of association as an incomplete execution of poetic vision, the poet was actually incredibly forward thinking in associating embodied language with nonlinear construction. In a letter to Yvor Winters, Crane characterizes the words of his poems as "hard little kernels," and this description of density parallels Fox's account of signs as "compact bundles of data."⁵⁹ In the memorable final stanza of "Voyages III," for example, the speaker describes the sea change of drowned bodies as "The silken skilled transmemberment of song."⁶⁰ Like a bundle of data, transmemberment accumulates meaning through a process of stacking (and comes about as close to vertical layering as is possible in written language). Around the body circulate associations of transformation, transmission, transubstantiation (a term that Crane uses to describe his own feelings about the poem in a letter to Waldo Frank and that also recalls the idea of the "Word made Flesh"), translation, remembrance, and re-membering (a putting back together of the body that challenges the association of this process with death).⁶¹ The body (or the body as sexual organ), the "member," is literally subsumed in this web, in the word, merged with language and reborn as something new, the communicative act of the song.

Throughout most of the poem, this alternative mode of communicating, one in which bodies appear in unexpected places, serves as a way for the speaker to attain greater understanding and to deepen the relationship with the lover. The process is halted in the penultimate section when the speaker begins to figure the sea's language in conventional terms, breaking the spell and returning himself (and us) to more standard communication. "What words / Can strangle this deaf moonlight?" the speaker asks and is almost instantly answered when the sea's language switches for the first time into dialogue.⁶² Rather than the passionate and revelatory interaction of previous sections, the language becomes banal, an imitation of sentiments exchanged by lovers throughout history: "'There's // Nothing like this in the world,' you say."⁶³ This is the first time in the poem we have communication represented with quotation marks, indicating speech, and the trite words drive a "tidal wedge" between the speaker and the sea that "no cry, no sword / Can fasten or deflect."⁶⁴

There is "Nothing so flagless as this piracy," this loss of meaningful communication, and the speaker bemoans the "Slow tyranny of moonlight, moonlight loved / And changed."[65] With the reversion to more conventional language comes the loss of intimate knowledge: "And never to quite understand!" to the speaker's projection of verbal speech onto the sea causes it to retreat, a process the speaker wistfully narrates through direct address: "Draw in your head . . . / Your eyes already in the slant of drifting foam; / Your breath sealed by the ghosts I do not know."[66] In acknowledgment of the fall-off from the ecstatic communication of previous sections, "Voyages VI" takes on more rigid formal attributes. Much of it falls into iambic tetrameter, and it adheres to a more formal rhyme scheme than the rest of the work (*abab* in the first stanza, then variations on *cded* for the rest). The identification of subjects with verbs again becomes a bit easier as we are taken back to a slightly more straightforward narrative with the speaker venturing out onto the water, seeking in vain to recover what has been lost.

As Crane demonstrates by situating it in opposition to the enforced standardization of communication, for him embodied language—with its nonlinear syntax and layered meanings—represented the future in terms of linguistic development. He perceived such nonnormative languages as having the potential to drastically change the ways human relationality was structured, specifically by creating a new level of intimacy through a merging of the semantic and the physical. In this way, he offers us insight into potential implications of manual languages, or any other nonnormative means of human expression, to fundamentally impact society by challenging our assumptions about how we all relate to one another through language.

## Juxtaposition

Understanding the ways in which the characteristic features of Crane's "hard little kernels" are constituent elements of actual embodied languages expands the range of interpretive possibilities we bring to his poems. A similar interpretive expansion occurs when we interrogate the relationship between signed languages and juxtaposition. Indeed, one way of understanding juxtaposition is as an attempt to produce some of the effects of simultaneity in necessarily linear language. We see this most vividly in art that investigates the relationship between the visual and the linguistic, in both of its most prominent modernist varieties: literary cubism and imagism. One of the benefits of considering modernist juxtaposition in relationship to the simultaneity of signed languages is that it enables us to connect these artistic experiments—experiments that have often been critiqued for their treatment of embodied subjects—to embodied language and to locate bodies in texts where they have heretofore been largely invisible. Both sets of examples I consider in the following sections—Gertrude Stein's *Tender Buttons* (1914) and theories of visual poetics; and William Carlos Williams's "The Great Figure" (1921) and Charles Demuth's 1929 *I Saw the Figure 5 in Gold*, described by the artist as a portrait of Williams—work at the intersection of words and images. As they demonstrate, it is precisely in such spaces that bodies have a habit of making unexpected appearances.

## Tender Bodies

Perhaps none of the famed "difficult" modernists is more closely associated with cubist literature than Gertrude Stein. A well-known patron and collector of visual art in her home in Paris, Stein's declarations of the impact of visual arts on modernist literature have shaped the ways critics have approached this intersection, as well as her own work. To begin, I examine some of what Stein herself said about the relationship between images and words and place both these and contemporary accounts of vision in conversation with what we have learned about visual languages from ASL linguistics. I then turn to Stein's *Tender Buttons*, a collection of textual portraits of objects, food, and rooms to argue that what this context helps reveal is the presence of bodies within the work.

Focusing on Stein's interest in the visual is far from a novel approach. Indeed, inspired by the writer's own commentary on her work, critical discussion of the relationship between Stein's texts and visual art has dominated the discourse. As Neil Schmitz argues, such an emphasis on Stein's relationship to cubism can be problematic because it "reduce[s] *Tender Buttons* [as well as Stein's other works] to the status of an exercise."[67] It also threatens to crowd out alternative approaches to the text; in particular, Schmitz is keen to direct attention toward the ways that Stein's work challenges "the primacy of *its* assumptions, *its* intelligibility, . . . *its* stability" through its indeterminacy.[68]

Conscious of the danger of beating a dead horse, however, I want to return (at least briefly) to the well-trod ground of Stein and the visual arts to make the case that placing her experiments in the context of actual visual (signed) languages enables us to identify the connection between her interest in cubist art and this indeterminacy. As ASL linguistics suggests, indeterminacy emerges as a necessary consequence of the structure of visual languages. Drawing out such connections enables us both to recognize in Stein's theories about the temporality of visual language ideas that can reframe our discussions of signed languages and to register the ghostly presence of bodies in her work.

For Stein, artistic composition, as well as modernity itself, emerges through the process of looking. As she explains in "Composition as Explanation," a lecture that was originally presented to the Cambridge Literary Club in 1926 as part of an effort instigated by Edith Sitwell to make Stein's largely unpopular experimental work more saleable,

> The only thing that is different from one time to another is what is seen and what is seen depends upon how everybody is doing everything. This makes the thing we are looking at very different and this makes what those who describe it make of it, it makes a composition, it confuses, it shows, it is, it looks, it likes it as it is, and this makes what is seen as it is seen. Nothing changes from generation to generation except the thing seen and that makes a composition.[69]

Art itself—the composition—by this account emerges as a consequence of a specifically modern way of looking.

The "what is seen" of modernity—at least the "what is seen" that was of interest to Stein—was specifically linked to the ideas of simultaneity that emerged both in cinema and in cubist painting. In her own writing method, which attempted to employ in written text ideas from the cinema about the collapse of series, she draws on the way a film projector takes a collection of celluloid images and plays them so quickly that they blur into one another; the eye sees only the moving picture, rather than each element in the series. As Stein explains in "Composition," "Beginning again and again is a natural thing even when there is a series."[70] This looping refuses the expected horizontal progression of a line, challenging our understanding of a "series" by stacking the images vertically. Stein's use of repetition accomplishes a similar effect in prose. Rather than moving the sentence forward, the repeated words make it loop back on itself. In troubling the linearity of the reading process, Stein also undermines the notion that there is particular meaning at all. If the semantic content of the words changes and one cannot move from one part of the sentence to the next along a predictable path, it can never be clear which version of the meaning of a word achieves primacy. Stein conceived of this democratization of words in specifically political terms. In "A Transatlantic Interview," she explains the process by which "words began to be for the first time more important than the sentence structure or the paragraph": "I was a little obsessed by words of equal value," a balance she likens to the "evenness of everybody having a vote."[71] Cubist art similarly attempted to collapse a series—in this case, generally of spatial perspectives of a subject—in a simultaneous presentation that refused to grant primacy to any particular perspective. In Marcel Duchamp's *Nude Descending a Staircase, No. 2*—a painting that both thrilled and enraged audiences when presented at the 1913 armory show in New York—for example, the action of moving down the stairs is collapsed into a single moment as the nude figure is presented as a series of geometric planes that suggest both the states of the movement and all angles from which such action could be viewed.[72]

As I have demonstrated, this kind of temporal compression is a feature that attends actual visual languages through the vertical rather than horizontal accumulation of information. Stein described the collapse of the multiple into a simultaneous moment in her own work as the enactment of "a continuous present," an expansion of the present through a return to ideas that was not a repetition in the same way that the diverse perspectives from which we see Duchamp's nude are not a repetition or, more precisely given the linguistic nature of Stein's work, the way that Valli's tear is never exactly itself.[73] It was this aspect of the potential for textual images that Stein latched onto in her own portraiture. It was not mimesis, in other words, that attracted Stein, but a deeper understanding of and excitement in the potential of visual language that went beyond realist representation as traditionally understood. As Jamie Hilder puts it, "this is what cubism was for Stein: a movement in language."[74] Stein was correct in her association of such movement and indeterminacy with visual languages. And in actual visual languages, juxtaposition and indeterminacy emerge as necessary byproducts of those languages' relationship with the body. What thinking about this context helpfully reveals in Stein are the traces of such bodies, specifically, as in sign languages, the bodies of individuals frequently marginalized.

On the surface, *Tender Buttons* is decidedly (and in defiance of expectations for portraiture) not about bodies at all. The book is divided into three sections—objects, food, and rooms—and is composed of a series of portraits of these inanimate things. In the book's focus on the inanimate rather than the animate, we already have a displacement of the body from where we might expect to find it. In "A Carafe, That Is a Blind

Glass," the piece that opens *Tender Buttons*, for example, the conventions of portraiture would suggest that we are being given a representation of a drinking vessel:

> A carafe, that is a blind glass.
>
> A kind in glass and a cousin, a spectacle and nothing strange a single hurt color and an arrangement in a system to pointing. All this and not ordinary, not unordered in not resembling. The difference is spreading.[75]

Ulla Haselstein argues that it is the referentiality provided by the pieces' titles that constitute the only convention of literary portraiture to which Stein adheres.[76] It is precisely this referentiality, however, that "A Carafe" challenges. What is the object at the center of this portrait? Recalling Stein's argument that there is no such thing as repetition, the doubling of the title deconstructs rather than pulls into coherence the supposed object of study. "A carafe" on its own is an object one can firmly imagine; "that is a blind glass" simultaneously undoes any clarity that might have been achieved with the first part of the title and introduces the language of vision—specifically an absence of vision—into the poem.

"Blind" as an adjective most logically amends an animate subject (a blind person, a blind animal), but here that subject is only an absent presence, called to mind as the reader attempts to work through the more challenging proposition of making "blind" attach to "glass." What does it mean for a glass to be blind? Does it suggest that the glass is partially full (that one cannot see through it)? That it does not reflect the image of the viewer? When objects are described as blind—as in a blind street—the most common, if obsolete, meaning is a dead end.[77] Here, however, we run into another problem. In what sense can a glass be a dead end? Is the reference a metatextual commentary on the audience, a kind of joke in which we begin a notoriously difficult book with a "dead end," a suggestion of the ways the following text will challenge our reading practices (which might be figured as looking through a glass to pull difficulty into focus)? If so, does this opacity where we expected clarity (in both the metaphor and reading of the poem) suggest the futility of interpretation writ large or merely that we need to adjust those practices, to find a different kind of glass to look through?

Even the relationship between the two parts of the title is ambiguous. Does the "that is" of the poem's title mean that "blind glass" is meant to clarify "carafe," an equivalent to "in other words"? Or are they meant to be read separately: "A carafe" and the observation that "that is a blind glass," perhaps made while looking at a separate object? Again, far from pointing us toward a singular subject of the portrait, the title, the thing that we might expect to be most stable about it, fractures out of our interpretive control in a proliferation of meaning reminiscent of Crane. Whereas Crane linked such indeterminacy explicitly to bodies, however, here Stein ties it more specifically to vision.

This association between whatever it is that is the poem's subject and vision continues in the first line with "spectacle"; perhaps the "spectacle" can "correct" the blindness of the glass. If so, we may not be at a dead end after all, and our own vision (our critical reading practices) can similarly be improved with adjustment. In this reading, the entire poem becomes a set of spectacles, realigning the way readers encounter words in preparation for the rest of the book.

In "spectacle," the glass that refocuses our vision, the corrective device that enables an enhanced kind of seeing, Stein also returns to the specters of bodies called to mind by "blind glass." Such nonnormative bodies, in the context of looking and "pointing," direct us to another of the meanings of "spectacle": "A specially prepared or arranged display of a more or less public nature (esp. one on a large scale), forming an impressive or interesting show or entertainment for those viewing it."[78] Such public demonstrations, particularly of individuals deemed to be oddities, were massively popular during the nineteenth and early twentieth centuries.

While the practice of exhibiting nonnormative bodies was not a uniquely modern phenomenon, it was at this time that the shows began to take on a specifically scientific significance. As Rosemarie Garland Thomson notes in her introduction to *Freakery*, the specific contribution of modernity to the freak show was to move "the freak from the embodiment of wonder to the embodiment of error."[79] Rather than being interpreted as fantastic oddities, such bodies were increasingly read as examples of nonnormative embodiment that modern society saw as its function to ameliorate through scientific processes suggested by the looking glasses of "A Carafe," as well as by references to classification ("A kind in glass," "a cousin," "an arrangement," "not unordered"). As I discussed in chapter 2, following on the popularity of freak shows, public demonstrations were also specifically employed by educators of deaf and blind children to make the case for the efficacy of a particular pedagogical method, and to gain public funds. This cluster of associations would explain both the association of "spectacle" and "strange" as well as the seemingly reflexive need to qualify that these spectacles are "nothing strange," as a comment both on the regularity of such "entertainments" and on the ways in which they had, by this point in time, begun to be recognized as distasteful.

The poem circles around vision and blindness. It is "arrange[d] in a system to pointing" us toward the marginalized bodies that never make a full appearance on the page. *The Oxford English Dictionary*'s secondary definition of "spectacle" similarly reminds us of the elision of such bodies through their objectification: "A person or thing exhibited to, or set before, the public gaze as an object either (a) of curiosity or contempt, or (b) of marvel and admiration."[80] The ease with which subject is turned into object, and the human (blind) subject made invisible in the spectacle that is ostensibly intended to provide greater understanding (where understanding is linked to vision), introduces a challenge to the idea of interpretation in the poem that invites an attentiveness to the ways language enables this elision to occur. If the "blind" object suggests a dead end to a particular kind of reading process and a push toward something new, perhaps it is in response to this slippery danger of the meanings we usually associate with particular signifiers.

In tackling vision (ways of looking), the poem challenges our ideas about bodies and about words. "Not unordered in not resembling" suggests a kind of redemption for the outlier (a version of difference as valid) at the same time that it metatextually comments on the writing itself, insisting that its failure to resemble other kinds of writing, or to present a version of portraiture that provides a more easily digestible description of the subject, does not constitute a lack of meaning. Similarly, the portrait's sly ending—"The difference is spreading"—points toward both a politics that draws focus back to marginalized bodies and new reading practices that reveal such possibilities to us.

"A Carafe, That Is a Blind Glass," that is, opens *Tender Buttons* by juxtaposing images that we cannot link to the poem's nominal subject (a carafe) through traditional reading practices. The refusal of this collage of images ("glass," "cousin," "color" "a system to pointing," "blind glass") to neatly cohere demands that readers wrestle with a radical level of indeterminacy, one that it explicitly links to vision and one that calls attention to bodies marginalized by traditional looking and reading practices.[81] Attentiveness to the embodied elements of visual languages enables us to bring these bodies into focus.

## Visual Texts and Textual Paintings: Charles Demuth and William Carlos Williams

A similar reemergence of suppressed bodies takes place in other kinds of word/image pairings from the period. A particularly rich example of what James E. Breslin calls the "cross-fertilization of the arts" occurs in the chain of influence that produced William Carlos Williams's "The Great Figure" and Charles Demuth's *I Saw the Figure 5 in Gold*.[82] As with Stein, in this space where the visual meets and merges with the textual, we witness an unexpected, and potentially ethical, appearance of bodies. Charles Demuth was a painter, best known for his association with the precisionist school of art that he helped establish and popularize. Also called cubist-realist art, precisionism was a specifically American take on ideas present in cubist and futurist works, one that celebrated the industrialization of American scenes by depicting them in geometric forms.

Much precisionism shared with cubism an interest in visually representing the totality of an object by collapsing space to present it from multiple perspectives simultaneously. This influence is decidedly recognizable in a series of nine portraits Demuth completed between 1924 and 1929 of his friends Georgia O'Keeffe (1924), Arthur Dove (1924), John Marin (1925), Eugene O'Neill (1927), Gertrude Stein (1928), and finally William Carlos Williams in 1929.[83] Inspired by Stein's take on portraiture, and the relationship between language and image, Demuth's paintings did not provide representations of the likenesses of these individuals; rather, they attempt to capture traits of their subjects through line, color, words, and juxtapositions. As Edward A. Aiken puts it, "unlike traditional portraiture, they do not beguile us by physiognomic verisimilitude into thinking we *know* the subject. To the contrary, they demand that we be willing to enter the game that the artist has established if we are to identify the subject."[84] As with so many other difficult modernist texts, the portraits rely on juxtaposition, as well as a combination of allusions to the subjects' other works and personality traits in order to make sense of them. It is up to the viewer to work through these webs of allusions and determine which are significant. Similar to the Eliot epigraphs I discussed at the beginning of the chapter, this mixture of personal and public referents contributes to interpretive indeterminacy.

These elements are particularly highlighted in Demuth's portrait of the American poet William Carlos Williams, his longtime friend and the subject of his *I Saw the Figure 5 in Gold*. Continuing the theme of cross-modal sharing, the painting draws on imagery from Williams's poem "The Great Figure," first published in the poet's 1921 collection *Sour Grapes*, as well as the artist's sense of Williams's oeuvre and his personality and experiences, particularly those that had influenced his creation of the poem. Williams recalls in his autobiography visiting a friend in Manhattan: "I heard a great clatter of bells and the roar of a fire engine passing the end of a street down Ninth Avenue. I turned just in time to see a golden 5 on a red background flash by. The impression was so sudden and forceful that I took a piece of paper out of my pocket and wrote a short poem about it."[85]

"The Great Figure" emphasizes the juxtaposition of sensory impressions provided by the engine:

> Among the rain
> and lights
> I saw the figure 5
> in gold
> on a red
> firetruck
> moving
> tense
> unheeded
> to gong clangs
> siren howls
> and wheels rumbling
> through the dark city.[86]

In a reversal of the challenge that Demuth was to face translating Williams's poem and poetic style into a visual image, in "The Great Figure," Williams attempts to communicate this visual information linguistically. Significant for our consideration of visual languages, one way the poem does this is to realign the traditionally horizontal sentence along a vertical axis. As Breslin notes of another Williams poem, the poet's realignment makes the poem multidirectional; it is an attempt to circumvent the necessary linearity of written language as much as possible so that the scene (and words) can be apprehended almost simultaneously.[87] There is also an attempt to collapse time in the juxtaposition of past and present; the poem gives us a specific moment in time, that in which the poet "saw" the fire truck. But the movement itself extends that present, "moving," "rumbling" forward in time.

"Among" similarly seeks to resist stasis, both for the truck, passing among the raindrops and lights, and for the viewer, whose perception is fragmented by them. The prismatic shattering of light through raindrops suggests the kind of perspectival multiplicity that Stein provided via syntactic bending and repetition. Also paralleling Stein, the poem gestures toward elided bodies not mentioned in the poet's fascination with the appearance of the truck itself. We are left with a tension between the speaker's specific (embodied) visual perception ("I saw") and the multiple perspectives implied by the poem's opening suggestion of a (multifaceted) prism. The "tense" truck stands in for the bodies written out of the poem, those who the truck is going to help, who have logical reason to be tense in ways neither the enthralled speaker nor the unheeding crowds do. The fascination with the mechanical, with the truck, invites a displacement of human qualities away from ignored bodies and onto the inanimate; they are elided and dehumanized in exact proportion to the move to personify the object.[88] On the surface, "The Great Figure" celebrates precisely that speed of "movement," of "wheels rumbling" through the city, the powerfully bright flashes of red and gold. But it also reveals the process of making invisible marginalized bodies that too often accompanies this kind of aestheticization.

Demuth's painting similarly explores the position of the subject in relation to modernist juxtaposition, fragmentation, and difficulty. The painting literalizes the fragmentation of perspective suggested by the absent present prism that opens the poem: the rays of light, darkness, and rain diagonally bisecting the canvas and shattering our perception of the engine, which, as in a cubist work, we see from multiple angles simultaneously. The canvas is dominated by the poem's reds and golds, lights and darks, as we perceive the engine coming at us, the repeated number fives moving closer and closer, the lights on the front growing larger and larger, the diagonally bisecting lines of rain and light suggesting the engine's hood at the same time that the horizontal thrust of the red rectangles present a view from the side. The combination of the frenetic movement of the light lines, the fives hurtling forward in space, and the headlights that seem simultaneously in front of and behind the train produce a sense of depth. The gray, black, and white rays of rain and shadow that move across the entire piece are arranged at the bottom of the canvas to parallel the grill lines of the front of the engine, further contributing to the feeling that it is simultaneously behind and in front of the viewer.

*I Saw the Figure 5 in Gold* offers a visual representation of the kind of layering of perceptions that Williams aims for with the vertical orientation of his poem. Together this layering and orientation function to

FIGURE 3.2. Black-and-white reproduction of Charles Demuth's *I Saw the Figure 5 in Gold* (1929). At the center of the canvas are three number fives, increasing in size so that they appear to be rushing toward the viewer. Behind them is a rectangular shape that evokes the outline of a train viewed from the side. In the upper half of the image are four circles that resemble headlights. Diagonal lines crisscross the canvas. Those at the bottom of the painting suggest both the shape of the grills found at the front of steam engines and refracted light. The word "Bill" appears at the top of the canvas, and the initials "C.D." and "W.C.W." at the bottom. (Oil on composition board, 36 × 29¾ in., The Alfred Stieglitz Collection, The Metropolitan Museum of Art. Photograph by the author.)

create a sense of action that exists in tension with the horizontal thrust of the red rectangles and, more specifically, the two-dimensional text of the piece. The references to "BILL," "CARLOS," and "W.C.W." direct viewers toward the portrait's subject in the same apparently transparent manner as the title of a Stein portrait. As in Stein's work, the idea that this is a portrait *of* Williams is deeply complicated by everything else in the piece, particularly the use of the same color and font (which appears like a printer's typeface) for the initials "W.C.W." and Demuth's own signature, "C.D.," both of which appear at the very bottom of the canvas, suggesting that Williams in some way exists inside and outside the painting, as both its subject and cocreator.

As Breslin points out, the painting's text functions as one of the more compelling examples of the piece's contradictory pull. It is primarily these two-dimensional textual signifiers that remind us of the work's subject (the poet and the poem), as well as the fraught relationships between movement and stasis and between two and three dimensions, which are at its heart. "It is important," Breslin notes, "to see how many features of the painting offer contradictory clues, like the multiple possibilities in a poem by Williams.... The point ... is not to select a 'correct' reading, but to suspend alternate possibilities simultaneously."[89] Significantly, it is the text in the painting—the intersection of images and words that point to the unmentioned, unimaged bodies of painter and poet, as well as those absent present bodies in the poem that inspired the work—that enable us to recognize this range of interpretive possibilities and suggest the necessity of holding all in suspension rather than selecting one.

Having developed a painting style through a careful consideration of the ways his peers had attempted to produce the effects of visual simultaneity within written works, Demuth then uses the written word within a visual work of art to signal back to that simultaneity, positing it as a necessary consequence of the collision of images and language. Over the course of this chapter, I have analyzed how such unexpected insights repeatedly emerge from texts that appear superficially to have very different stakes and interests. Whether by revealing the connection between indeterminacy and simultaneity in engagements with bodies, as in the work of Valli and Crane, or by enabling us to recognize the presence of bodies in works that do not foreground them, as in Eliot, Stein, Williams, and Demuth, Deaf epistemology highlights unexpected ways that the body aligns with aspects of modernist difficulty—indeterminacy and juxtaposition—that have tended to be read as either decidedly un- (and even anti-) corporeal or that have reductively made use of disabled bodies as a metaphor for brokenness. In the next chapter, I continue to explore more productive implications of the intersection of images, bodies, and texts by returning to the question of temporality and its relationship to space in modernist conceptions of the image.

# 4 / The Image: Cinematic Poetics and Deaf Vision

The work of Crane, Stein, Williams, and Demuth demonstrates how knowledge of actual visual and embodied languages allows us to make a surprising link between the concrete (the material body) and the abstract (the indeterminacy that languages in the visual mode deploy). This connection turns out to be very useful in understanding some of the competing ways images were thought of at the beginning of the twentieth century. In this chapter, I continue exploring what ASL might contribute to an ontology of the linguistic image by focusing on the qualities of movement and temporality and argue that the expanded description of the image suggested by such an ontology enables us to reconsider classifications of modernist works, specifically the apparent abandonment of imagism by H.D. and the supposed emphasis of sonority over vision in William Faulkner's *The Sound and the Fury*.[1]

While I continue to focus primarily on understandings of the image specific to the context of modernist art and writing, considerations of what emerges in the spaces where words intersect with images are highly relevant to broader discussions of the visual culture we inhabit and the visual literacies it demands.[2] Despite the prevalence of images in our society and the significant role they play in shaping our culture, as W. J. T Mitchell argues in his groundbreaking study *Picture Theory*, "we still do not know exactly what pictures are, what their relation to language is."[3] This is a discussion, I argue, to which ASL can provide crucially relevant perspectives. ASL itself has long been seen, at times reductively, as a language of pictures. The fundamentally visual way in which most deaf individuals process language has had, as I discussed in chapter 3, specific effects on the development of ASL's grammar.[4] It has also influenced the culture that has developed around this language. As the former president of the National Association of the Deaf and early sign language filmmaker George W. Veditz declared in 1910, "[Deaf people] are first, last and of all time the people of the eye."[5] The literature of this "people of the eye" provides a reservoir of knowledge about the potential cultural and linguistic meanings of the image that can help illuminate modernists' own negotiations with these questions.

## Modernist Images

*The age demanded an image*
*Of its accelerated grimace* —EZRA POUND, "Hugh Selwyn Mauberly"

Like most deaf people, modernists tended to identify their culture as a visual one, and many took a specific interest in the ways this impacted language use and aesthetics. We get some sense of the extent of writers' emphasis on the visual in the wide range of ways they attempted to represent ideas about vision in textual form. From the handcrafted texts of small outfits such as Cuala Press (which incorporated decoration to call readers' attention to the materiality of the works) to typographical experimentation such as that of book III of William Carlos Williams's *Paterson* (which produced a similar effect through the manipulation of the visual arrangement of words on the page) to concrete poetry (which turned these arrangements into pictures) to the development of techniques such as montage (which famously borrowed ideas about transitions and cutting from the cinema), much experimental modernist aesthetic practice probed the implications suggested by new technologies on the relationship between words and images.[6] Despite the widespread recognition of the significance of images to literary practice, however, people had radically divergent ideas about what images were and how they produced meaning.

One approach to the image developed out of a long tradition of associating visual images with truth and knowledge. As demonstrated by the etymologies of terms such as "enlightenment" or the fact that "seeing something with one's own eyes" has long held a privileged status as a means of acquiring knowledge, an ontological status has tended to be transferred to objects visually perceived; we can see them, therefore they are real.[7] This association between truth and sight has ancient roots. As Adriana Cavarero explains, "Greek philosophy understands thought—and therefore the entire realm of truth that lies in its purview—in terms of vision, ... a stable, immobile, objective world that lies in front of us."[8] And this privileged status of that which we can see has shaped a diverse array of cultural practices and beliefs, from the scientific revolution's investment in visible evidence to the use of visual surveillance to determine the "truth" of bodies as chronicled by Michel Foucault. In the post-Enlightenment world, "visible" has become a near synonym for "verifiable."

To secure this verifiability, the images that appear in the field of vision are imagined as "stable," "immobile," and "objective"; they are singular and precise. Behind these descriptions lies the assumption that there is such a thing as "stable," "immobile," and "objective" truth to which vision gives us access. It was such truths, fixed before our eyes, that photography seemed to present. Originally invented in the eighteenth century by Thomas Wedgewood and developed throughout the nineteenth, it was in the twentieth century that photography became inexpensive enough to be available to the masses. George Eastman's 1901 Kodak Brownie enabled people without specialist training to preserve images. The widespread use of such devices enabled a prosthetic extension of the eye, as it could see, apparently for itself, visual records of people and places brought back from around the world. These developments also had a major impact on the establishment of academic fields such as anthropology, which was distinguished from other areas of study around the same time precisely through its emphasis on direct observation, the primacy it afforded to documentary visual evidence.[9]

One of the key ways in which these circulating images impacted modernist writing was related to how they appeared to disrupt linear temporality. The word "photography" itself suggests a kind of written image, a writing of light that preserved a moment in time, held in stasis, removed from the processes of entropy. Snapshots such as those offered by the Brownie enabled viewers to see time appearing to stand still. It was this sense of the fragmentation of time that attracted Ezra Pound to the visual image as he thought about new approaches to poetry. In "A Retrospect," the essay in which he most extensively lays out his understanding of imagism, he defines "an Image [as] that which presents an intellectual and emotional complex in an instant of time."[10] In the same way that both photographic and later cinematic vision involve compressing an image onto a two-dimensional plane, Pound was interested in condensation, a preference he emphasized with his insistence that such poetry involve "direct treatment of the 'thing'" and "use absolutely no word that does not contribute to the presentation."[11]

For Pound, such dictums were an attempt to direct modernist verse away from aspects of symbolist writing he perceived as overly florid and out of step with the speed and steel of the modern world. Imagist poetry was to be "harder and saner, . . . 'nearer the bone.' It will be as much like granite as it can be, its force will lie in it truth, . . . austere, direct, free from emotional slither."[12] "Emotional slither" is intended as a dig at the kind of nineteenth-century poetry Pound wanted to distinguish himself and his cohort from, but it also links this new kind of poetry—and its understanding of the image—to a lack of movement, something that does not slither, that is "harder," more specific, more still. As Pound put it, "It will be as much like granite as it can be," and this stability and hardness would be linked to its accuracy: "its force will lie in its truth."[13] Imagist poetry, like many people's interpretation of the photographic image, sought to access truth by freezing a visual image in an instant of time.

While on the surface this account of images appears dialectically opposed to that of the period's next major development in visual technology, the cinema, moving pictures (or "series production," as Stein referred to them) were in fact just series of such images; looked at carefully, motion pictures were really discrete snapshots, fragments, that had been run through a projector quickly enough to create the illusion of movement.[14] On the screen, a medium that always already flattened the images it represented, scenes were further broken into bits by jump cuts, and bodies were fragmented as the camera zoomed in or out or as scenes cut from one to the next.[15] Such disjunction, based on the recognition of a series of discrete images, provided an irresistible parallel for writers interested in incorporating the visual into their work to the turbulent and rapidly changing world that Marshall Berman, quoting Karl Marx, describes as an environment in which "all that is solid melts into air."[16]

This idea of the image as granite and stable represented one approach to vision, one that was directly linked to the development of imagist verse. As both modern and contemporary cultural commentators have noted, however, this was not the only set of ideas in circulation regarding the meaning of the visual image and how it might be linked to language. If images were privileged through a belief that associated them with truth, the very fact of their exponential proliferation seemed to undermine the link. Martin Jay makes precisely this argument in his influential *Downcast Eyes*, in which he provides a genealogy of vision from ancient Greece to modern France, describing the modern period as marking a shift *away* from what he terms the "scopic regime" of Cartesian perspectivism, a concept he uses to link Renaissance ideas about perspective with Cartesian notions of subjective rationality that privileged vision as a means to acquire truth. By contrast, he argues, in France in particular, modernity witnessed a turn away from occularcentricity and toward "a profound suspicion of vision and its hegemonic role."[17]

Michael North makes a similar argument in *Reading 1922*, in which he points to the very proliferation of images, the thing that would seem to make the age more occularcentric, as evidence of their ontological instability. As he contends, "Newer and more powerful media simply made audiences more aware than ever of the fact of mediation. In so doing, they accomplished for a vast public what philosophy, anthropology, and psychology were accomplishing for an intellectual elite."[18] For North, this realization is at the root of modernist literature's characteristic self-reflexivity. If photographs and then film enabled people to extend the reach of their eyes, the constant technological presence also made them increasingly aware of the process that went into producing that image; even as such images appeared to provide access to the real, they deconstructed the notion of a real by blurring the lines between fact and manipulation, by demonstrating that something could appear other than it was.

As Stein observed in her book-length portrait of Pablo Picasso, "the truth that the things seen with the eyes are the only real things, had lost its significance."[19] Her own approach to vision, as I illustrated in chapter 3, involved challenging what we mean by sight, fragmenting the subject of our gaze in ways that call attention to the conventionality of our usual methods of looking. Like cubist paintings, which aspired to provide more realistic images by showing them from multiple perspectives at once, such self-reflexive works denaturalize sight. The proliferation of visual images, according to this argument, achieved precisely the opposite effect of making them "stable, immobile, [and] objective," of converting them into truths "nearer the bone." It is this apparent contradiction that has kept the visual approaches of H.D. and Gertrude Stein from being read in relation to each other, despite a number of significant similarities.[20] Because of the artificial binary created between these models of visual poetics (collapsed in an instant versus extended in time, hard versus fluid, granite versus indefinite), Stein came to be associated with greater complexity and an enhanced ability to speak to the complex political realities of modernity.

In a study of the modernist long poem, a genre associated with this latter set of characteristics, Margaret Dickie explains that such works appeared more engaged with the world because they were "openly didactic.... The poets set out to teach not necessarily difficult lessons, but simple precepts that required new and complex forms of expression responsive to the conditions of the modern world."[21] In contrast to the sweeping social and political pronouncements of longer works, earlier poems seemed small and bounded, even escapist. This shifting preference led to a movement away from the short verses that had dominated early experimental modernism and toward longer works such as *The Cantos*, *Paterson*, and *Trilogy*. These later texts presented themselves as "poem[s] including history," to borrow Pound's definition of "epic," suggesting that their earlier experimental forms were not up to this task.[22] It was, in other words, the fact that epics were apparently better suited to presenting ideas that were extended in time that made them seem more relevant. History is context; it is an understanding of the story across time. Snapshots and the poetic styles associated with them purport to freeze a single instant, while epic works off the notion of protraction. Despite what seems to be a neat division, however, both movement and temporal expansion, key components of writing aimed at including history, are actually present in visual poems. ASL provides us with a way of reconciling both these versions of what images are, especially in the spaces where they interact with language.

## Dewdrops and Moon Beams

While a great deal of early research into ASL had the aim of establishing its similarities to spoken or written language for the very pragmatic reason that it was frequently dismissed as not being a "real" language at all, what is most interesting about ASL is precisely what it does not share with other modes of language. Because of the visual nature of ASL poetry, it has the ability to produce four-dimensional words and images that link aspects of each of the apparently contradictory interpretations of images described earlier. To be clear, ASL is not a pictorial or iconographic language. As in other languages, words (signs) are comprised of smaller abstract units similar to phonemes in spoken languages. The ways in which aesthetic uses of ASL manipulate images, however, provides insight into how we might think about the possibilities of imagistic language more broadly.

Nearly as long as there has been formal analysis of ASL grammar, it has been described as cinematic. As William Stokoe, the Gallaudet linguist credited with formally establishing that ASL was a complete language in his 1965 *A Dictionary of American Sign Language on Linguistic*

*Principles*, explained, "In a signed language ... narrative is no longer linear and prosaic. Instead, the essence of sign language is to cut from a normal view to a close-up to a distance shot to a close-up again, and so on, even including flashback and flash-forward scenes, exactly as a movie editor works. Not only is signing itself arranged more like edited film than like written narration, but also each sign is placed very much as a camera: the field of vision and angle of view are directed but variable."[23] Images within ASL can be presented from varying perspectives analogous to camera angles. As I explained in my discussion of the Flying Word Project's "Poetry" in chapter 1, the signer can zoom in or out of a particular scene or sign. These perspectives can be stitched together employing methods that parallel those of editing; H-Dirksen L. Bauman identifies dialogue editing, parallel editing, and cutaway as specific film techniques that appear in ASL.[24] They can be made to run fast or presented in slow motion, as demonstrated in Austin Andrew's "Deaf Ninja," in which the slow-motion establishing shots of the ninja's positions and individual falling raindrops are intercut with much faster frenetic movements of his fight.[25]

As all of these techniques suggest, movement is vital to both the grammar and vocabulary of ASL, a dynamic most readily observable in its poetry. To begin to analyze the thematic implications of this movement, I look at a poem that perhaps comes closest to the ideas about imagism expressed by Pound; it presents an image without interpretation, using "absolutely no word that does not contribute to the presentation," as Pound describes in "A Retrospect."[26] Indeed, in this regard, it surpasses even his briefest imagist poem, "In a Station of the Metro"—"The apparition of these faces in the crowd / Petals on a wet black bough"—in which "apparition" introduces a subjective (and interpretive) framework through which the image that Pound presents is read (associating it with death, the underworld, Persephone, immateriality).[27]

In Bernard Bragg's "Flowers and Moonlight on the Spring Water," by contrast, the body of the poem consists of nothing but the images. Rather than direct us toward the context in which we are meant to read it, Bragg uses the relationship between the title and the body of the poem to open a space for contemplating the ontology of the linguistic image itself. He begins by signing the title, which he renders in signed English as follows: QUOTATION MARKS FLOWER M-O-O-N-L-I-G-H-T ON SPRING RIVER.[28] Translated into English, the poem's title is perhaps the closest approximation of its contents, but the difference is striking; it demonstrates the distinction between describing a visual image, as the tile does, and presenting or enacting it. As the poem begins, the signer looks up as night falls, the sign for RIVER emerging from the sign for EVENING. "River," as opposed to "water," renders the vague image more precise. Spring flowers grow from the landscape. The moonlight rides along the ripples of the water as reflections of the stars twinkle around it, before both light and water fade off into the distance.

The brief poem is, as Bragg explains in his introduction to it, "so very visual." It presents, in deceptive simplicity, a cluster of associated images. Framed by the opening temporal marker of night, it then introduces a series of nouns that interact with one another: the moon, the stars, flowers, the river. What is notably absent from this account is description. The poem consists of no adjectives, nor does it append additional information to that which the title provided. Instead, it uses the relationality of these nouns, along with verbs: (night) falling, (flowers) blooming, (moonlight) riding, and (stars) twinkling on the water as it flows. Repeatedly, the poem connects visual images with action and movement. Unlike the moving pictures of the cinema, however, here motion is no trick but rather is a fundamental element of the being of both the poem's words and, it suggests, the objects they represent.[29]

As well as through the verbs that constitute the poem's most memorable visuals, the action that is the signing of the poem—the signer's hands moving through space as he produces the signs—creates a connection between them that becomes part of the meaning of the image. Night is not a static backdrop for the poem; it actively falls on the river that emerges from it as though the two were linked, as though this specific river only comes into being as a result of the fall of night, its being in flux like Stein's continuous present. Similarly, the flowers bloom, as though they too owe their existence to nightfall. The river flows, the light from the moon and stars glittering across its rippled surface as it moves along. Nothing in this still life is actually still; all of the poem's nouns are characterized by action.[30] It is this action that produces the piece's aesthetic pleasure—the round fullness of the flowers swelling, the delicate shimmer of light.

"Flowers and Moonlight" also demonstrates another aspect inherent in signed languages such as ASL: their mimetic potential. Representational art has long had a problem with dimensions, specifically the fact that the canvas (or the film screen or the parchment) has fewer of them to work with than does the subject it depicts. The significance of this seemingly trivial observation can be observed most clearly in the history of trompe l'oeil art, which aspires to mimetic realism through a deception of the eye intended to make it perceive more dimensions than are actually present.³¹ As a visual, embodied art form, ASL literature escapes this problem, operating in the same number of dimensions as the things it represents. Signs themselves have presence; they move through time and space, they can be seen and felt. The different kinds of light produce textured patterns on the ripples of the water. The flowers swell and have shape that can be read tactilely.

This presence does not, of course, mean that literal flowers or rivers magically burst into existence as the poet signs. But if the signs do not produce *the* real, they do produce *a* real; the words possess a multidimensional presence that impacts the way visual poetics engages temporality. The first sign of the poem marks the time, but it, like the rest of the piece, is already in motion. Night moves, it falls on the signer's face and the river. Like everything else in the poem, it refuses to stay still. Through this constant movement, the poem presents a challenge to ideas of the visual image (or of visual poetics) as capturing a singular moment in time. The implications of such temporal expansion are explored even further in Clayton Valli's "Dew on a Spiderweb," which identifies this extension as a fundamental component of ASL's mimetic capabilities. "Dew" opens with the signer encountering a spiderweb and explaining it to viewers.³² The web emerges out of the fog on tree branches, all of which are visually (and physically) linked with the repetition of "5" and "4" handshapes. The web is backlit by the moon, which causes the dewdrops dotted across it to glisten. The speaker is enthralled with the image and addresses the audience directly to explain that she has never seen anything like it before. Desiring to preserve the image, she turns back to it with a camera, snapping photos from multiple angles.

Upon opening the camera, however, she realizes that she has forgotten to wind the film. Distraught, the signer explains that the image is destroyed, that she will never see anything like it again. The assertion, however, contradicts itself. To communicate this, the signer has visually reproduced the web, identical in all but pace to the first one. The web's image *has* been preserved, made present on the signer's hands. More than just describing how the web looks, the signer has created a thing in the air—not identical to the web but nevertheless physically, tangibly present, no more ephemeral than the web itself.³³

This present-ing of the web is significant to a broader consideration of the relationship between words and images; indeed, it directly challenges assumptions about the separation between them. As W. J. T. Mitchell argues, "A verbal representation cannot represent—that is, make present—its object in the same way a visual representation can. It may refer to an object, describe it, invoke it, but it can never bring its visual presence before us in the way that pictures do."[34] For Mitchell, this is a foundational difference between the media. But here, the web, like the flowers and river of "Flowers and Moonlight," *are* made present, are subject to a being there in language.[35]

Again, this presence enables a different relationship to temporality than more traditional understandings of the connection between visual images and words might allow, a relationship that the signer becomes increasingly aware of throughout the rest of the poem. The process of explaining the web's destruction (the gap between the first and second presentations of the image) enables a self-reflexivity that causes the signer to analyze the way she has accomplished this. Whereas in the first presentation of the web, the signs pointed outward toward an (invisible) object, in the second stanza, the signer begins attempting to describe the web but realizes that she has produced it; the image becomes a thing itself, an object extended in space and time, always already disrupting the signer's desire to capture it in a photo, to freeze it in time and press it between the pages of an album. Structurally, the presence of the physical body and the visual perception of it extends the signs in time. The final stanza of "Dew on a Spiderweb" drives home this notion, again playing on the distinction between the poem's title—which pins down the image with a stable name—and the way the image is signed in the body of the text, requiring the signer to recognize the thingliness of the words themselves.

The temporal aspect of this dynamic, marked in "Flowers and Moonlight" by the movement of night, is represented here through the different pacing of the image presentation in each stanza (normal, fast, slow).[36] The poem's primary revelation about the nature of the linguistic image, in other words, is that operating in four dimensions enables the image produced in language to replicate many of the effects of the original image. Unlike a static image captured in the signer's photo album, this image has dimension; it can be manipulated in space and time and therefore has a material reality that is satisfying to the signer in a way a flat image would not be even if she had remembered to wind the camera. Significantly for the purposes of analyzing modernist images, the poem demonstrates how in visual languages the ability to manipulate temporality is not opposed to a present image but rather derives from the language's ability to produce things in the world.

These features—the indeterminacy I discussed in the previous chapter, the movement and engagement with temporality I describe here—provide us with new and relevant ways for thinking about what visual language is and can be. In highlighting this element of visual presentation in art, ASL poetry helps reconcile the modernist fascination with the image as something inescapably tangible and present and its potential to be multifaceted, shifting, and indeterminate. Moreover, unlike other accounts that have attempted to bridge this divide, it remains attentive to actual properties of visual languages.

## Alternative Images

Analysis of the relationship between indeterminacy and the concrete in manual languages is especially useful in understanding the poetic movement most directly linked with the first approach to the visual image: imagism. Within early literary modernism, perhaps no approach to poetics expressed more explicit interest in the intersection between words and images than the famous (and famously short-lived) imagism. Despite the ongoing fascination with all things visual throughout the period, imagism is often undervalued, read as a less successful precursor to subsequent developments.[37]

The story of imagism's founding is well rehearsed: after editing H.D.'s "Hermes of the Ways," Ezra Pound scrawled "H.D. Imagiste" at the bottom of the page before sending it to Harriet Monroe at *Poetry* for publication in 1912. The story, and the ways it has been retold, speaks to the limited lenses through which the movement was perceived from the start, namely as a marketing technique for H.D. to get published.[38] This perspective on what was at stake for writers associated with the movement—H.D., Pound, Richard Aldington, F. L Flint—was also seen as contributing to its "failure."

As I have highlighted in Pound's manifestos, descriptions of imagist poetry suggested that images should be presented as something fixed. Despite fierce disagreement with Pound over nearly everything else associated with the movement, this core understanding was shared by Amy Lowell, who both wrote in and did much to publicize the new style. As she describes in a preface to the 1915 *Some Imagist Poets*, imagism was about exactitude. The aim was "to present an image (hence the name: 'Imagist'). . . . We believe that poetry should render particulars exactly and not deal in vague generalities, however magnificent and sonorous. . . . To produce poetry that is hard and clear, never blurred nor indefinite."[39] To Pound's granite, then, we may add another cluster of associated ideas: "hard and clear," definite, rendering particulars exactly.

During the nineteen-teens, imagism was publicized as a fresh new approach that broke away from the verbosity that Pound found distasteful in Romantic verse. The excitement over poetry that was hard and clear, however, did not last long. Almost as soon as it emerged, the emphasis on precision started to read a bit too much like restriction, out of touch with the "variety and complexity" that Eliot identified as defining characteristics of the modern age.[40] Tensions arose over both style and marketing. In the preface to *Some Imagist Poets*, Lowell—who by this point was in a battle with Pound for control of the movement—alludes to "differences of taste and judgment" and "growing tendencies . . . forcing them [contributors] along different paths."[41] And by the 1930 printing of the *Imagist Anthology*, the note prefacing the edition opens with the premise that imagism was already dead: "To prevent any possible misunderstanding, the announcement is here made that this volume is not intended as an attempt to revive Imagism."[42] Instead, the book was meant as a collection of the work of individuals who had formerly written imagist verse but had "developed along varying lines," though they "still feel friendly."[43] Similarly, Ford Maddox Ford begins his foreword to the volume by wistfully reflecting, "those were the days."[44]

If writers invested in the movement quickly became dismissive, so too did people on the outside. As Joseph Frank argues, "Imagism was important not so much for any actual poetry written by Imagist poets—no one knew quite what an Imagist poet was—but rather because it opened the way for later developments."[45] Within literary history, imagism became a footnote, a set of ideas about images and words that were perceived as less significant than the later work that writers such as Pound and H.D. produced in the genre of the epic long poem, whose temporal expansion was seen as capable of capturing more complexity.

Just as imagism was considered over almost before it began, so too was H.D. perceived to be gone before her time. H.D. Imagiste's intimate association with imagism led scholars such as Randall Jarrell to declare in 1945—at which point H.D. was still actively writing and publishing—that "H.D. is History."[46] H.D. disappears (excepting references to Pound's poems to her), for example, from the pages of Hugh Kenner's influential *The Pound Era* after the "fall" of imagism. Even among those who respect and study H.D.'s work, the tendency is to read her earlier imagist and later epic poems as representing two utterly distinct branches of thought, the later signaling a complete break from and disavowal of her earlier fascination with the intersection of language and vision.

Although it was Pound's reading of H.D.'s poem "Hermes of the Ways" that led to the codification of the imagist movement, her ideas about images were never reducible to his, as evidenced by her few published comments on vision. Significantly, though, in critical accounts that have sought to rediscover H.D., her differences from Pound are always coded as a movement away from literal vision; the indeterminacy of her work is interpreted as something that has to be explained away using nonliteral vision (psychoanalytic and prophetic). In *H.D. and the Image*, for example, Rachel Connor convincingly makes the case that H.D.'s reputation has been diminished by the fact that scholars and readers have been too quick to box her into Pound's idea of the image and, when that was found to be lacking, to assume she must be as well.[47] The way Connor makes her case is by investigating H.D.'s involvement in alternative kinds of vision: psychoanalysis (through her sessions with Freud and her *Tribute to Freud*, in which she discusses them), psychic (linked to her Moravian heritage, which she discusses in *The Gift*), and cinematic (particularly through her involvement with the POOL production company and her role as actress in Kenneth Macpherson's 1930 *Borderline*).

While this approach enables us to connect H.D.'s earlier imagist work with her later long poems and epics, a distinct gain, it often does so at the expensive of a complex presentation of the image. In other words, H.D.'s ideas about vision are only permitted to become complex when they move away from the visual and toward more metaphysical ideas about vision (psychic and spiritual). In the few places she publishes explicitly about vision, however, H.D. never separates the two. In *Notes on Thought and Vision*, she describes the connections between "vision of two kinds—vision of the womb and vision of the brain," the former signifying prophecy and the latter more literal sight.[48] Similarly, in a rare review of John Gould Fletcher's *Goblins and Pagodas*, H.D. dissociates vision from stability: "[Fletcher] uses the direct image, it is true, but he seems to use it as a means of evoking other and vaguer images."[49] Here, H.D. links the direct image, which we might associate with Pound's vision, to "vaguer" ones that refused to be pinned down. While she expands on the idea of the image, that is, exploring its many meanings, she does not disavow the actual visual image, working instead to expand the possibilities of it. In reading poems from both H.D.'s earliest published volume, *Sea Garden* (1916), and her 1946 *Trilogy*, widely regarded as a move away from her imagist roots, I want to use the elements of movement and temporality that are operative in ASL poetry to link the two in an embrace, rather than an abandonment, of the literal visual image.

If Pound's understanding of the image relies on a certain stillness, H.D's is full of motion. While H.D. rarely wrote explicitly of her aesthetic principles in the way that Pound did, the opening poem *Sea Garden* provides her own version of a poetics of the image, one that is specifically associated not with fixity but with dynamic change. The poem reads as follows:

> Rose, harsh rose,
> marred and with stint of petals,
> meager flower, thin,
> sparse of leaf,
>
> More precious
> than a wet rose
> single on a stem—
> you are caught in the drift.
>
> Stunted, with small leaf,
> you are flung on the sand,
> you are lifted
> in the crisp sand
> that drives in the wind.
>
> Can the spice-rose
> drip such acrid fragrance
> hardened in a leaf?[50]

Here, H.D. provides a rehabilitation of what is perhaps the most clichéd symbol in all of literature, the rose, so often used to represent romantic love, delicacy, and beauty. In "Sea Rose," however, that general image is replaced with a much more specific one: it is a sea rose that H.D. is interested in, a flower that resists the connotations of the more romanticized image, not gently offered to a lover but "flung on the sand, / you are lifted / in the crisp sand / that drives in the wind," the verbs actively emphasizing its shifting condition.

The rose's beauty, that which makes it "more precious" to the speaker "than a wet rose / single on a stem," is the fact that it is "caught in the drift"—the elemental forces that tear away at the flower, rendering it "harsh," "marred," "stint of petals," "meager," "thin," and "sparse of leaf." It is this unexpected set of qualities that are identified as desirable. They are indications of strength, the ability to literally weather the storm. This depiction also functions to introduce readers to the poet's idea of images; the sea rose works for H.D. as a visual because it is not idealized, because it is rough around the edges. The frailty of the more realistic rose as opposed to the symbol is emphasized by the whiteness that surrounds the words on the page, like the frothing sea rushing in around the flower.

In addition to being a poem about nature (and a different kind of natural beauty), and like Stein's "A Carafe, That Is a Blind Glass," "Sea Rose" is also a commentary on the ways we usually read images, the kinds of roses that tend to appear in our poetry, and why these easy symbolic associations are problematic. Avoiding the poetic tropes associated with roses, H.D. presents us with a prosaic, imperfect flower, calling our attention to the ways actual flowers interact with their environments, ways that rarely lead to that idealized form. Roses are delicate. The world moves around them, tearing at them. It is that resilience that H.D. celebrates here. She also opens this, her first volume of verse, with a strong message: her images will not be idealized but will be linked to objects in the world, objects that move and are damaged by that movement.

Throughout the book, H.D. returns to this concept of the image: one marked by imperfections that suggest experience. In what is perhaps H.D.'s most famous imagist poem, "Hermes of the Ways," the beauty of the image is again presented through its movement, a movement conditioned by interaction with natural elements:

The hard sand breaks,
and the grains of it
are clear as wine.

Far off over the leagues of it,
the wind,
playing on the wide shore,
piles little ridges,
and the great waves
break over it.[51]

The sand may be hard and tiny (à la Pound), but it is a hardness in constant motion, caught in a cycle of being blown (one might imagine it slithering) into ridges by the wind, then swept away by the waves breaking over it before being returned to shore with the next swell, only to be swept up by the wind again.[52]

Following on this theme, "Sheltered Gardens" offers an explicit critique of images divorced from their surroundings, from their time. "For this beauty," the beauty of the static image, of the sheltered garden, the speaker notes,

> beauty without strength,
> chokes out life.
> I want wind to break,
> scatter these pink-stalks,
> snap off their spiced heads,
> fling them about with dead leaves—
> spread the paths with twigs[53]

The diction is violent, ripping through the delicate images of pink petals like the winds the speaker describes wanting to fling them into. As in the previous two poems, emphasis is placed on activity, suggesting an actual state of affairs in the world—the ravages of time and elemental forces—rather than the stillness of Platonic essences. Nearly each line of the stanza begins with a verb that attempts to keep the flowers in motion, in which state the speaker finds them more agreeable both as things in the world and as poetic images.[54]

The most classically imagist of H.D.'s poems, in other words, take great effort to elaborate an image specifically marked by movement, by change occurring over time. This is a version of the image that the poet carried with her throughout her career, across her so-called break with imagism and into her work with longer poetic forms. In "Tribute to the Angels," the second book of her war epic *Trilogy*, H.D. demonstrates a continued interest in the problem of stasis, of using language to fix things. Pressed to undertake precisely such a task with regard to an image that the speaker understands as multifaceted, alive, and extended in time, she balks:

> "What is the jewel colour?"
> green-white, opalescent,
>
> with under-layer of changing blue,
> with rose-vein; a white agate
>
> with a pulse uncooled that beats yet,
> faint blue-violet;
>
> it lives, it breathes,
> it gives off—fragrance?
>
> I do not know what it gives,
> a vibration that we can not name
>
> for there is no name for it;
> my patron said, "name it";

I said, I can not name it,
there is no name[55]

The quotation marks around the patron's demands situate them within a formalized linguistic tradition, as opposed to the speaker's words, which, even when in direct reply to the interlocutor, are free from standardized punctuation. Even before the speaker of the opening question is identified as being in a position of financial power over the poem's primary speaker ("patron"), he is already been associated with a system of rules. This link to finance invites a rereading of the implications of his description of the color as a "jewel," tying the aesthetic observation to objects with monetary value.

Significantly, once identified in line 12 as the patron, the character immediately shifts from the interrogative to the imperative mode. Calling the words that the primary speaker has just finished using to communicate about the color into question, he demands that she ascribe to it a singular name. The primary speaker's description actively avoids this move to stabilize, referencing both colors that refuse to be pinned down ("green-white," "opalescent," "under-layer of changing blue," "blue-violet") and descriptors that ascribe movement ("changing," "vibration") and life ("rose-vein," "pulse uncooled that beats yet," "it lives, it breaths"). Against the impulse to stabilize and commodify, the primary speaker insists that visual impressions are multivalent and changing.

This presentation of the visual image deliberately points to a failure of conventional language to capture what the speaker finds significant about it. And this becomes a central thematic strand of the poem. When the Lady, who becomes Mary through the alchemic transmutation of language—"Now polish the crucible / and set the jet of flame // under, til *marah-mar* / are melted, fuse and join // and change and alter, / mer, mere, mère, mater, Maia, Mary, // Star of the Sea, Mother"—arrives, apparently to provide "Holy Wisdom" that will "retrieve / what she lost the race, // given over to sin, to death," the "Book of Life" she carries is specifically "not / the tome of the ancient wisdom" but rather "the blank pages / of the unwritten volume of the new."[56]

Significantly, this wisdom, like the image of Valli's spiderweb, cannot be captured in the pages of a book and is linked to vision. "This is no rune nor riddle," the poem's speaker cryptically explains; "it is happening everywhere ... but you have seen for yourself ... you have seen for yourself."[57] She insists that the truth is engaged experientially, visually, and that in the same way that the color that fascinates the speaker cannot be named and the pages of the book cannot be filled, it cannot be explained. The blank pages of the book also, and unexpectedly, link H.D.'s understanding of vision to silence, to something that escapes fixed knowledge. The refrain of "we have seen" is picked up in the twenty-ninth section of the poem, in which the various incarnations of the Lady are presented:

> we have seen her, an empress,
> magnificent in pomp and grace,
>
> and we have seen her
> with a single flower
>
> or a cluster of garden-pinks
> in a glass beside her;
>
> we have seen her snood
> drawn over her hair,
>
> or her face set in profile
> with the blue hood and stars;[58]

The catalogue continues for eighteen more couplets (and two sections) before the speaker reveals, "none of these, none of these / suggest her as I saw her."[59] The description of the Lady, that is, does not provide the kind of seeing or understanding that the speaker is after. She comes closest when she compares what she has witnessed to movement: the "gracious friendliness / of the marble sea-maids in Venice, // who climb the altar-stair"—in other words, when she moves away from more traditional, static visual description.[60]

## The Past in the Present

*Enter H.D., wrapped in a palimpsest* —HARRY CROSBY, "Aeronautics"

The presentation of the visual image as indeterminate and in motion resonates with H.D.'s primary literary trope for discussing the temporal expansiveness of her later work: the palimpsest. H.D.'s interest in the figure has frequently been analyzed in relation to her spiritualism, read as a metaphor for her belief in a metaphysical relationship between past and present, but rarely in terms of actual sight. What is most striking about the palimpsest is that the temporal leaps it allows are decidedly *not* metaphysical; they are physically, visually present. If H.D.'s first volume of poetry, the one most associated with imagism, begins with a poetics—indeed, an ethics—of the image as moving, so too does her work engage the other unexpected aspect of visual language: time. As we saw, one of the interesting elements that ASL as visual language adds to the discussion is an expansion of time, a quality usually ascribed to the long poem. Even in work that has been described as falling neatly in this period of H.D.'s career, however, she ties this expansion to literal visual images.[61]

H.D. begins her 1926 novel *Palimpsest* with a definition suggesting her understanding of the concept:

> a palimpsest, i.e., a
> parchment from which one writing has been
> erased to make room for another.[62]

Palimpsests provide visible trace of the past in the present, appearing on parchment or paper that has been written on several times, earlier versions having been imperfectly erased. Past marks leave visible traces that poke through the most recent writing, shading its meaning with their presence, in addition to any semantic significance it might be possible to make out. Palimpsests enable, to return to Eliot, a literal presentness of the past, an extension of it into the present. Significantly for our purposes, H.D. connects such presence to her experimentation with the intersection between visual images and words.

*Trilogy* is driven by a sense of the palimpsestic, of the past becoming visible when one scrapes away at the text. "How can you scratch out // indelible ink of the palimpsest / of past misadventure?" the speaker asks, suggesting visual figure as a means of engagement in, rather than escape from, the present.[63] *Trilogy* opens with a nontextual palimpsest drawn from the poet's own experience of living in London during the bombings of the Second World War. Contemplating the ruins of a hollowed-out structure, where layers of the past have been made literally visible, the speaker describes,

> An incident here and there,
> And rails gone (for guns)
> From your (and my) old town square:
>
> . . . . . . . . . . . . . . . . . . . . . . . . . . . . .
>
> there, as here, ruin opens
> the tomb, the temple; enter,
> there as here, there are no doors:

> the shrine lies open to the sky,
> the rain falls, here, there
> sand drifts; eternity endures:
>
> ruin everywhere, yet as the fallen roof
> leaves the sealed room
> open to the air,
>
> so, through our desolation,
> thoughts stir, inspiration stalks us
> through gloom[64]

Deploying "ruin" as a verb, rather than a noun, emphasizes the activity (and culpability) inherent in the image of buildings whose roofs have been blasted away, leaving them open to the sky. This active process of ruin is everywhere part of eternity, disallowing stasis. It is this reality that people become aware of when encountering the bombed-out buildings, their minds stirred into motion just as elemental forces (shifting sand, falling rain) alter those no-longer-sealed rooms.

Whatever metaphorical associations the speaker draws from this visual image, the political force of the poem remains linked to its status as a literal image. Bits of older buildings are actually made visible by the violent removal of that which had covered them. Setting contemporary violence in the context of earlier cycles of destruction is H.D.'s most directly political use of the palimpsest. Significantly, and in defiance of critiques that suggested the visual image was too bounded to perform effective socially aware work, neither this political engagement nor the temporal expansiveness she invokes to make her point draws her away from optical vision.

In a letter to Norman Holmes Pearson, H.D. recounts an actual encounter with the destroyed home of a neighbor that may have provided the inspiration for this particular image: "The house next door was struck another night. We came home and simply waded through glass. . . . One of the group found some pleasure in the sight of the tilted shelves and the books tumbled on the floor. He gave a decisive football kick with his army boot to the fattest volume. It happened actually to be Browning. He demanded dramatically, 'what is the use of all this now?'"[65] In some ways, the entirety of *Trilogy* can be interpreted as a response to this question: What is the use of language in the face of the real-world palimpsests violently produced in the context of war? As I suggested in my discussion of movement, one answer that H.D. provides in the poem is the refusal of stasis, the embrace of an indeterminacy that enables a certain amount of personal control in how one interprets events or images and the disavowal of a politics that would seek to use the idea of definitive truth to impose its will on others. "Ruin opens / the tomb" suggests both activity and, homonymically, language—the sound of "rune" resonating through "ruin," connecting movement and language to this particular visual image.

Another way H.D. develops this notion of playful and liberating indeterminacy is through the palimpsestic nature of words themselves. Analogous to Crane's linguistic density, as the poem's speaker explains later in the first book, individual words function as poems in and of themselves, "anagrams, cryptograms, / little boxes, conditioned // to hatch butterflies."[66] Words as butterflies again ties language to motion, as well indeterminacy. H.D. actively "melt[s], fuse[s] and join[s]" the bitter *"marah-mar"* into "mer, mere, mère, mater, Maia, Mary."[67] Similarly, she moves from "venery" to "Venus whose name is kin // to venerate, / venerator" and the inaccurate identification of "word" as the root of "sword."[68] These traces are actually (or at least they actually appear to be) present in the words themselves, histories of their roots and etymologies visible in the letters on the page. At the heart of indeterminacy and slippage, that is, H.D. again brings us back to a concrete, visual image. As in her earlier work, these superficially opposing ideas about what the image can mean are presented as intrinsically interconnected.

## Palimpsestic Fiction

In addition to enhancing our reading of works that have long been associated with the visual image, the suggestion of the relationship between movement, temporality, and the image in the context of language helps us to uncover visual structures of works not typically associated with vision at all, including those of William Faulkner. It has become a critical commonplace when describing the work of Faulkner to focus on his lyrical or musical use of language, his attention to elements of aurality and orality in language.[69] As William E. H. Meyer Jr. summarizes the near consensus, "Faulkner's Southern lyricism and historicism continue to promote aurality over hard-nosed vision in novels including *The Sound and the Fury* and *Light in August.*"[70] As I have demonstrated through the history of imagism, there is a pervasive attempt in modernist studies to separate off modes of writing specifically perceived as visual from other (usually—though strikingly not in Meyer's article—more critically valued) approaches to modernist aesthetics. The assumption behind such divisions is that the visual image is something concrete and specific ("hard-nosed"), that it is inextricably bound to a particular moment and place. Both modernist epic and aurally focused work, by contrast, tend to be associated with expansiveness through time and space. These biased assumptions about the possibilities of visual language have limited perception of explicitly visual poetics. They have also occluded the significance of the visual within texts such as *The Sound and the Fury*.[71]

*The Sound and the Fury* is famous for being a difficult text, a difficulty that derives in large part from its structure: the novel is presented from a variety of perspectives—those of Benjy, Quentin, Jason, and a third-person narrator who focuses primarily on events concerning Dilsey. Unlike the simultaneity of perspectives of a cubist painting or a Stein poem, these perspectival shifts in Faulkner are associated with the epic sweep of his narrative and are therefore read as unrelated to imagism.[72] As I have argued in both this chapter and chapter 3, however, both imagism in particular and an understanding of visual language more generally can and do incorporate temporality in ways that resonate with *The Sound and the Fury*.

This is most apparent in the novel's first section, "April Seventh, 1928," which is told from the perspective of the Compsons' thirty-three-year-old intellectually disabled son, Benjy. It is within Benjy's section that Faulkner is most formally experimental, especially in the ways he represents time. The section contains multiple scenes occurring over several decades, which the novel moves between with no warning apart from an inconsistent use of italics. This juxtaposition has made the first section the most challenging part of the text for most readers to follow. Indeed, Faulkner's original plan was to color code each of the fourteen separate scenes he identified.[73] In 1929, when the novel was initially published, such a color scheme was expensive and impractical, and the text instead registered some of these jumps in italics, although, as George R. Stewart points out, the typographical shifts do not necessarily indicate a separate scene, often leading to more confusion than they resolve.[74]

The difficulties of the text's first section, in other words, arise in part from Faulkner's engagement with the modernist techniques of fragmentation and juxtaposition that we encountered in chapter 3 and in part because of pragmatic limitations of printing. Despite having multiple extratextual explanations, however, they have most commonly been attributed to Benjy's disability. The connection was made first and most famously by Faulkner himself. In an interview with Jean Stein vanden Heuve, Faulkner dismissively suggests, "You can't feel anything for Benjy because he doesn't feel anything. . . . He was an animal."[75] Similarly, despite admitting to conceiving the entire novel based around Benjy's section, Faulkner describes its nonlinear structure to a group of undergraduates in 1957 as "part of the failure": "It seemed to me that the book approached nearer the dream if the groundwork of it was laid by the idiot, who was incapable of relevancy."[76]

Alongside the novel's title, taken from Macbeth's final soliloquy, in which the character describes life as "a tale / Told by an idiot, full of sound and fury / Signifying nothing," these comments have been taken to mean that Benjy's status as an intellectually disabled individual, marked in particular by his repeated bellowing, renders him incapable of producing meaning.[77] Beyond the fact that Macbeth, particularly at this point in the play, is an odd authority to turn to for rational wisdom and that, in any case, the "tale / told by an idiot, full of sound and fury" refers to life, that is, something of immense complexity, the character has been more often interpreted, as Stacy Burton notes, "as a passive, blank slate upon which events are written."[78] Trapped by biases regarding intellectual disability that restrict readings of disabled characters such as Benjy to particular (and predictable) tropes—markers of displeased deities, punishments for familial sin, evildoers whose disability becomes an apparently legible index of their own malfeasance—Benjy and his narrative voice are interpreted as convenient symbols for the "corrupted" blood of his once-prosperous family, the corporeal evidence of their descent.

Using disabled characters as narrative prostheses, to return to Sharon Snyder and David Mitchell's argument, is always problematic, but it is particularly counterproductive here as it disallows a recognition of the solutions that Benjy's voice offers to some of the novel's (and the Compsons') central problems: the passing away of the old South and the related fall of the family's fortunes. As more careful readers have noted, it is factually inaccurate to suggest that Benjy's section lacks an internal coherence. Even if the writer does not provide typographical (or colored) hints to the reader, the supposedly irrelevant Benjy repeatedly demonstrates a photographic recollection of precise experiences and exchanges of dialogue that are linked through clear logical patterns, as in the following series of scenes from the very beginning of the novel:

> "Wait a minute." Luster said. "You snagged on that nail again. Cant you never crawl through here without snagging on that nail."
>
> *Caddy uncaught me and we crawled through. Uncle Maury said to not let anybody see us, so we better stoop over, Caddy said. Stoop over, Benjy. Like this, see. We stooped over and crossed the garden, where the flowers rasped and rattled against us. The ground was hard. We climbed the fence, where the pigs were grunting and snuffing. I expect they're sorry because one of them got killed today, Caddy said. The ground was hard, churned and knotted.*
>
> *Keep your hands in your pockets, Caddy said. Or they'll get froze. You don't want your hands froze on Christmas, do you.*
>
> "It's too cold out there." Versh said. "You don't want to go out doors."[79]

These synchronic scenes are linked to specific sensory experiences, which allow readers who are looking to identify the moment the scene shifts: Benjy's feeling of catching his clothing on a nail while trying to climb under the fence, the cold of the winter days. Also significant is the clarity of these memories of events, which, we piece together later, occur decades apart. Benjy is able to report the specific sounds of the pigs, the movements of the flowers, the texture of the ground, the sound of Luster's and Caddie's dialects. Rather than making the character appear to have no mind, or a mind that is unknowable, presenting Benjy's impressions in this manner functions to align him with other, non-intellectually-disabled characters whose thoughts are narrated through the style of stream of consciousness. In this way, and against Faulkner's intentions, Benjy's portrayal can be read in conversation with Sherwood Anderson's and Charlie Chaplin's depictions of the dangers of communicative norms; readers see that Benjy has complex and meaningful thought processes. He is unable to express them in conventional speech, however, and it is this that leads to his castration and institutionalization.

The sensory links that provide this logical lattice also function to establish a relationship between past and present that is productively distinct from those experienced by the other characters. While Benjy tends to be read as having no conception of time, his family is seen to be overburdened by it. For Quentin and Jason, the other Compsons granted their own sections of the text, the past functions as something that one is either trapped in or haunted by. In an analysis of Faulkner's novel, Jean-Paul Sartre argues that "time is, above all, *that which separates.*"[80] It is what fragments the novel into these difficult slivers, what makes it impossible for the characters to connect with one another at the moments they most need support, what estranges the Compsons from the more illustrious history of their family.

Sartre describes such temporal collapse as a process by which "the hero's consciousness 'sinks back into the past' and rises only to sink back again. The present is not, it becomes. Everything *was*."[81] In this reading, the blurred chronology becomes a problem, not merely for readers struggling through the text but for the characters who are prohibited from moving forward by an intense connection to what came before that shatters the present, bleeding it of its potential, disallowing its wholeness. The reflection of this temporal instability onto form is perceived as a haunting from which no one is permitted to escape.

But as I have argued, this account does not accurately reflect Benjy's experience of time, in which events across years are knitted together. As the passage quoted earlier demonstrates, time as experienced by Benjy is decidedly *not* separation. The collapse of past into present enables him to experience Caddy, to inhabit a time when she and he were taking a wintry walk, rather than being confined to a present when she has always already gone. Reversing Sartre's suggestion that "everything has already happened" in the novel, such a model suggests that perhaps everything is happening now.[82] Readers experience this continuous present tense; the lack of paragraph differentiation between time periods collapses all of time in an undifferentiated palimpsest on the page. Benjy's responses to these events suggest that he similarly does not distinguish between them. Coming out of a section in which he was sent to deliver a letter to Mrs. Patterson from his uncle Maury (with whom Mrs. Patterson was having an affair), for example, Benjy panics when he is intercepted by Mr. Patterson and runs down the hill. The description of this event and what happens next reads as follows: "*He took the letter. Mrs Patterson's dress was caught on the fence. I saw her eyes again and I ran down the hill.* 'They aint nothing over yonder but houses. . . . We going down to the branch.'"[83] As Luster's dialogue after the italics reveals, in the text's present Benjy is still running from the couple, despite the fact that the action in this context lacks the logic it had in the earlier scene. For Benjy, the scene jumps function not as recollections of time gone by but as an enactment of Stein's continuous present.

As these brief examples demonstrate, in Benjy's section we are presented with an alternative, nonlinear model of temporality, one that resonates strongly with the ways H.D.'s palimpsest imagines nonlinear processing as a movement away from totalizing models of fixed knowledge. It is precisely such an alternative way of interacting with their cultural and familial past that the Compsons desperately need. Read in this way, Benjy opens the novel not as metaphor of the family's fallen status but as a structural alternative to the tragic logic that insists on a particular, teleological descent into destruction. Because of their own biases, however, both the characters and Faulkner fail to pick up on it. And it is this failure to recognize the alternative to their own temporality offered by Benjy's worldview, rather than the "degraded" genes that his difference is interpreted as representing, that makes the family's tragedy inevitable.

While *The Sound and the Fury* is not an obviously visual novel in that it is not characterized by lengthy descriptions of what things look like, its similarities to the work of H.D. suggest that it might be read as structurally visual in its approach to temporality, as well as in the ways it engages with elements of nonlinearity and indeterminacy that the ASL poetry of Bernard Bragg and Clayton Valli demonstrates are fundamental components of visual language. In addition to expanding the contexts in which we might think about Deaf culture and language to include works such as *The Sound and the Fury*, *Trilogy*, or H.D.'s imagist poetry, that is, Deaf epistemology reveals the connections between modernists' interest in visual thinking (the image) and temporality (epic expansion, often expressed through techniques such as stream of consciousness), which have nearly always been approached as entirely separate projects. As I hope to have demonstrated in this chapter, as well as those that precede it, complicating the idea of this difference as a tension has wide-reaching implications for both our understanding of specific texts or authors and our approach to modernist aesthetics more broadly.

# Epilogue: The Textual Body

*The living is. The living communicates. It
transforms and reinvents itself in, and through, its
own language. The genetic code becomes flesh.*

—LOUIS BEC, "Life Art"

As we move further into the twenty-first century, the importance of understanding the implications of visual and embodied languages has only increased, and the insights into them offered by both Deaf and modernist studies become all the more relevant. One of the most dramatic developments in discourses surrounding embodied language occurred on April 14, 2003, when the Human Genome Project (HGP) completed its thirteen-year effort to identify the twenty to twenty-five thousand genes present in human DNA and to sequence their three billion chemical bases. The publication of the genome ushered in an era in which gene sequences can be read, if not yet interpreted, either off a computer screen or in the 130 volumes required to print it in its entirety. And that language of reading has been an important part of the discourse surrounding the HGP in ways that have shaped our understanding of its significance.[1] As the National Human Genome Research Institute's website describes the achievement, "Having the complete sequence of the human genome is similar to having all the pages of a manual needed to make the human body. The challenge now is to determine how to read the contents of these pages."[2]

Part of the appeal of the textual metaphor is that it functions at multiple levels. As James C. Wilson explains, the sequence is frequently referred to as the "Book of Life": "digitization/alphabetization of the genetic body-text has fostered the much used analogy of DNA as a molecular language where the 'letters' are bases, the 'words' are genes, and the 'book' is the complete genome."[3] Replication errors, by extension, become misspellings or misreadings. These descriptions have provided a useful tool that enables science communicators to explain genetics to a broad audience. But despite the ease of the metaphor, the parallels to textuality have, as Wilson himself notes, limitations.[4] At its most basic level, metaphor enables us to understand something unfamiliar (in this case, the genome) through a direct comparison with something we recognize (here, text and the reading practices associated with it). While this is both pragmatic and necessary as a means of navigating novel experiences and contexts, it risks glossing over ways in which the new concept might significantly differ from what we are comparing it to.

As I have argued throughout the book, modernism offers alternative ways of thinking about reading, interpretation, and, specifically, metaphoric relationality that have deep investments in the embodiment of text. When we talk about reading genetic text, in terms of both the processes our bodies already use to decode genetic information and the understanding we are now trying to develop of these processes, our activities may well be more in line with the interpretive practices necessary to read a difficult modernist poem than an instruction manual. At present, the genome is in some sense both readable and illegible; as in a modernist text, recognizing the constituent parts (words, genes) does not equate to understanding the ways they work together to produce (semantic or corporeal) meaning. The genome represents perhaps the purest example of Hart Crane's idea of the "genetic" text, which Crane believed would provide "a new *word*, never before spoken and impossible to actually enunciate."[5] Just as conventional spoken language failed to provide satisfactory communicative exchanges in Crane's poetry, determining the ways our bodies decode genetic information involves working out new approaches for conceptualizing how bodies interact with information we have transcribed as text.

As I outline in my earlier discussion of his work, Crane understood metaphor as an "organic principle" that connects one thing to another through "associational meanings."[6] His interest lay in how this process disrupts authorially dictated meaning (which would restrict reader engagement with text to a kind of scavenger hunt to try and uncover it) by implicitly shifting the meaning-making power onto readers, who bring their own associations to the table. There are ways the analogy fails, but there is a potentially productive parallel in the amount of instability Crane's conception of metaphor introduces into reading. As it turns out, and like Crane's own stacked words, genes can have multiple, potentially contradictory meanings. Richard Lewontin and Richard Levins provide one example: "the code sequence

GTAAGT is sometimes read by the cell as an instruction to insert the amino acids *valine* and *serine* in a protein, but sometimes it signals a place where the cell machinery is to cut up and edit the message, and sometimes it may be only a spacer."[7] The fact that humans have far fewer genes than most geneticists were expecting (early estimates put the number in the hundred thousands; in reality, we have something like twenty-one thousand, which is less than the number necessary to make a cabbage) means that there are aspects of the reading process that we do not understand. Whether we call that process reading (or decoding, interpreting, or anything else) is itself not the crucial issue. What is important is that we come to understand the complexities of the process, the ways in which it complicates our assumptions about the relationship between signifier and signified. Modernism's fascination and experimentation with the unexpected ways that parts can combine not only to produce but also to destabilize meaning may well prove useful in thinking through how information is processed, especially when that information is represented as text.

There is an obvious danger here of pushing a point too far. But whether or not modernist interpretive practices provide helpful ways of thinking about reading the language of genetics, the HGP and the discourse that has surrounded it point to an abiding, indeed increasing, interest in the intersection of bodies and text. The preceding chapters have traced some of the ways that consideration of Deaf culture, history, linguistics, and literature productively bears on these issues, specifically by reframing questions that have been central to the field of modernist studies: the tension between an emerging celebrity culture and theories of impersonality, the apparent paradox of an aesthetic simultaneously fascinated with primitivism and making it new, the juxtaposition and indeterminacy at the heart of modernist difficulty, and the perceived disjunction between imagism and epic in the careers of many prominent modernist writers. In discussing Deaf and disability studies in these contexts, it has been my aim to make the case for the widespread relevance of the field to suggest some nonidentitarian directions in which literary disability studies might move. As conversations surrounding the HGP illustrate, far from being a niche concern of writers and artists at the beginning of the twentieth century, the implications of bodies conceived of as text are likely to shape the direction of scientific developments as well as ethical conversations and art practices surrounding them in the coming century. By excavating modernism's investments in these ideas, Deaf epistemology reveals surprising ways that modernist studies might contribute to these areas of inquiry.

One place we can already observe this contribution is in art practices that play at the border of the sciences and the humanities, between genetic bodies and words. One of the best known series of such works is Eduardo Kac's *Genesis*, described by the artist as "transgenic artwork" that began with the creation of an "artist's gene" by translating a sentence from the book of Genesis—"Let man have dominion over the fish of the sea, and over the fowl of the air, and over every living thing that moves upon the earth"—into Morse code and converting the Morse code into DNA base pairs.[8] Like Randy Garber's *Made in Translation*, with which I began this book, *Genesis* highlights the processes of translation and transcription in the transmission of information and the creative potential of what emerges in the spaces of semantic slippage. Kac's 1999 exhibit of *Genesis* consisted of a petri dish containing the bacteria, a camera that enabled participation via the Internet, and an ultraviolet light box. People watching online were invited to activate the light, which caused mutations in the bacteria. At the end of the exhibition, the DNA was translated back through Morse code into English. The mutated sentence read: "LET AAN HAVE DOMINION OVER THE FISH OF THE SEA AND OVER THE FOWL OF THE AIR AND OVER EVERY LIVING THING THAT IOVES UA EON THE EARTH."[9]

The effect of the radiation on the words "man" (AAN), "moves" (IOVES), and "upon" (UA EON) provides rich interpretive possibilities. Rather than exerting dominion over the fish or fowl, it is man himself that is altered in the reverse translation, through an embodied linguistic process that is linked to movement. The word "moves" itself is morphed into a cypher visually resembling "love." "Upon," formerly signifying a fixed point of reference, the location of man, is changed into a word that resembles a temporal marker—"eon"—an extension across geological time. As in "Salt in the Basement," in which gaps in translation are emphasized in order to encourage reflection on the material specificity of language (the slippage between the father's explanation of the salt and the boy's understanding that emerges out of the different ways their languages present information), *Genesis* highlights the indeterminacy produced through and around processes of translation, particularly as they encounter living organisms. The alteration of "man," "moves," and "upon" also points toward a shift in the relationship between humans and the natural world, undercutting the notion that the earth is something inert, a backdrop against which man is free to exert biblically authorized dominion over other living things. Instead, "upon," the word initially meant to link man to that world, also comes alive, shifting, interpenetrating, in a version of the ecological ethic that Sherwood Anderson gestured toward in his poetry.

This first stage of *Genesis* suggests that at the heart of considerations of (bacterially) embodied language, of living words, lies motion and indeterminacy that, as I discussed in chapters 3 and 4, ASL reveals to be foundationally linked to embodied language. These ideas also drive the second phase of *Genesis*, in which Kac used a protein produced by the Genesis gene to create three-dimensional sculptures, translating the genetic-text into visual art. This process of increasing dimensions is crucial to what Bec describes in the epigraph to this epilogue as "the genetic text becom[ing] flesh." In a 2003 news report, the BBC science editor David Whitehouse explained, "An organism's genome is a two-dimensional and static description of a living creature. To come to life it must be translated into action, rather like a screenplay must be turned into acting."[10] What enable that shift are the ways that the "text" is expressed in and through a living body (acting, signing, or just being).

Throughout *Deafening Modernism*, I have highlighted some of the pragmatic, ethical, philosophical, relational, political, and aesthetic implications of this interdimensional translation (the new modes of being together that emerge when semantic content cannot be separated from a human body signifying, the literary and artistic forms made possible by a language that moves through three spatial dimensions as well as time). It is the ethical and philosophical consequences of text "coming to life" that motivate this second part of *Genesis*, titled "Transcription Jewels." As Kac explains, the piece highlights the commodification of biological material and the "intersemiotic resonances that contribute to expand the historically rich intertextuality between word, image, and spatial form. The process of biological mutation extends it into time."[11] Like Valli's "Dew on a Spiderweb" or Bragg's "Flowers and Moonlight on the Spring Water," the apparently fixed visual image is recognized as shifting, fluctuating, temporally expanding not only coincident with these intersections but as a result of them.

The sculptures' appearance reinforces these ideas. Set within a wooden box, the first is a gold cast of the model of the protein structure, and the second is a glass bottle containing Genesis DNA. Viewed together, the shape of the glass and the twisting gold of the protein model resemble a genie being released, a visual allusion that resonates at multiple levels. As Kac suggests in the preceding quote, and as the visual reference to mythology supports, the three-dimensional rendering gestures toward temporal extension, both forward (into the future of biotechnology) and backward (to the ancient stories, as well as to the primitive form of life that the bacteria represents). Part of the irony that Kac highlights by referencing commodification (the precious glass bottles and gold referred to as jewels) is that the Genesis protein, while alive, is not natural. It is our ability to "read" the bacteria's DNA that enables the commodification, a process that suggests some of the ethical complications of reading bodies.[12]

If bodies can be conceptualized as language—sequenced and even "rewritten"—so too can text be considered alive. In the 2012 book *Animacies*, Mel Chen argues, "Language is as much alive as it is dead, and it is certainly material.... It is a corporeal, sensual embodied act. It is, by definition, animated."[13] As both her book and Kac's transgenic art suggest, the recognition of this fact and the process of unpacking its implications for the ways we conceptualize relationality between one another and the world in and through language will likely drive developments across a range of fields in coming years.

Throughout this book, I have worked to develop a Deaf epistemology that helps to highlight examples of writers, artists, and theorists thinking through similar complexities. Whether by modeling an ethics of relationality through embodied impersonality, the noncontradictory ways discourses can move simultaneously toward the past and the future, interpretive strategies for navigating indeterminacy that engage the body, or analyses of the visual image that invite us to register the movement and temporal expansion embedded within, Deaf epistemology provides a range of interpretive possibilities for engaging modernism that also gesture outward, offering surprising insight into conversations, including those surrounding contemporary genetic art, in which modernist studies has a great deal to contribute. By expanding the contexts in which we consider all of these fields, it is my hope that *Deafening Modernism* has revealed some of the approaches that analysis of the significances and possibilities of embodied language might take in the coming years.

# Notes

## Introduction

1. Randy Garber, "Conversing and Reversing," *Contemporary Impressions* 10.2 (2002): 2.

2. Lennard J. Davis, *Enforcing Normalcy: Disability, Deafness, and the Body* (London: Verso, 1995), 100.

3. "Deafen, v. 1–2," *The Oxford English Dictionary Online* (2011), http://www.oed.com/view/Entry/47692?redirectedFrom=deafen#eid.

4. Davis 100–101.

5. "Deafen, v. 1–2," *OED Online*.

6. For additional insights into what such crip epistemologies might look like, see the special double issue of the *Journal of Literary and Cultural Disability Studies* on "Cripistemologies," edited by Robert McRuer and Merri Lisa Johnson (vol. 8, nos. 2–3).

7. Davis 124. Following the convention, I use "Deaf" to refer to the cultural minority and "deaf" to refer to the audiological condition of deafness, as well as to describe individuals for whom (either because of age or the time in which they lived) it would not make sense to talk about a Deaf cultural identity. As this book makes clear, however, the distinction between deafness as physical state and deafness as cultural identity is not always (or ever) a clear one. For an excellent critique of this binary division, see Brenda Jo Brueggemann's *Deaf Subjects: Between Identities and Places* (New York: New York UP, 2009).

8. Within Deaf studies, the term "Deaf gain" has sometimes been used to counteract the sense of "hearing loss" as a negative experience by developing deafness as a valued identity category. There are times when ideas of Deaf gain overlap with those of Deaf insight or epistemology, but in my reading, Deaf gain functions primarily as a valorization of Deaf people and identity. I focus instead on Deaf epistemology because my interest in this project lies in emphasizing the ways such insight enhances our understanding of culture, history, and language broadly, regardless of hearing status.

9. Signed languages are not, of course, the only languages that are embodied. What I want to emphasize in using the term is the fact that unlike spoken languages, which can be recorded and played back without any reference to the original speaker, signed communication cannot be separated from the body. I return to this idea at the end of this chapter and elaborate on its implications in chapters 1 and 2, but I would just note here that the politics surrounding this embodiment have dramatically shaped perceptions of ASL in ways that have impacted its usage and development. Perceptions of signed languages have also been shaped by their insistent visibility. As I elaborate on in chapter 1, vision is not the only avenue for accessing signed information. Many DeafBlind individuals communicate using a language called Tactile ASL, which involves signing into the hands of another person. While similar, however, ASL and Tactile ASL are not identical. Because the majority of Deaf signers experience ASL visually and describe both their language and culture in these terms, it is the visual version of the language that is my primary focus.

10. Christopher Krentz's 2007 *Writing Deafness*, which examines deaf-authored nineteenth-century texts, as well as deaf characters that appear in the work of hearing writers, and Jennifer Esmail's 2013 *Reading Victorian Deafness*, which similarly focuses on the nineteenth century and, where it turns to literary analysis, on deaf characters and authors, are the notable exceptions to an almost complete lack of work on the intersections between English-language literature and Deaf studies. Christopher Krentz, *Writing Deafness: The Hearing Line in Nineteenth-Century American Literature* (Chapel Hill: U of North Carolina P, 2008); Jennifer Esmail, *Reading Victorian Deafness: Signs and Sounds in Victorian Literature and Culture* (Athens: Ohio UP, 2013).

11. While I refer to both deafness and disability as critical modes for engaging with literature throughout the book, I do not mean to entirely conflate the two. Many culturally Deaf people consider themselves members of a linguistic minority and very pointedly do not identify as disabled. This disidentification is itself problematic, as it establishes a new hierarchy in which "Deaf" emerges as a privileged term over "disabled." There remains a great deal of stigma associated with the term "disabled" in common parlance from which it may make pragmatic sense to distance oneself. The deployment of the term within disability studies, however, attempts to overturn such biases, emphasizing the productive force of the concept in ways that often apply to Deaf, as well as other kinds of disability, experiences. It is in this spirit that I use the terms and, at times, permit them to overlap.

12. Toni Morrison, *Playing in the Dark: Whiteness and the Literary Imagination* (New York: Vintage Books, 1993), 5.

13. Lennard J. Davis, introduction, *The Disability Studies Reader*, 2nd ed., ed. Lennard J. Davis (New York: Routledge, 2006), xv.

14. The transitory nature of ability is sometimes registered in disability studies by referring to people as TAB, or temporarily able bodied.

15. Sharon L. Snyder and David T. Mitchell, *Cultural Locations of Disability* (Chicago: U of Chicago P, 2006), 7.

16. Lennard J. Davis, *Bending Over Backwards: Disability, Dismodernism, and Other Uncomfortable Positions* (New York: New York UP, 2002), 2.

17. Tobin Siebers, *Disability Theory* (Ann Arbor: U of Michigan P, 2008), 25.

18. For a history of the rise of institutional medicine, see Michel Foucault, *The Birth of the Clinic*, 3rd ed. (New York: Routledge, 2003).

19. Tom Shakespeare, "The Social Model of Disability," *The Disability Studies Reader*, 3rd ed., ed. Lennard J. Davis (New York: Routledge, 2010), 269–270.

20. Ibid., 270.

21. Siebers 24. Under the rubric of complex embodiment, I would include nonnormative sensory and intellectual, as well as physical, ways of being.

22. Even within the Deaf community, there was initially resistance to this idea. Deaf people were so accustomed to the mistaken ways hearing linguistics described signed languages that many did not immediately side with Stokoe.

23. William Stokoe, *A Dictionary of American Sign Language on Linguistic Principles* (Washington, DC: Gallaudet UP, 1965).

24. Brueggemann 25.

25. The Clarke School, an oral school for deaf children, for example, advertises its success in providing "children who are deaf and hard of hearing with the listening, learning and spoken language skills they need to succeed." The school's philosophy of teaching "children to listen and speak, rather than use sign language," is intended "to prepare children to succeed in mainstream classrooms alongside their hearing peers," suggesting a correlation between educational success (as well as the ability to "listen") and oral language skills. Clarke Schools for Hearing and Speech, home page, 2013, http://www.clarkeschools.org/. There is a direct link between these kinds of messages and the disinclination of parents to teach deaf children to sign or to learn sign language themselves. The numbers are difficult to come by, but it is estimated that only between 3 and 25 percent of hearing parents of deaf children can sign. For more information on the lasting impacts of communication gaps between parents and children, see Cyril Courtin, "The Impact of Sign Language on the Cognitive Development of Deaf Children: The Case of Theories of Mind," *Journal of Deaf Studies and Deaf Education* 5.3 (2000): 266.

26. For a complication of the idea that novelty functioned as a motivation for aesthetic innovation in the twentieth century, see chapters 6 and 7 of Michael North's *Novelty: A History of the New* (Chicago: U of Chicago P, 2013).

27. Richard W. Bailey, *Speaking American: A History of English in the United States* (Oxford: Oxford UP, 2012), 17. Translation brought close to three hundred new words into English, though significantly fewer remain in usage.

28. Stamp Act, 1765, http://ahp.gatech.edu/stamp_act_bp_1765.html.

29. Alexis de Tocqueville, *Democracy in America* (New York: Penguin, 2003), 554.

30. Bailey 14.

31. As David Mitchell, Georgina Kleege, and others have importantly pointed out, the English language problematically uses the verb "to see" to refer to both vision and understanding, a conflation that suggests a general lack of comprehension (or intelligence) on the part of individuals with visual impairments; not "seeing" visually is all too frequently implicitly equated with not "seeing" the meaning of an idea. Throughout *Deafening Modernism*, I have tried to avoid this usage. Because we have yet to develop a sufficient range of alternative options for expressing the sentiment and its permutations, however, and because repetitive diction is frowned on in publishing, there are moments, such as this one, when I could not find a suitable alternative.

32. U.S. Bureau of the Census, *Historical Statistics of the United States, Colonial Times to 1970* (Washington, DC: U.S. Bureau of the Census, 1975).

33. This impulse to colonize was not new. The same cultural narratives of exceptionalism and manifest destiny had driven westward expansion and the subjugation

of indigenous peoples throughout the nineteenth century. What changed in 1989 was that these ideologies increasingly came to be directed overseas, an impulse that only intensified a year later with the closing of the frontier.

34. James W. Schepp, *Shepp's New York City Illustrated* (Chicago: Globe Bible Publishing Company, 1894), 455.

35. Ctd. in Bailey 144.

36. Joshua L. Miller, *Accented America: The Cultural Politics of Multilingual Modernism* (Oxford: Oxford UP, 2011), 9. Perhaps the fiercest proponent of a specifically "American" language was H. L. Mencken, whose 1921 *The American Language* outlines its benefits as a distinct idiom. See, in particular, the introduction. H. L. Mencken, *The American Language: An Inquiry into the Development of English in the United States*, 4th ed. (New York: Knopf, 1984).

37. Theodor Roosevelt, 1919, qtd. in James Crawford, *At War with Diversity: US Language Policy in an Age of Anxiety* (Clevedon, UK: Cromwell, 2000), 8.

38. Chap. 127, par. 177, sec. 1. The reference to "American" as the state's official language remained on the books until 1969, when the legislation was quietly amended to refer to "English."

39. Theodor Roosevelt, "Americanism," *Works of Theodore Roosevelt: Memorial Edition*, vol. 20 (New York: Scribner, 1926), 464–465.

40. Miller 36.

41. The ongoing desire to associate American identity with English monolingualism was most recently evidenced by the outcry over the 2014 Coca-Cola Super Bowl commercial, which featured a series of young girls singing "America the Beautiful" in English, Spanish, Tagalog, Mandarin, Hindi, Hebrew, Keres, Senegaleese-French, and Arabic. For more on the controversy, see Ethan Sacks, "Coca Cola's 'America the Beautiful' Super Bowl Commercial Angers Conservative Pundits," *New York Daily News* 3 February 2014, http://www.nydailynews.com/entertainment/tv-movies/coca-cola-super-bowl-ad-angers-conservatives-article-1.1600849.

42. Edward P. Smith, *Annual Report of the Commissioner of Indian Affairs to the Secretary of the Interior* (Washington, DC: United States Bureau of Indian Affairs, 1874), 8.

43. Qtd. in Amelia V. Kantanski, *Learning to Write "Indian": The Boarding School Experience and American Indian Literature* (Norman: U of Oklahoma P, 2007), 3.

44. For an analysis of the implications of using bodily metaphors to discuss governmental and other nonhuman entities, see David T. Mitchell and Sharon L. Snyder, *Narrative Prosthesis: Disability and the Dependencies of Discourse* (Ann Arbor: U of Michigan P, 2000). I discuss the theory in more detail at the end of this introduction.

45. Qtd. in Kantanski 4.

46. Ibid.

47. Ibid., 21.

48. Ibid.

49. Ibid.

50. Miller 270.

51. George Veditz, "The Preservation of Sign Language," trans. Carol Padden and Eric Malzkuhn, *Deaf World: A Historical Reader and Primary Sourcebook*, ed. Lois Bragg (New York: New York UP, 2001), 83.

52. Plato, *Cratylus*, trans. C. D. C. Reeve (Indianapolis: Hackett, 1998), 1. The fact that Plato's reference to the signers appears in the context of his discussion of names that express essences suggests fascinating ways in which sign languages might inform our understanding of language more broadly. Unfortunately for the history of philosophy and linguistics, this is his only reference to sign, and these connections go unexplored. For more on Plato's discussion of the deaf, see H-Dirksen Bauman's "On the Disconstruction of (Sign) Language in the Western Tradition: A Deaf Reading of Plato's *Cratylus*," *Open Your Eyes: Deaf Studies Talking*, ed. Bauman (Minneapolis: U of Minnesota P, 2008), 127–145.

53. Leonardo da Vinci, *Treatise on Painting*, vol. 1, trans. Philip McMahon (Princeton: Princeton UP, 1956), 14.

54. René Descartes, *Discours de la method* (1636), *Oeuvres de Descartes*, vol. 5, ed. Charles Adam and Paul Tannery (Paris: Cerf, 1913), 57–58.

55. Qtd. in Jonathan Rée, *I See a Voice: Deafness, Language, and the Senses—A Philosophical History* (New York: Metropolitan Books, 1999), 124.

56. Étienne Bonnot de Condillac, *Cours d'instruction du Prince de Parme*, vol. 1 (Parma, 1793), 13.

57. Jean-Jacques Rousseau and Johann Gottfried Herder, *On the Origin of Language*, trans. John H. Moran and Alexander Gode (Chicago: U of Chicago P, 1986), 6.

58. Simultaneous Communication (SimCom) is a mode of communication by which one signs and speaks at the same time. Because it is not possible to simultaneously produce two distinct grammars, the signs follow English word order and grammar. SimCom overlaps with Pidgin Signed English (PSE), which mixes ASL signs with English grammar but is not accompanied by speech. The terminology is problematic because it suggests that simultaneous communication is taking place; in practice, what is called SimCom involves a breaking of the grammatical rules of at least one of the languages involved (almost always ASL). Despite this, the phrase is still widely used.

59. Nora Ellen Groce, *Everyone Here Spoke Sign Language: Hereditary Deafness on Martha's Vineyard* (Cambridge: Harvard UP, 1985), 53.

60. Helmer R. Myklebust, *Psychology of Deafness: Sensory Deprivation, Learning, and Adjustment* (New York: Grune and Stratton, 1957), 241–242.

61. Qtd. in Margalit Fox, *Talking Hands* (New York: Simon and Schuster, 2007), 18–19.

62. E. A. Fay, "Tabular Statement of American Schools for the Deaf, 1889," *American Annals of the Deaf and Dumb* 35 (1890).

63. Jonathan Sterne, *The Audible Past: Cultural Origins of Sound Reproduction* (Durham: Duke UP, 2003), 2.

64. Ibid., 16–17.

65. Bell's father, Alexander Melville Bell, was a scholar of physiological phonetics who created Visible Speech, a method of notation that allowed one to record the movement of the throat, tongue, and lips that an individual made while speaking, as a means to help the deaf learn to speak.

66. Qtd. in Charles Snyder, "Clarence John Blake and Alexander Graham Bell: Otology and the Telephone," *Annals of Otology, Rhinology, and Laryngology* 83.4 (1974): 30.

67. Sterne 40.

68. Bell's interest in deaf education was personal as well as professional; both his mother and wife were deaf. Having grown up watching his mother struggle to communicate with a world that did not understand her signs, his faith in oralism was cemented by his perception that his wife, an oral deaf adult, was more easily able to interact in the hearing world.

69. Qtd. in Jack R. Gannon, *Deaf Heritage: A Narrative History of Deaf America* (Silver Springs, MD: National Association of the Deaf, 1981), 79.

70. Bell was deeply involved with the American eugenics movement. Between 1912 and 1918, he was chairman of the board of scientific advisers to the Eugenics Record Office, and his 1883 lecture *Memoir upon the Formation of a Deaf Variety of the Human Race* expressed a specific plan for breeding deafness out of the human race. Alexander Graham Bell, *Memoir upon the Formation of a Deaf Variety of the Human Race* (Washington, DC: Alexander Graham Bell Association for the Deaf, 1969).

71. Of the 164 delegates at the 1880 conference, only one, James Denison, was deaf. The resolutions passed at the conference were not formally overturned until the 21st International Conference on Education of the Deaf, held in 2010 in Vancouver, Canada. In America, the National Association of the Deaf (NAD) was founded in direct response to the conference's attack on signed languages.

72. *Audism Unveiled*, prod. Benjamin Bahan, H-Dirksen Bauman, and Facundo Montenegro (Dawn Sign, 2008), DVD.

73. James William Sowell, "The Oralist," *Deaf American Poetry: An Anthology*, ed. John Lee Clark (Washington, DC: Gallaudet UP, 2009), 88, lines 13–14.

74. Carol Padden and Tom Humphries, *Inside Deaf Culture* (Cambridge: Harvard UP, 2005), 13.

75. In this way, Deaf kinship might be thought of as more akin to queer identification than to the experience of linguistic, ethnic, or racial minorities.

76. Toni Morrison, *Lecture and Speech of Acceptance, upon the Award of the Nobel Prize for Literature, Delivered in Stockholm on the Seventh of December, Nineteen Hundred and Ninety-three* (New York: Knopf, 1993), 15–16.

77. Kantanski 8.

78. Ibid., 11–12.

79. Willy Conley, "Salt in the Basement: An American Sign Language Reverie in English," *Deaf American Poetry: An Anthology*, ed. John Lee Clark (Washington, DC: Gallaudet UP, 2009), 195–197, lines 1–18.

80. Ibid., lines 33–35.

81. Ibid., lines 48–52.

82. Ibid., line 12.

83. Juan A. Suarez, "T. S. Eliot's *The Waste Land*, the Gramophone, and the Modernist Discourse Network," *New Literary History* 32.3 (2001): 751.

84. Walt Whitman, "A Song of the Rolling Earth," *Walt Whitman: Complete Poetry and Collected Prose* (New York: Library of America, 1982), 363.

85. In *Extraordinary Bodies*, Rosemarie Garland Thomson coins the term "normate" to denaturalize assumptions about normalcy and signal the construction of the "identity of those who, by way of the bodily configurations and cultural capital they assume, can step into a position of authority and wield the power it grants them." Rosemarie Garland Thomson, *Extraordinary Bodies: Figuring Physical Disability in American Culture and Literature* (New York: Columbia UP, 1997), 8. As Lennard

Davis argues in chapter 2 of *Enforcing Normalcy*, the application of the idea of norming to human behavior was a nineteenth century development, one that was linked to industrial development, as well as the emerging fields of statistics and eugenics. Davis, *Enforcing Normalcy* 23–49.

86. Sarah Wilson, *Melting Poet Modernism* (Ithaca: Cornell UP, 2010), 49.

87. Ibid., 10.

88. Michael North, *The Dialect of Modernism: Race, Language and Twentieth-Century Literature* (Oxford: Oxford UP, 1994), 1.

89. Hart Crane, "Episode of Hands," *The Complete Poems of Hart Crane: The Centennial Edition*. Ed. Marc Simon (New York: Liveright, 2001), 73, lines 11–15.

90. This work is discussed in greater detail in subsequent chapters.

91. Helen Gilbert, "Dance, Movement and Resistance Politics," *The Post-Colonial Reader*, ed. Bill Ashcroft, Gareth Griffiths, and Helen Tiffin (London: Routledge, 1995), 342. Gilbert's argument was made in reference to Australian Aboriginal dance.

92. Hart Crane, *The Bridge*, *The Complete Poems of Hart Crane: The Centennial Edition*, ed. Marc Simon (New York: Liveright, 2001), 42–108, IV.133–135.

93. Gertrude Stein, "Portraits and Repetition," *Stein 1932–1946* (New York: Library of America, 1998), 294.

94. Virginia Woolf, "Pictures," *The Essays of Virginia Woolf: 1925–1928*, ed. Andrew McNeillie (London: Hogarth, 1994), 243.

95. Rebecca Beasley, *Ezra Pound and the Visual Culture of Modernism* (Cambridge: Cambridge UP, 2008), 4.

96. Martin Jay, *Downcast Eyes: The Denigration of Vision in Twentieth-Century French Thought* (Berkeley: U of California P, 1993), 69. This description is, as Jay himself notes, only a "shorthand way to characterize the dominant scopic regime," and is not meant to homogenize the diverse approaches to vision that individuals have always had. Ibid., 69–70.

97. P. Adams Sitney, *Modernist Montage: The Obscurity of Vision in Cinema and Literature* (New York: Columbia UP, 1990), 2. Italics in original.

98. Ibid.

99. Michael North, *Reading 1922: A Return to the Scene of the Modern* (Oxford: Oxford UP, 1999), 110.

100. Gertrude Stein, *Picasso* (New York: Dover, 1984), 10.

101. Various attempts have been made over the years to develop written forms of ASL, but none to date have achieved widespread popularity or use.

102. Mitchell and Snyder 6.

1 / Impersonality: Tradition and the Inescapable Body

1. H.D., *Notes on Thought and Vision* (San Francisco: City Lights Books, 1982), 59.

2. Critiques of this divide begin with Andreas Huyssen's *After the Great Divide: Modernism, Mass Culture, Postmodernism* (Bloomington: Indiana UP, 1986).

3. T. S. Eliot, "Tradition and the Individual Talent," *The Sacred Wood and Other Essays* (Mineola, NY: Dover, 1998), 32.

4. Ibid., 28.

5. Ibid., 31.

6. Ibid., 32.

7. Homer, *The Odyssey*, trans. Robert Fagles (New York: Penguin, 1996), 1–3.

8. Jane Chance Nietzsche surveys representations of such genius figures and their relationship to the poetic arts in *The Genius Figure in Antiquity and the Middle Ages* (New York: Columbia UP, 1975).

9. Maud Ellmann, *The Poetics of Impersonality: T. S. Eliot and Ezra Pound* (Cambridge: Harvard UP, 1987). For more on spiritualism and automatic writing in the early twentieth century, see Charlotte Elizabeth Dresser and Fred Rafferty's *Spirit World and Spirit Life: Automatic Writing* (New York: J. F. Rowny, 1922).

10. Eliot, "Tradition," 33, 30.

11. Ibid., 33.

12. Sharon Cameron, *Impersonality: Seven Essays* (Chicago: U of Chicago P, 2007), ix.

13. Ellmann 34.

14. Ibid., 4. Sharon Cameron makes a similar argument when she notes, "we don't know what the *im* of impersonality means" (ix).

15. Yeats explains his theory in "A Packet for Ezra Pound," printed in *A Vision* (New York: Kessinger, 2003).

16. Ellmann 197.

17. Rochelle Rives, *Modernist Impersonalities: Affect, Authority, and the Subject* (New York: Palgrave Macmillan, 2012), 14–15.

18. In *The Death and Return of the Author: Subjectivity in Barthes, Foucault, and Derrida* (Edinburgh: Edinburgh UP, 1998), Seán Burke argues that far from rendering writers dead, the shift toward author functions has given them a life after death and that, moreover, the continued circulation of authorial personalities was directly linked to the cultural circulation of their bodies.

19. Roland Barthes, "The Death of the Author," *Image/Music/Text*, trans. Stephen Heath (New York: Hill and Wang 1978), 3, 5.

20. Michel Foucault, "What Is an Author?," *Aesthetics, Method, and Epistemology*, ed. James D. Faubion, trans. Robert Hurley et al. (New York: New Press, 1994), 205.

21. Galow argues that the emergence of this culture significantly impacted "'literary' writing in the decades before World War II" and that it contributed to a "new landscape" in which writers needed to "construct[] . . . public personae." Galow, *Writing Celebrity: Stein, Fitzgerald, and the Modern(ist) Art of Self-Fashioning* (New York: Palgrave Macmillan, 2011), xi.

22. Ibid., 19.

23. For a detailed account of the economics of these tours and their relationship to expansions of literary markets, see chapter 5 of Joan Shelley Rubin's *Songs of Ourselves: The Uses of Poetry in America* (Cambridge: Harvard UP, 2007), 74–91.

24. Melissa Bradshaw, *Amy Lowell: Diva Poet* (Aldershot, UK: Ashgate, 2011), 5.

25. Galow 28.

26. Amy Lowell, "Spring Day," *The Complete Poetical Works of Amy Lowell* (Boston: Houghton Mifflin, 1925), 145.

27. Witter Bynner nicknamed Lowell "the Hippopoetess," a moniker picked up on by Ezra Pound, who wrote to Margaret Anderson, "And poor dear Amy. It is only a month ago that I heard someone manifestly NOT an enemy refer to the 'Hippopoetess.'" Ezra Pound, *The Letters of Ezra Pound to Margaret Anderson: The Little Review Correspondence*, ed. Thomas L. Scott and Melvin J. Friedman (New York: New Directions, 1988), 116. Qtd. in Bradshaw 32.

28. Margaret Widdemer, "The Legend of Amy Lowell," *Texas Quarterly* 2 (1963): 196. Qtd. in Bradshaw 29.

29. Conrad Aiken, "An Anatomy of Melancholy," *New Republic* (1923): 294. Eliot added a set of notes to the poem for its first American publication in response to critiques that the work was too difficult. Far from clarifying, however, the notes themselves extend the poem's challenge; they provide a mixture of erudite source materials (which do not in all cases have a readily apparent link to the lines they propose to illuminate), other works in a variety of disciplines that readers are instructed to read, and flippant remarks by Eliot that identify particular portions as incidentally overheard dialogue or emphasize the liberties he has taken in adapting references to suit his purpose.

30. "Shantih, Shantih, Shantih: Has the Reader Any Rights before the Bar of Literature?," *Time* 3 March 1923: 12; Charles Powell, "So Much Waste Paper," *Manchester Guardian* 31 October 1923: 7.

31. Malcolm Cowley, "The Dilemma of *The Waste Land*," *The Waste Land: A Norton Critical Edition*, ed. Michael North (New York: Norton, 2001), 163.

32. Qtd. in Lawrence Rainey, *Institutions of Modernism: Literary Elites and Public Culture* (New Haven: Yale UP, 1998), 89. At the time, Wilson was considering publishing the poem himself. James Sibley Watson Jr. to Scofield Thayer, 19 August 1922, Box 44, Folder 1260, The Dial Papers, Yale Collection of American Literature, Mss. 34, Beinecke Rare Book and Manuscript Library, Yale University, New Haven, CT.

33. W. B. Yeats, "Among School Children," *The Collected Poems of W. B. Yeats*, 2nd ed., ed. Richard J. Finneran (New York: Scribner, 1989), 215–217, VIII.1–8.

34. Ibid., I.8.

35. For additional information on the social dynamics of storytelling in contemporary Deaf cultures, see Ben Bahan, "Face-to-Face Tradition in the American Deaf Community: Dynamics of the Teller, the Tale, and the Audience," *Signing the Body Poetic: Essays on American Sign Language Literature*, ed. H-Dirksen L. Bauman, Jennifer L. Nelson, and Heidi M. Rose (Berkeley: U of California P, 2006), 21–50; and Cynthia Peters, *Deaf American Literature: From Carnival to Canon* (Washington, DC: Gallaudet UP, 2000).

36. Heidi M. Rose, "The Poet in the Poem in the Performance: The Relation of Body, Self, and Text in ASL Literature," *Signing the Body Poetic: Essays on American Sign Language Literature*, ed. H-Dirksen L. Bauman, Jennifer L. Nelson, and Heidi M. Rose (Berkeley: U of California P, 2006), 136.

37. There is not a great deal of consistency with regard to terminology surrounding DeafBlindness. Throughout *Deafening Modernism*, I have elected to use "DeafBlind" (as opposed to "Deaf blind," "deaf-blind," or any of the other numerous variants) in recognition of the identification with the Deaf community that many signing Deaf-Blind individuals—those I focus on in this book—feel and to suggest that DeafBlindness itself constitutes both a cultural and experiential reality that is distinct from being "just" Deaf or blind separately and that is also more than the sum of those two identity components. For more information on Tactile ASL, see Johanna Mesch, *Tactile Sign Language* (Washington, DC: Gallaudet UP, 2002) or visit Pro-Tactile: The DeafBlind Way, http://www.protactile.org/.

38. The tendency to exclude DeafBlind individuals from the Deaf community through this emphasis on vision when talking about Deaf gain is a problem that has only recently begun to be addressed within Deaf studies.

39. The potential ethical implications of this contact parallel (though, again, may not be identical to) those I outline here.

40. Michael Davidson, *Concerto for the Left Hand: Disability and the Defamiliar Body* (Ann Arbor: U of Michigan P, 2008), 119.

41. Peter Cook and Kenneth Lerner, "Poetry," *Signing the Body Poetic: Essays on American Sign Language Literature*, ed. H-Dirksen L. Bauman, Jennifer L. Nelson, and Heidi M. Rose (Berkeley: U of California P, 2006), DVD. Translated by the author. Direct transliterations from ASL to English do not reflect the complexity of the language used by the signer. For this reason, throughout the book, I have attempted to provide more conceptually accurate summaries of the poems that hopefully gesture toward their linguistic complexity, some of which occurs in modes and dimensions for which there is no exact written-language equivalent.

42. Role shifting enables a signer to communicate from the perspective of various characters in a story and to differentiate between them through body shifting, changes in eye line, nonverbal behaviors, and facial expressions.

43. Rose 140.

44. Perhaps, intriguingly, this also means that one cannot point to a "Cook's body" distinct from "Poetry."

45. Significantly, because of the ways these poetic experiments diverged from disembodied models of impersonality, they have frequently been perceived as unsophisticated and are largely ignored by general readers and critics alike. Only a few scholarly articles have ever been published on the subject of Anderson's poetry, as well as one master's thesis, "The Significance of Sherwood Anderson's Poetry" by Winfield Scott Lewis, completed in 1961 at Loyola University. A collection of Anderson's selected works was not available until 2007 (*American Spring Song: The Selected Poems of Sherwood Anderson*, ed. Stuart Downs [Kent, OH: Kent State UP, 2007]). In terms of scholarly resources, the Modern American Poetry website (companion to Oxford University Press's *Anthology of American Poetry*) does not even list Anderson as a poet. Nor does the seventh edition of *The Norton Anthology of American Literature* (in which he is described solely as a fiction writer) or the third edition of *The Norton Anthology of Modern and Contemporary Poetry*.

46. Eve Feder Kittay, *Love's Labor: Essays on Women, Equality, and Dependency* (New York: Routledge, 1998), xii.

47. Kelly Oliver, "Subjectivity as Responsivity: The Ethical Implications of Dependency," *The Subject of Care: Feminist Perspectives on Dependency*, ed. Eve Feder Kittay and Ellen K. Feder (Lanham, MD: Rowman and Littlefield, 2002), 330.

48. Within the context of disabled bodies and the individuals who take care of them in particular, it is specifically suggested that this ethics of care could help to bring about better living and working conditions for the individuals who engage in caretaking work as a major component of their lives, individuals who are predominantly poor women of color. For more on this, see Eva Kittay's "Dependency, Equality, and Welfare," *Feminist Studies* 24.1 (1998): 32–43.

49. Leo Bersani, *Intimacies* (Chicago: U of Chicago P, 2010), 96.

50. Leo Bersani, "Is the Rectum a Grave?," *AIDS: Cultural Analysis / Cultural Activism* 43 (1987): 217. Tim Dean describes a similar pleasurable annihilation in Hart Crane's poem "Legend," in which, he argues, "the 'transmemberment' of *poesis* necessitates a metaphysical . . . death, a shattering of the self that paradoxically is attained

through the self-acknowledgment rendered by kisses." Tim Dean, "Hart Crane's Poetics of Privacy," *American Literary History* 8.1 (1996): 95.

51. Michel Foucault, "The Social Triumph of the Sexual Will," *The Essential Works of Michel Foucault: Ethics, Subjectivity and Truth*, ed. Paul Rabinow (New York: New Press, 1994), 160; Foucault, "Friendship as a Way of Life," ibid., 138. Foucault continues that the goal is to "escape as much as possible from the types of relations that society proposes for us and try to create in the empty space where we are new relational possibilities" (Foucault, "Social," 160).

52. Bersani, *Intimacies*, 642.

53. Luce Irigaray, "The Path toward the Other," *Beckett after Beckett*, ed. S. E. Gontarski and Anthony Uhlmann (Gainesville: UP of Florida, 2006), 50.

54. Sherwood Anderson, "A Poet," *A New Testament* (New York: Boni and Liveright, 1927), 59, lines 1–8.

55. Sherwood Anderson, "Manhattan," *Mid-American Chants* (New York: Quale, 2006), 18, lines 12–14.

56. Ibid., lines 18–19.

57. Ibid., line 8.

58. Sherwood Anderson, "Song of Theodore," *Mid-American Chants* (New York: Quale, 2006), 15–17, lines 3–8.

59. Ibid., lines 62–63.

60. Ibid., lines 75–79.

61. Sherwood Anderson, "The Healer," *A New Testament* (New York: Boni and Liveright, 1927), 26–27, lines 1–6.

62. Ibid., lines 7, 26.

63. Sherwood Anderson, "Song for Lonely Roads," *Mid-American Chants*(New York: Quale, 2006), 49, lines 4–6, 19–22.

64. *Leaves of Grass* opens with the assertion, "I celebrate myself, / And what I assume you shall assume, / For every atom belonging to me as good belongs to you," and later inquires, "Who need be afraid of the merge?" Walt Whitman, *Leaves of Grass 1855*, *Walt Whitman: Complete Poetry and Collected Prose* (New York: Library of America, 1982), 27, 33.

65. Sherwood Anderson, "The Cornfields," *Mid-American Chants* (New York: Quale, 2006), 1–2, lines 16–18.

66. Anderson, "Manhattan," lines 18–19.

67. Sherwood Anderson, "Word Factories," *A New Testament* (New York: Boni and Liveright, 1927), 85–88, lines 1.

68. Ibid., lines 21–22, 22–26.

69. Ibid., lines 43–46.

70. Ibid., lines 54–60.

71. Anderson, "The Healer," lines 1–11.

72. Bahan, 43.

73. For more information on the role of eye movement in ASL, see Clayton Valli, Ceil Lucas, and Kristin J. Mulrooney, *Linguistics of American Sign Language: An Introduction*, 4th ed. (Washington, DC: Gallaudet UP, 2005).

74. Emmanuel Levinas, *Entre Nous: On Thinking-of-the-Other*, trans. Michael B. Smith and Barbara Harshav (New York: Columbia UP, 1998), 145; Levinas, *Humanism of the Other*, trans. Nidra Poller (Urbana: U of Illinois P, 2006), 67.

75. To be clear, "human" and "language user" are not equivalent terms. While not all humans use language, however, all language users are human, enabling the recognition.

76. Jennifer Esmail, "The Power of Deaf Poetry: The Exhibition of Literacy and the Nineteenth-Century Sign Language Debates," *Sign Language Studies* 8.4 (2008): 350.

77. George Oppen, "Of Being Numerous," *George Oppen: Selected Poems*, ed. Robert Creeley (New York: New Directions, 2001), 83–109, VII.1–5.

78. Debbie Rennie, "Missing Children," *Signing the Body Poetic: Essays on American Sign Language Literature*, ed. H-Dirksen L. Bauman, Jennifer L. Nelson, and Heidi M. Rose (Berkeley: U of California P, 2006), DVD. "Missing Children" was composed in collaboration with Kenny Lerner. Translated by author. I discuss the poem in the context of philosophies of the voice in Rebecca Sanchez, "'Human Bodies Are Words': Towards a Theory of Non-verbal Voice," *College English Association Critic* 73.3 (2012): 32–46.

79. Classifiers are specific handshapes used to indicate additional information about nouns and verbs, including location, shape, size, and style of movement.

80. To emphasize the multiple levels of layering occurring at this point in the poem, Rennie is mimicking a child who is mimicking an adult character. In a strategy that gestures toward the section's moral ambiguities, the intertwined bodies of the subjects inhabited by Rennie stand in for the bodies not shown: those twisted by the explosion of the bombs.

2 / Primitivism: Communicative Norms and the Ethics of the Story

1. Sieglinde Lemke, *Primitivist Modernism: Black Culture and the Origins of Transatlantic Modernism* (Oxford: Oxford UP, 1998), 5.

2. Filippo Tomaso Marinetti, "The Founding and Manifesto of Futurism 1909," *Modernism: An Anthology of Sources and Documents*, ed. Vassiliki Kolocotroni, Jane Goldman, and Olga Taxidou (Chicago: U of Chicago P, 1998), 251.

3. As Michael North points out in *Novelty: A History of the New* (Chicago: U of Chicago P, 2013), the phrase "make it new" was a translation of an ancient Chinese source, and its use by Pound postdated the period typically thought of as "high" modernist.

4. Phyllis Rose, *Jazz Cleopatra* (New York: Random House, 1989), 47.

5. Carole Sweeney, *From Fetish to Subject: Race, Modernism, and Primitivism, 1919–1935* (New York: Praeger, 2004), 51.

6. Robert Goldwater, *Primitivism in Modern Art* (New York: Belknap, 1986), 35.

7. Sweeney 51.

8. Elazar Barkan and Ronald Bush, introduction, *Prehistories of the Future: The Primitivist Project and the Culture of Modernism*, ed. Barkan and Bush (Stanford: Stanford UP, 1995), 2.

9. Qtd. in Stephen Kern, *The Culture of Time and Space, 1880–1915* (Cambridge: Harvard UP, 2003), 206.

10. Theodor Adorno, *Minima Moralia: Reflections on a Damaged Life*, trans. E. F. N. Jepheott (London: Verso, 2005), 47.

11. "Norm, n. 1," *The Oxford English Dictionary Online* (2011), http://www.oed.com/view/Entry/128266?rskey=rsFvLW&result=1&isAdvanced=false.

12. Lennard J. Davis, introduction, *The Disability Studies Reader*, 2nd ed., ed. Davis (New York: Routledge, 2006), 6.

13. For more on the relationship between disabled bodies and the American body politic, see Emily Russell, *Reading Embodied Citizenship: Disability, Narrative, and the American Body Politic* (New Brunswick: Rutgers UP, 2011).

14. For more on the impact of boarding schools on American Indian literature and language use, see Amelia V. Katanski, *Learning to Write "Indian": The Boarding School Experience and American Indian Literature* (Norman: U of Oklahoma P, 2007).

15. Qtd. in Alan Taylor, *Writing Early American History* (Philadelphia: U of Pennsylvania P, 2006), 24.

16. David Appelbaum, *Voice* (Albany: State U of New York P, 1990), 13.

17. Lennard J. Davis, *Enforcing Normalcy: Disability, Deafness, and the Body* (London: Verso, 1995), 20.

18. Qtd. in Fatimah Tobing Rony, *The Third Eye: Race, Cinema, and Ethnographic Spectacle* (Durham: Duke UP, 1996), 3.

19. Qtd. in Douglas C. Baynton, "A Silent Exile on This Earth: The Metaphorical Construction of Deafness in the Nineteenth-Century," *The Disability Studies Reader*, 2nd ed., ed. Lennard J. Davis (New York: Routledge, 2006), 42. Garrett was a graduate of Alexander Graham Bell's program for instructing teachers of the deaf.

20. Qtd. in ibid.

21. Qtd. in ibid., 43.

22. Qtd. in Douglas Baynton, *Forbidden Signs: American Culture and the Campaign against Sign Language* (Chicago: U of Chicago P, 1996), 43.

23. In an excellent chapter analyzing the issue of deaf intermarriage in the Victorian period, Jennifer Esmail argues that it was the emergence of eugenics that propelled the sign-language debates from a private issue pertaining to deaf people and educators into a public threat. Jennifer Esmail, *Reading Victorian Deafness: Signs and Sounds in Victorian Literature and Culture* (Athens: Ohio UP, 2013), 136.

24. Qtd. in Carol Padden and Tom Humphries, *Inside Deaf Culture* (Cambridge: Harvard UP, 2005), 106. For more information on how this history impacted the development of a distinct Black ASL, see Carolyn McCaskill, Ceil Lucas, Robert Bayley, and Joseph Hill, *The Hidden Treasure of Black ASL: Its History and Structure* (Washington, DC: Gallaudet UP, 2011).

25. Baynton, *Forbidden Signs*, 46.

26. Qtd. in Albert Ballin, *The Deaf Mute Howls* (Washington, DC: Gallaudet UP, 1998), 78.

27. See Henri Bergson, *Laughter: An Essay on the Comic* (New York: Arc Manor, 2008).

28. Winston Churchill, "Everybody's Language," *Collier's* 26 October 1935, rpt. *The Essential Chaplin: Perspectives on the Life and Art of the Great Comedian*, ed. Richard Schieckel (Chicago: Ivan R. Dee, 2006), 210. Churchill's description of Chaplin's pantomimic skills was close to Chaplin's own assessment, in his 1964 autobiography. Describing his reluctance to move into the world of talking films, Chaplin explains, "I was determined to continue making silent films, for I believed there was room for all types of entertainment. Besides, I was a pantomimist, and in that medium I was unique and, without false modesty, master. So I continued with the production of another silent picture, *City Lights*." Charles Chaplin, *My Autobiography* (New York: Simon and Schuster, 1964), 325.

29. Churchill 214.

30. Ibid., 212.
31. R. P. Blackmur, *Language as Gesture: Essays in Poetry* (New York: Harcourt Brace Jovanovich, 1952), 6.
32. Ibid., 7.
33. Ibid., 22.
34. Ibid., 12–13.
35. Ibid., 19.
36. Mikhail Bakhtin, *Rabelais and His World*, trans. Helene Iswolsky (Bloomington: Indiana UP, 1984), 48.
37. Sherwood Anderson, *Winesburg, Ohio* (New York: Penguin, 1992), 24.
38. Ibid., 71.
39. Ibid., 103.
40. Ibid.
41. Ibid.
42. Ibid., 197.
43. Ibid., 198.
44. Ibid., 130.
45. Ibid., 141.
46. Ibid., 135, 137.
47. Ibid, 142.
48. Ibid., 167–168.
49. Ibid., 169.
50. Ibid.
51. Ibid., 170.
52. Ibid., 171.
53. Ibid., 87.
54. Ibid., 91.
55. Ibid., 96.
56. In doing so, Anderson anticipates the social model, which, as I discussed in the introduction, locates disability in restrictive social conditions that limit individuals' access, rather than in the bodies of individuals themselves. This thinking about disability has been incredibly important in the disability rights movement but has more recently come under criticism for failing to fully account for the lived realities of those who do consider their bodies to be disabled.
57. Bill Solomon, "The Novel in Distress," *Novel* 43.1 (2010): 130.
58. E.M. Forster, *Aspects of the Novel* (New York: Harcourt, Brace and World, 1954), 45–46.
59. Sherwood Anderson, "The Modern Writer," *Homage to Sherwood Anderson, 1876–1941*, ed. Paul P. Appel (Mamaroneck, NY: Paul P. Appel, 1970), 174.
60. Solomon 124.
61. Karl Kroeber, *Retelling/Rereading: The Fate of Storytelling in Modern Times* (New Brunswick: Rutgers UP, 1990), 4.
62. While Deaf culture is not an obvious site for discussion of oral cultures, it can illuminate the ways in which the elements of oral cultures that intrigued Anderson might play out in modern, literate ones. As J. P. Gee argues, "ASL exists in an 'oral' culture, a culture based on face-to-face signed interaction. Like many other such cultures, it has an active tradition of folklore and performance-centered 'oral'

(signed) narratives, encapsulating traditional values, and passed down from generation to generation." J. P. Gee and Walter J. Ong, "An Exchange on American Sign Language and Deaf Culture: J. P. Gee and Walter J. Ong," *Language and Style: An International Journal* 16.2 (1983): 232. Part of what examining such contemporary cultures emphasizes is the radical destabilization that occurs when the text and the author's body become inseparable, as was the case in ancient oral cultures and remains so in modern Deaf ones.

63. Anderson, *Winesburg, Ohio*, 27.
64. Ibid., 28.
65. Thomas Yingling, "*Winesburg, Ohio* and the End of Collective Experience," *New Essays on Winesburg, Ohio*, ed. John W. Crowley (Cambridge: Cambridge UP, 1990), 115.
66. Ibid.
67. As Robert McRuer insightfully points out in *Crip Theory*, "compulsory heterosexuality is contingent on compulsory able-bodiedness, and vice versa." The two function as "wedded but invisible" manifestations of modern society's obsession with the establishment and maintenance of physical norms. Robert McRuer, *Crip Theory: Cultural Signs of Queerness and Disability* (New York: New York UP, 2006), 2.
68. Anderson, *Winesburg*, 32.
69. Ibid., 32.
70. Ibid., 27.
71. Ibid., 32, 30.
72. Ibid., 29.
73. Ibid., 28–29.
74. Ibid., 28.
75. Ibid., 194.
76. Ibid., 28.

## 3 / Difficulty: Juxtaposition, Indeterminacy, and the Linguistics of Simultaneity

1. Joshua L. Miller's *Accented America: The Cultural Politics of Multilingual Modernism* (Oxford: Oxford UP, 2011) and Sarah Wilson's *Melting-Pot Modernism* (Ithaca: Cornell UP, 2010), for example, both give excellent accounts of the impact of attempts to standardize American English on various ethnic and linguistic minorities without touching on the ways these same pressures affected disabled Americans.

2. In *The Dialect of Modernism*, Michael North cites the careers of Claude McKay and T. S. Eliot as examples of the dramatically different outcomes faced by writers who engaged in high levels of formal experimentation, on of the basis of their subject positions. In the 1930s, Eliot was celebrated as a well-respected representative of modernism, while McKay found so few opportunities for publication that he ended up in a state work camp. Michael North, *The Dialect of Modernism: Race, Language and Twentieth-Century Literature* (Oxford: Oxford UP, 1994), 127.

3. Tim Armstrong, *Modernism, Technology and the Body* (Cambridge: Cambridge UP, 1998), 4–5.

4. David T. Mitchell and Sharon L. Snyder, *Narrative Prosthesis: Disability and the Dependencies of Discourse* (Ann Arbor: U of Michigan P, 2000), 9. In the introduction to the book, Mitchell and Snyder define four components of narrative prosthesis:

First, narrative prosthesis refers to the pervasiveness of disability as a device of characterization in narrative art. Second, it enables a contrast between the prosthetic leanings of mainstream discourses that would disguise or obliterate the evidence of physical and cognitive differences, and literary efforts that expose prosthesis as an artificial, and thus, re-signifiable relation. Third, it refers to the problematic nature of the literary transgressive ideal in relation to social violence that often issues from the repetition of a representational formula (or anti-formula).... Finally, it acknowledges that literary representation bears on the production and realization of disabled subjectivities.

One of the best-known examples of this phenomenon in relation to the First World War is Septimus Warren Smith in Virginia Woolf's *Mrs. Dalloway*, whose inability to reintegrate into London life after serving is used to highlight the deep fissures and traumas running throughout the city and characters even as they go about their daily routines.

 5. T. S Eliot, "The Metaphysical Poets," *Selected Prose of T. S. Eliot*, ed. Frank Kermode (San Diego: Harcourt, 1975), 65.

 6. Leonard Diepeveen, *The Difficulties of Modernism* (New York: Routledge, 2003), xiii.

 7. T. S. Eliot, "The Waste Land," *T. S. Eliot: The Complete Poems and Plays, 1909–1950* (New York: Harcourt Brace, 1950), 37. Significantly, the epigraph remains untranslated and unattributed in the poem's notes.

 8. Andreas Huyssen, *After the Great Divide: Modernism, Mass Culture, Postmodernism* (Bloomington: Indiana UP, 1986), viii. As Huyssen explains, "Modernism constituted itself through a conscious strategy of exclusion, an anxiety of contamination by its other: an increasingly consuming and engulfing mass culture."

 9. Eliot, *The Waste Land*, 37. Significant for thinking about the tension between personality and impersonality in Eliot's work, this passage from *Purgatorio* moves increasingly away from the notion of the author as individual genius and toward the idea of a lineage of great writers. The pilgrim encounters Guinizelli and is somewhat starstruck. Guinizelli in turn identifies Daniel as "the better craftsman." Dante Alighieri, *The Divine Comedy*, trans. Robert Kirkpatrick (New York: Penguin, 2013). In *The Spirit of Romance* (1910), Pound similarly acknowledges his indebtedness to both Daniel and Dante. Ezra Pound, *The Spirit of Romance* (Norfolk: New Directions, 1929).

 10. Eliot, *The Waste Land*, 37. For analysis of Pound's role in the composition of *The Waste Land*, as well as reproductions of his editing marks, see T. S. Eliot, *The Waste Land: A Facsimile and Transcript of the Original Drafts Including the Annotations of Ezra Pound*, ed. Valerie Eliot (San Diego: Harcourt Brace, 1971).

 11. Marjorie Perloff, *The Poetics of Indeterminacy: Rimbaud to Cage* (Evanston, IL: Northwestern UP, 1999), 16, 18.

 12. Hart Crane, "A Letter to Harriet Monroe," *Hart Crane: Complete Poems and Selected Letters*, ed. Langdon Hammer (New York: Library of America, 2006), 165.

 13. This is, significantly, not the only way to read the poem. But it has remained, coming up to a century after its publication, the predominant interpretation attached to it. Early reviews of the work set the tone. Although Conrad Aiken found the poem ultimately successful, he described it as "an anatomy of melancholy." Conrad Aiken, "An Anatomy of Melancholy," *The Waste Land: A Norton Critical Edition*, ed. Michael

North (New York: Norton, 2001), 148. Malcolm Cowley, who again is careful to celebrate the poem as a paragon of modernist qualities, finds it a "problem" because, according to him, it situates all dignity and meaning in the past. "Our age," by contrast, "was prematurely senile and could not even find words of its own in which to bewail its impotence; that it was forever condemned to borrow and patch together the songs of dead poets." Malcolm Cowley, "The Dilemma of *The Waste Land*," *The Waste Land: A Norton Critical Edition*, ed. Michael North (New York: Norton, 2001), 164.

14. This involvement of the reader in the process of creating poetry was explicitly acknowledged by Crane, if not by Eliot. In Crane's explanation of his particular flavor of difficulty, he notes, "It implies (this *inflection* of language) a previous or prepared receptivity to its stimulus on the part of the reader. The reader's sensibility simply responds by identifying this inflection of experience with some event in his own history or perceptions—or rejects it altogether. The logic of metaphor is so organically entrenched in pure sensibility that it can't be thoroughly traced or explained outside of historical sciences, like philology and anthropology." Crane, "Letter to Harriet Monroe," 166.

15. Diepeveen, xiv–v.

16. Structural linguistics had a particularly significant impact on the development of close reading practices associated with New Criticism.

17. Ferdinand de Saussure, *Course in General Linguistics*, ed. Perry Meisel and Haun Saussy, trans. Wade Baskin (Peru, IL: Open Court, 1972), 69–70.

18. Ibid., 70.

19. Signed languages constitute languages because they are complex, arbitrary systems of symbolic communication that employ standardized grammatical and syntactical rules.

20. Some people have argued that shifts in intonation and gesture constitute additional channels through which information can be communicated during a spoken utterance. The general consensus, however, is that these channels represent extralinguistic information and that spoken languages operate through fewer articulators than do manual ones. As Bencie Woll puts it, "the linearity of spoken language and the simultaneity of signed languages are artifacts of the modalities in which they occur." Bencie Woll, "Perspectives on Linearity and Simultaneity," *Simultaneity in Signed Languages: Form and Function*, ed. Myriam Vermeerbergen, Lorraine Leeson, and Onno A. Crasborn (New York: John Benjamins, 2007), 340.

21. There is a parallel in the way the tactile system functions for signing DeafBlind individuals. While tactile ASL incorporates fewer channels than visually processed sign—the majority of the linguistic information is expressed through the hands and arms—backchanneling can be used to encode grammatical information from the face that is not being visually processed. Backchanneling involves using the non-receiving hand—usually through a series of taps on the receiver's arm or leg—to provide information to that which would otherwise be registered visually. Much more research needs to be done to investigate the similarities between backchanneling and the simultaneous reception of multiple channels of information in visually received signing.

22. Howard Poizner, Edward S. Klima, and Ursula Bellugi, *What the Hands Reveal about the Brain* (Cambridge: MIT Press, 1987), 30.

23. Margalit Fox, *Talking Hands* (New York: Simon and Schuster, 2007), 101.

24. Ibid., 159.

25. Padden has also identified a subclass of words she terms "backwards verbs," which move through space from object to subject. This group includes words such as "copy" and "invite." Carol A. Padden, *Interaction of Morphology and Syntax in American Sign Language* (New York: Garland, 1988).

26. Fox 169.

27. For more information on adverbs in ASL, see D. E. Anderson and J. S. Reilly, "Pah! The Acquisition of Adverbials in ASL," *Sign Language and Linguistics* 1.2 (1998): 117–142.

28. David Cornia, Ursula Bellugi, and Judy Reilly, "Neuropsychological Studies of Linguistic and Affective Facial Expressions in Deaf Signers," *Language and Speech* 42.203 (1999): 310.

29. Clayton Valli, "Tears of Life," *ASL Poetry: Selected Works of Clayton Valli* (San Diego: Dawn Pictures, 1995), DVD. Translated by the author. A version of the poem, signed by Vivienne Simmons, can be found on YouTube: Peter Quint, "Poem—Tears of Live.mov," YouTube, 15 July 2010, http://www.youtube.com/watch?v=_A5KIyg-q88.

30. In "Portraits and Repetition," Stein explains, "I am inclined to believe there is no such thing as repetition. And really how can there be. . . . There can be no repetition because the essence of that expression is insistence, and if you insist you must each time use emphasis and if you use emphasis it is not possible while anybody is alive that they should use exactly the same emphasis." Gertrude Stein, "Portraits and Repetitions," *Stein: Writings 1932–1946* (New York: Library of America, 1998), 288.

31. W. J. T. Mitchell, "Preface: Utopian Gestures," *Signing the Body Poetic: Essays on American Sign Language Literature*, ed. H-Dirksen L. Bauman, Jennifer L. Nelson, and Heidi M. Rose (Berkeley: U of California P, 2006), xx.

32. The title of the section occurs in Hart Crane, "The Wine Menagerie," *The Complete Poems of Hart Crane: The Centennial Edition*, ed. Marc Simon (New York: Liveright, 2001), 23–24, line 29.

33. Elisa New, "Hand of Fire: Crane," *The Regenerate Lyric: Theology and Innovation in American Poetry* (Cambridge: Cambridge UP, 1993), 184.

34. In "Hart Crane's Poetics of Privacy," Tim Dean links Crane's distinct version of difficulty to an ontological difficulty derived from the poet's experiences of private gay-male codes of behavior. As Dean explains, "The poems in *White Buildings* [the collection in which "Voyages" first appeared] are constructed not according to the logic of a more or less legible homosexual code but according to the logic of a radical privacy that attempts to circumvent the very possibility-condition of such a code by constructing a form of privacy alternate to that of the closet." Tim Dean, "Hart Crane's Poetics of Privacy, *American Literary History* 8.1 (1996): 101.

35. Harold Bloom, introduction, *The Complete Poems of Hart Crane: Centennial Edition*, ed. Mark Simon (New York: Liveright, 2001), xii.

36. Edward J. Brunner, *Splendid Failure: Hart Crane and the Making of "The Bridge"* (Urbana: U of Illinois P, 1985); R. P. Blackmur, *Language as Gesture: Essays in Poetry* (New York: Harcourt Brace Jovanovich, 1952), 316.

37. Joseph Riddel, "Hart Crane's Poetics of Failure," *ELH* 33.4 (1966): 473.

38. Hart Crane, "General Aims and Theories," *Hart Crane: Complete Poems and Selected Letters*, ed. Langdon Hammer (New York: Library of America, 2006), 161.

39. Ibid., 163, 164.

40. Crane, "The Wine Menagerie," line 29; Crane, "Voyages," *The Complete Poems of Hart Crane: The Centennial Edition*, ed. Marc Simon (New York: Liveright, 2001), 34–40, IV.17.

41. Like "The Wine Menagerie" and "Voyages," "At Melville's Tomb" was originally published in Crane's 1926 *White Buildings*. Hart Crane, "At Melville's Tomb," *The Complete Poems of Hart Crane: The Centennial Edition*, ed. Marc Simon (New York: Liveright, 2001), 33.

42. Crane, "General Aims and Theories," 163.

43. Crane, "Letter to Harriet Monroe," 165; "General Aims and Theories," 163.

44. "General Aims and Theories," 163; Hart Crane, "The Broken Tower," *The Complete Poems of Hart Crane: The Centennial Edition*, ed. Marc Simon (New York: Liveright, 2001), 161–162, line 23; Crane, "Voyages," VI.29.

45. Hart Crane, *O My Land, My Friends: The Selected Letters of Hart Crane*, ed. Langdon Hammer and Brom Weber (New York: Four Walls Eight Windows, 1997), 186.

46. Crane, "Voyages," I.2–16.

47. Evelyn J. Hintz, "Hart Crane's 'Voyages' Reconsidered," *Contemporary Literature* 13.3 (1972): 323.

48. Crane, "Voyages," II.1–5.

49. Bloom xxi; Crane, "Voyages," II.25.

50. Perloff, 16.

51. Crane, "Voyages," II.16.

52. Ibid., II.17–18.

53. Ibid., II.14–15.

54. Ibid., IV.12–13.

55. Ibid., IV.17–19.

56. Ibid., VI.23, VI.21.

57. Thomas Yingling, *Hart Crane and the Homosexual Text: New Thresholds, New Anatomies* (Chicago: U of Chicago P, 1990), 30.

58. Ibid.

59. Crane, *O My Land, My Friends*, 287.

60. Crane, "Voyages," III.18.

61. Crane, *O My Land, My Friends*, 186.

62. Crane, "Voyages," V.8–9.

63. Ibid., V.13–14.

64. Ibid., V.11–12.

65. Ibid., V.20, V.12–13.

66. Ibid., V.22–24.

67. Neil Schmitz, "Gertrude Stein as Post-Modernist: The Rhetoric of 'Tender Buttons,'" *Journal of Modern Literature* 3.5 (1974): 1205.

68. Ibid., 1206.

69. Gertrude Stein, "Composition as Explanation." *Stein: Writings 1903–1932* (New York: Library of America, 1998), 520.

70. Ibid., 522.

71. Gertrude Stein, "A Transatlantic Interview," *The Norton Anthology of Modern and Contemporary Poetry*, 3rd ed., vol. 1, ed. Jahan Ramazani, Richard Ellmann, and Robert O'Clair (New York: Norton, 2003), 988.

72. Marcel Duchamp, *Nude Descending a Staircase, No. 2*, 1912, oil on canvas, 147 cm × 89.2 cm, Philadelphia Museum of Art, Philadelphia.

73. Stein, "Composition as Explanation," 524. Stein defines a "continuous present" as follows: "A continuous present is a continuous present. I made almost a thousand pages of a continuous present. Continuous present is one thing and beginning again and again is another thing."

74. Jamie Hilder, "'After All One Must Know More than One Sees and One Does Not See a Cube in Its Entirety': Gertrude Stein and Picasso and Cubism," *Critical Survey* 17.1 (2005): 81.

75. Gertrude Stein, *Tender Buttons*, Stein: *Writings 1932–1946* (New York: Library of America, 1998), 313.

76. As Haselstein notes, Stein avoids "description, condensation, and the 'iconic' form of encompassing categorization, but also narrativization, empathy, and psychological theorizing." Ulla Haselstein, "Gertrude Stein's Portraits of Matisse and Picasso," *New Literary History* 34.4 (2003): 727.

77. The most famous example of this from modernist literature can be found in the opening of James Joyce's "Araby": "North Richmond Street, being blind, was a quiet street except at the hour when the Christian Brothers' School set the boys free." James Joyce, *Dubliners: A Norton Critical Edition*, ed. Margot Norris (New York: Norton, 2006), 20.

78. "Spectacle, noun," *The Oxford English Dictionary Online* (2009), http://www.oed.com/view/Entry/186057?rskey=PqPMmz&result=1&isAdvanced=false#eid.

79. Rosemarie Garland Thompson, introduction, *Freakery: Cultural Spectacles of the Extraordinary Body*, ed. Thompson (New York: New York UP, 1996), 13.

80. "Spectacle, noun," *OED Online*.

81. For more on the politics of looking, see Rosemarie Garland Thomson, *Staring: How We Look* (Oxford: Oxford UP, 2009).

82. James E. Breslin, "William Carlos Williams and Charles Demuth: Cross-Fertilization in the Arts," *Journal of Modern Literature* 6.2 (1977): 248.

83. Ibid.

84. Edward A. Aiken, "'I Saw the Figure 5 in Gold': Charles Demuth's Emblematic Portrait of William Carlos Williams," *Art Journal* 46.3 (1987): 179.

85. William Carlos Williams, *The Autobiography of William Carlos Williams* (New York: New Directions, 1967), 172.

86. William Carlos Williams, "The Great Figure," *William Carlos Williams: Selected Poems*, ed. Charles Tomlinson (New York: New Directions, 1985), 36.

87. Breslin 256.

88. A similar ironic displacement occurs after the suicide of Septimus Smith in Virginia Woolf's *Mrs. Dalloway*, as the text jerks abruptly away from the bloody end of the young man's life to focus on Peter Walsh, who, seeing the ambulance carrying Septimus's body to hospital, muses, "One of the triumphs of civilization. . . . It is one of the triumphs of civilization, as the light high bell of the ambulance sounded," despite the fact that it is precisely "civilization" that has led to Septimus's demise. As in Williams's poem, whatever personal calamity required the summoning of the emergency response vehicle is swept away in the face of the speaker's identification of the symbol of modern speed and efficiency. Virginia Woolf, *Mrs. Dalloway* (San Diego: Harcourt, 1981), 151.

89. Breslin 263.

## 4 / The Image: Cinematic Poetics and Deaf Vision

1. As Georgina Kleege explains, while some specialists distinguish between sight (as something pertaining to the eye) and vision (as a result of the eye interacting with the brain), most do not. For this reason, I use these terms interchangeably. Georgina Kleege, *Sight Unseen* (New Haven: Yale UP, 1999), 22.

2. "Visual culture" is not, of course, a specifically modern or contemporary descriptor. The earliest uses of the phrase seem to occur in Michael Baxandall's *Painting and Experience in Fifteenth-Century Italy: A Primer in the Social History of Pictorial Style* (Oxford: Oxford UP, 1988) and Svetlana Alpers's *The Art of Describing: Dutch Art in the Seventeenth Century* (Chicago: U of Chicago P, 1984). As the titles of both works suggest, visual images have long played a significant role in shaping culture. What considerations of modernism contribute to these discussions is a new range of visual technologies (in particular, photography and cinema) that affect these relationships.

3. W. J. T. Mitchell, *Picture Theory: Essays on Verbal and Visual Representation* (Chicago: U of Chicago P, 1995), 13.

4. For more information on nonvisual means of processing ASL, see my discussion of Tactile ASL in chapter 1.

5. George Veditz, 1910, qtd. in Douglas C. Baynton, *Forbidden Signs: American Culture and the Campaign against Sign Language* (Chicago: U of Chicago P, 1996), 10.

6. For more on the history of small presses in the context of visual modernism, see the introduction to Jerome McGann's *Black Riders: The Visible Language of Modernism* (Princeton: Princeton UP, 1993).

7. In the introduction to *Downcast Eyes*, Martin Jay demonstrates the prevalence of visual metaphors by incorporating twenty-one of them into his first paragraph. Martin Jay, *Downcast Eyes: The Denigration of Vision in Twentieth-Century French Thought* (Berkeley: U of California P, 1993), 1. As Georgina Kleege has pointed out, such associations necessarily marginalize individuals who are blind or have limited vision. Kleege 18–23.

8. Adriana Cavarero, *For More than One Voice: Toward a Philosophy of Vocal Expression* (Stanford: Stanford UP, 2005), 250.

9. For more on the specific role that photography plays in anthropology, see John Collier Jr.'s *Visual Anthropology: Photography as a Research Method* (Albuquerque: U of New Mexico P, 1986).

10. Ezra Pound, "A Retrospect," *Literary Essays of Ezra Pound*, ed. T. S. Eliot (New York: New Directions, 1918), , 4.

11. Ibid., 3.

12. Ibid., 12.

13. Ibid.

14. Gertrude Stein, "Portraits and Repetition," *Stein: Writings 1932–1946* (New York: Library of America, 1998), 294. "I cannot repeat this too often, . . . any one is of one's period and this our period was undoubtedly the period of the cinema and series production."

15. For an elaboration of the relationship between bodily fragmentation and the cinema, see Brigitte Peucker's *Incorporating Images: Film and the Rival Arts* (Princeton: Princeton UP, 1995) and Susan McCabe's *Cinematic Modernism: Modernist Poetry and Film* (Cambridge: Cambridge UP, 2005).

16. Marshall Berman, *All That Is Solid Melts into Air: The Experience of Modernity* (New York: Penguin, 1988), 5.

17. Jay, *Downcast Eyes*, 14.

18. Michael North, *Reading 1922: A Return to the Scene of the Modern* (Oxford: Oxford UP, 1999), 18.

19. Gertrude Stein, *Picasso* (New York: Dover, 1984), 10.

20. When Stein and H.D. are discussed together, it is nearly always in relation to their gender or sexuality, rather than in comparisons of their comments on the meaning of linguistic images.

21. Margaret Dickie, *On the Modernist Long Poem* (Iowa City: U of Iowa P, 1986), 8.

22. Ezra Pound, "Date Line," *Literary Essays of Ezra Pound*, ed. T. S. Eliot (New York: New Directions, 1918), 86.

23. William Stokoe, "Syntactic Dimensionality: Language in Four Dimensions," paper presented at the New York Academy of Sciences, 1979. Qtd. in Oliver Sacks, *Seeing Voices* (New York: Random House, 2000), 71–72.

24. For more on Bauman's analysis of the cinematic elements of ASL, see H-Dirksen L. Bauman, "Getting out of Line: Toward a Visual and Cinematic Poetics of ASL," *Signs and Voices: Deaf Culture, Identity, Language, and Arts*, ed. Kristin A. Lindgren, Doreen DeLuca, and Donna Jo Napoli (Washington, DC: Gallaudet UP, 2008), 163–176. In the chapter, he provides a cinematic (shot-by-shot) analysis of Clayton Valli's poem "Snowflake." For more on the historical development of film (particularly recording technology) and its impact on Deaf culture, see Christopher Krentz's "The Camera as Printing Press: How Film has Influenced ASL Literature," *Signing the Body Poetic: Essays on American Sign Language Literature*, ed. H-Dirksen L. Bauman, Jennifer L. Nelson, and Heidi M. Rose (Berkeley: U of California P, 2006), 51–70.

25. Austin Andrews, "Deaf Ninja," YouTube, accessed 16 February 2009, http://www.youtube.com/watch?v=L91KVUXRBq8, video. Because so little ASL poetry has been published in any format, many of the sources I cite are videos that have been posted to YouTube. The lack of an archive for ASL poetry is a problem that the advent of video and digital recording technology has not entirely ameliorated. I would argue that this speaks simultaneously to the ongoing failure to recognize sign language as a language and, therefore, sign-language literatures as worthy of preservation and to the role of face-to-face interaction in ASL poetry that I analyzed in chapter 2. For a detailed analysis of the politics and pragmatics surrounding the accessibility of ASL literature, as well as a list of resources available, see chapter 3 of Brenda Jo Brueggemann, *Deaf Subjects: Between Identities and Places* (New York: New York UP, 2009).

26. Pound, "A Retrospect," 3.

27. Ezra Pound, "In a Station of the Metro," *Norton Anthology of Modern Poetry*, 3rd ed., ed. Jahan Ramazani, Richard Ellmann, and Robert O'Clair (New York: Norton, 2003), 351.

28. Bernard Bragg, "Flowers and Moonlight on the Spring Water," YouTube, updated 16 July 2010, http://www.youtube.com/watch?v=MHDO8d6url4, video. Translated by author. In glosses of ASL, separating individual letters with a hyphen indicates that they are finger-spelled. ASL gloss is a written English transliteration of signs produced. As with all word-for-word translations, it does not accurately reflect the actual meaning of the language used by the signer. As I explained in chapter 1, I have attempted to provide more conceptually accurate interpretations of the poems

that hopefully gesture toward some of their linguistic complexity. Glossing that is not contextualized can be controversial because it suggests that the signer is producing broken English, reaffirming the mistaken belief that ASL is nothing more than "English on the hands." I use glossing here to draw a distinction between Bragg's presentation of the title (in signed English) and the poem (in ASL), as well as the distinctions between description and enactment or presentation suggested by this contrast.

29. In a brief but important discussion of imagism and ASL in *Concerto for the Left Hand*, Michael Davidson emphasizes the significance of the ability of ideogram (as inaccurately interpreted first by Ernest Fennollosa and later, through him, Ezra Pound) to "fuse both temporality (the characters map a sequence of actions) and space (the character combines several discrete images) in a single sign." Michael Davidson, *Concerto for the Left Hand: Disability and the Defamiliar Body* (Ann Arbor: U of Michigan P, 2008), 105. Going on to describe a series of translations of Fennollosa's images by the Flying Words Project into ASL, Davidson suggests that this "unit[y of] subject and object through the visual image" is similar to the unity in ASL "realized in a poet whose body is itself both the producer and text of his poem." Ibid., 107. This particular set of translations (as in all ASL poems) do indeed collapse text and signer, but I would argue that this is not the same thing as the unity of space and temporality, the latter of which is expanded, rather than condensed, in an ASL poem or a linguistic image.

30. The signer's hands bring action to the scene, calling attention to its flux and movement. In contrast to the idea of still life as a form of fixture or death—as in the French *nature morte*—this night scene is very much alive.

31. Trompe l'oeil techniques have appeared in painting, architecture, sculpture, and other art forms. Famous examples include Pere Borrell del Caso's 1874 *Boy Escaping Criticism*, murals from Pompeii that depict open windows or doors, appearing to lead onto larger spaces, and the fake dome painted on the ceiling of the church of Sant'Ignazio in Rome by Andrea Pozzo in 1658.

32. Clayton Valli, "Dew on a Spiderweb," signed by Ella Mae Lentz, *ASL Poetry: Selected Works of Clayton Valli* (San Diego: Dawn Pictures, 1995), DVD. The poem can be viewed on YouTube at http://www.youtube.com/watch?v=YaHChvFWegQ.

33. Translation by author.

34. Mitchell, *Picture Theory*, 152.

35. Heidegger describes a similar relation between language and being in "The Nature of Language" when he postulates, "Experience means *eundo assequi*, to obtain something along the way, to attain something by going on a way. What is it that the poet reaches? Not mere knowledge. He obtains entrance into the relation of word to thing.... The word itself is the relation which in each instance retains the thing within itself in such a manner that it 'is' a thing." Martin Heidegger, "The Nature of Language," *On the Way to Language*, trans. Peter D. Hertz (New York: HarperCollins, 1971), 66. Similarly, in "The Origin of the Work of Art," he asserts, "language, by naming beings for the first time, first brings beings to word and to appearance." Heidegger, "The Origin of the Work of Art," *Poetry, Language, Thought*, trans. Albert Hofstadter (New York: HarperCollins, 1971), 71. For Heidegger, it is this experience of thinging that relates art (and specifically poetry) to the kind of truth that the structural indeterminacy of signed languages challenges. While providing a useful vocabulary for thinking about the relationship between signed words and things (or signed words

as things), the conclusions he draws from these relationships move off in a different direction from those suggested by signed languages.

36. The varying speeds of the poem's sections are the only things commented on in the analysis of the poem's poetic features provided on the DVD of Clayton Valli's collected works.

37. For an excellent and exhaustive account of imagism, see Helen Carr, *The Verse Revolutionaries: Ezra Pound, H.D. and the Imagists* (London: Jonathan Cape, 2009).

38. According to Hugh Kenner, as early as September 1917, Pound wrote, "the whole affair [the imagism movement] was started not very seriously chiefly to get H.D.'s five poems a hearing without its being necessary for her to publish a whole book." Qtd. in Hugh Kenner, *The Pound Era* (Berkeley: U of California P, 1973), 177.

39. Amy Lowell, "Preface to *Some Imagist Poets*," *Norton Anthology of Modern and Contemporary Poetry*, 3rd ed. ed. Jahan Ramazani, Richard Ellmann, and Robert O'Clair (New York: Norton, 2003), 927.

40. T. S. Eliot, "The Metaphysical Poets," *Selected Prose of T. S. Eliot*, ed. Frank Kermode (San Diego: Harcourt, 1975), 656.

41. Lowell, "Preface," 926. A first anthology, *Des Imagistes*, was published in 1914.

42. Glenn Hughes, "Note," *Imagist Anthology 1930* (New York: Heinemann, 1929), 12.

43. Ibid.

44. Ford, Ford Maddox, "Foreword: 'Those Were the Days,'" *Imagist Anthology 1930* (New York: Heinemann, 1929), 13.

45. Joseph Frank, "From *Spatial Form in Modern Literature*," *Theory of the Novel: A Historical Approach*, ed. Michael McKeon (Baltimore: Johns Hopkins UP, 2000), 787.

46. Randall Jarrell, *Kipling, Auden and Co.: Essays and Reviews, 1935-1964* (New York: Farrar, Straus and Giroux, 1980), 130.

47. As Connor explains in the introduction to the book, her title—*H.D. and the Image*—is playfully ironic; throughout the text, it is her project to challenge the notion of the image as a singular conception. Rachel Connor, *H.D. and the Image* (Manchester: Manchester UP, 2004).

48. H.D., *Notes on Thought and Vision* (San Francisco: City Lights Books, 1982), 20.

49. H.D., "Review of John Gould Fletcher's *Goblins and Pagodas*," *Egoist* 3 (1916): 183.

50. H.D., "Sea Rose," *Collected Poems 1912-1944*, ed. Louis L. Martz (New York: New Directions, 1983): 5, lines 1-16.

51. H.D., "Hermes of the Ways," *Complete Poems 1912-1944*, ed. Louis L. Martz (New York: New Directions, 1983), 37-39, lines 1-9.

52. Indeed, the granite that Pound celebrated is named from the Latin *granum* (grain), for its coarse structure.

53. H.D., "Sheltered Garden," *Complete Poems 1912-1944*, ed. Louis L. Martz (New York: New Directions, 1983), 19-21, lines 41-47.

54. H.D. repeats these ideas throughout the volume, particularly in the poems "Sea Lily," "Evening," "Sea Poppies," "Sea Violet," "Evening," "Night," and "Orchard."

55. H.D., *Trilogy* (1946; New York: New Directions, 1998), 2.13.

56. Ibid., "Tribute to the Angels," 8.8-15, 36.1, 36.9-11, 36.12, 38.10-12.

57. Ibid., 21.1-2, 8, 10.

58. Ibid., 29.8-15.

59. Ibid., 31.1-2.

60. Ibid., 31.5-7.

61. In *On the Modernist Long Poem* (1986), Margaret Dickie explains the use of the term "long poem" in reference to modernist works as follows: "Bare and simple as it is, *the long poem* as a term identifies nonetheless the single feature that most attracted the poet and made his work most problematic. Long in the time of composition, in the initial intention, and in the final form, the Modernist long poem is concerned first and last with its own length" (6).

62. H.D., *Palimpsest* (New York: New Directions, 1998), i.

63. H.D., "Walls," *Trilogy*, 2.26–28.

64. Ibid., 1.1–3, 10–21.

65. Qtd. in Donna Krolik Hollenberg, "Introduction: 'A Whole Deracinated Epoch,'" *Between History and Poetry: The Letters of H.D. and Norman Holmes Pearson*, ed. Hollenberg (Iowa City: U of Iowa P, 1997), 9.

66. H.D., "Walls," *Trilogy*, 39.7–9.

67. H.D. "TTA," *Trilogy*, 8.12.

68. H.D., "TTA," *Trilogy*, 12.8–10, H.D., "Walls," *Trilogy*, 11.2–3.

69. For examples, see Paul R. Lilly Jr., "Caddy and Addie: Speakers of Faulkner's Impeccable Language," *Journal of Narrative Technique* 3.3 (1973): 170–182; and Karl F. Zenders, "Faulkner and the Power of Sound," *PMLA* 99.1 (1984): 89–108.

70. William E. H. Meyer Jr., "Faulkner, Hemingway, et al.: The Emersonian Test of American Authorship," *Journal of American Culture* 21.1 (1998): 37.

71. In 1961, Eben Bass published a short note arguing that "the growth of certain images helps restore order, or time, to the novel," focusing in particular on the series of relationships that develop from Caddy's wedding slipper, the pear tree, the mirror, and the fire. Eben Bass, "Meaningful Images in *The Sound and the Fury*," *Modern Language Notes* 76.8 (1961): 728. The article points toward, but is too brief to fully explore, the implications for these significant visual images as an overarching structural principle, which is what I argue for here.

72. I use the term "epic" here in the Poundian sense of a work "including history." While the novel is more limited in its scope than some of Faulkner's other works, the text is deeply concerned at both a structural and a thematic level with the relationship between the present and the past. The term "epic" also helps differentiate texts that incorporate multiple perspectives and time periods from works whose focus is on a singular character, image, or setting.

73. For graphs and other visual representations of the various scenes that constitute the novel, see Joel Deshaye and Peter Stoicheff, comp., "*The Sound and the Fury*: A Hypertext Edition," http://drc.usask.ca/projects/faulkner/main/index.html.

74. George R. Stewart, "'Each in Its Ordered Place': Structure and Narrative in 'Benjy's Section' of *The Sound and the Fury*," *American Literature* 29.4 (1958): 446. Given this confusion, Stewart suggests that "the actual method of printing causes greater confusion than if Faulkner had used no 'gimmick' at all." Ibid. In 2012, the Folio Society produced a limited (1,480 copies) run of the text following Faulkner's original color plan. It cost $345 and almost instantly sold out.

75. William Faulkner, "Interview with Jean Stein vanden Heuvel," *The Sound and the Fury: Norton Critical Edition*, ed. David Minter (New York: Norton, 1994), 233.

76. William Faulkner, "Class Conferences at the University of Virginia," March 13, 1957, *The Sound and the Fury: Norton Critical Edition*, ed. David Minter (New York: Norton, 1994), 236.

77. The full stanza in *Macbeth* reads as follows: "Life's but a walking shadow, a poor player / That struts and frets his hour upon the state / And then is heard no more. It is a tale / Told by an idiot, full of sound and fury / Signifying nothing." William Shakespeare, *Macbeth*, 5.5.27–31. The line was also (and quite problematically, given its original implications) the source for the title of the 2002 documentary about cochlear implants, *Sound and Fury* (dir. Josh Aronson, 2002, DVD).

78. Stacy Burton, "Rereading Faulkner: Authority, Criticism, and *The Sound and the Fury*," *Modern Philology* 98.4 (2001): 619.

79. William Faulkner, *The Sound and the Fury* (New York: Vintage, 1990), 4–5.

80. Jean-Paul Sartre, "On *The Sound and the Fury*: Time in the Work of Faulkner," *The Sound and the Fury: Norton Critical Edition*, 2nd ed., ed. David Minter (New York: Norton, 1994), 269.

81. Ibid., 267.

82. Ibid.

83. Faulkner, *The Sound and the Fury*, 14.

Epilogue: The Textual Body

1. As early as 1995, according to Mary Rosner and T. R. Johnson, there were already three dominant metaphors in place for discussing the Human Genome Project and modes of interpreting the genome: "nature as book or library; scientist as collector and interpreter," "nature as machine; scientist as mechanic," and nature as the unexplored country; scientist as explorer." Mary Rosner and T. R. Johnson, "Telling Stories: Metaphors of the Human Genome Project," *Hypatia* 10.4 (1995): 107, 110, 115.

2. National Human Genome Research Institute, National Institute of Health, "Human Genome Project," March 2014, http://report.nih.gov/NIHfactsheets/ViewFactSheet.aspx?csid=45&key=H#H.

3. James C. Wilson, "(Re)Writing The Genetic Body-Text: Disability, Textuality, and the Human Genome Project," *Cultural Critique* 50 (2002):25. The biologist Steve Jones similarly explains genetics in linguistic terms: "The language of the genes has a simple alphabet, not with 26 letters but just four. These are the four different DNA bases . . . (A, G, C and T for short). The bases are arranged in words of three letters such as CGA or TGG. . . . It is possible to write a meaningful sentence with 25 letters instead of 26, but only just. Life manages with a mere four." Steve Jones, *The Language of Genes* (New York: Doubleday, 1995), 15–16.

4. Wilson is primarily concerned with the ways that describing genetic variance in terms of textual errors reinscribes the medical model by positioning disability as a mistake in need of editing.

5. Hart Crane, "General Aims and Theories," *Hart Crane: Complete Poems and Selected Letters*, ed. Langdon Hammer (New York: Library of America, 2006), 161.

6. Ibid.

7. Richard Lewontin and Richard Levins, *Biology under the Influence: Dialectical Essays on Ecology, Agriculture and Health* (New York: Monthly Review P, 2007), 245.

8. Genesis 1:26. Eduardo Kac, *Genesis*, March 2014, http://www.ekac.org/geninfo2.html. Kac has explained that he selected Morse code because, "as first employed in radiotelegraphy, it represented the dawn of the information age—the genesis of global communications." (Genesis website)

9. The mutated genetic coding and Morse code read as follows:

CTCCGCGTACTGCTGTCACCCCGCTGCCCTGCATCC
GTTTGTTGCCGTCGCCGTTTGTCATTTGCCCTGCGC
TCATGCCCCGCACCTCGCCGCCCGCCCCATTTCCTC
ATGCCCCGCACCCGCGCTACTGTCGTCCATTTGCCC
TGCGCTCATGCCCCGCACCTCGTTTGCTTGCTCCAT
TTGCCTCATGCCCCGCACTGCCGCTCACTGTCGTCC
ATTTGCCCTGCGCTCACGCCCTGCGCTCGTCTTACT
CCGCCGCCCTGCCGTCGTTCATGCCCCGCCGTCGTT
CATGCCCCGCTGTACCGTTTGCCCTGCGCCCACCTG
CTACGTTTGTCATGCCCCGCACGCTGCTCGTGCCCC

.-.. . -/.- .- -./.... .-..- ./-..—-—.. -. ..—- -./—-... . .-./-.... ./..-. .... ..../—-..-./-....
./......-/.- -. -../—-... .- . .-./-.... ./..-.—- .—.-../—- ..-/-..... ./.- .. .-./.- -. -../—-... .
.-./..... - .-. -.—/.-.. .....- .. -.—/-..... .. -.—./-..... .- -/..—-... ..../..- .-/.— -./-....
./. .- -.-.—....

Kac Web, "Genesis: Translated from the Mutated Gene to English," n.d., http://www.ekac.org/translated.html.

10. David Whitehouse, "Scientists Hail New 'Map of Life,'" BBC News, 20 November 2003, http://news.bbc.co.uk/2/hi/science/nature/3223318.stm.

11. Eduardo Kac, "Life Transformation—Art Mutation," *Educating Artists for the Future: Learning at the Intersection of Art, Science, Technology and Culture*, ed. Mel Alexenberg (Bristol, UK: Intellect Books, 2008), 205.

12. *Genesis* consists of four other sets of art: "Encryption Stones," "Fossil Folds," "In Our Own Image I" and "In Our Own Image II," all of which continue the exploration of the indeterminacy that unexpectedly lies at the intersection of bodies, images, and language.

13. Mel Y. Chen, *Animacies: Biopolitics, Racial Mattering, and Queer Affect* (Durham: Duke UP, 2012), 53.

# Bibliography

Adorno, Theodor. *Minima Moralia: Reflections on a Damaged Life.* Trans. E. F. N. Jepheott. London: Verso, 2005.
Aiken, Conrad. "An Anatomy of Melancholy." *New Republic* (1923): 294–295. Rpt. *The Waste Land: A Norton Critical Edition.* Ed. Michael North. New York: Norton, 2001. 148–152.
Aiken, Edward A. "'I Saw the Figure 5 in Gold': Charles Demuth's Emblematic Portrait of William Carlos Williams." *Art Journal* 46.3 (1987): 178–182.
Alighieri, Dante. *The Divine Comedy.* Trans. Robert Kirkpatrick. New York: Penguin, 2013.
Alpers, Svetlana. *The Art of Describing: Dutch Art in the Seventeenth Century.* Chicago: U of Chicago P, 1984.
Anderson, D. E., and J. S. Reilly. "Pah! The Acquisition of Adverbials in ASL." *Sign Language and Linguistics* 1.2 (1998): 117–142.
Anderson, Sherwood. *American Spring Song: The Selected Poems of Sherwood Anderson.* Ed. Stuart Downs. Kent, OH: Kent State UP, 2007.
———. "The Cornfields." *Mid-American Chants.* New York: Quale, 2006. 1–2.
———. "The Healer." *A New Testament.* New York: Boni and Liveright, 1927. 26–27.
———. "Manhattan." *Mid-American Chants.* New York: Quale, 2006. 18.
———. *Mid-American Chants.* 1918. New York: Quale, 2006.
———. "The Modern Writer." *Homage to Sherwood Anderson, 1876–1941.* Ed. Paul P. Appel. Mamaroneck, NY: Paul P. Appel, 1970. 173–190.
———. *A New Testament.* New York: Boni and Liveright, 1927.
———. "A Poet." *A New Testament.* New York: Boni and Liveright, 1927.
———. "Song for Lonely Roads." *Mid-American Chants.* New York: Quale, 2006. 49.

———. "Song of Theodore." *Mid-American Chants*. New York: Quale, 2006. 15–17.
———. *Winesburg, Ohio*. New York: Penguin, 1992.
———. "Word Factories." *A New Testament*. New York: Boni and Liveright, 1927. 85–88.
Andrews, Austin. "Deaf Ninja." YouTube. Accessed 16 February 2009. http://www.youtube.com/watch?v=L91KVUZRBq8. Video.
Appelbaum, David. *Voice*. Albany: State U of New York P, 1990.
Armstrong, Tim. *Modernism, Technology and the Body*. Cambridge: Cambridge UP, 1998.
*Audism Unveiled*. Prod. Benjamin Bahan, H-Dirksen Bauman, and Facundo Montenegro. Dawn Sign, 2008. DVD.
Bahan, Benjamin. "Face-to-Face Tradition in the American Deaf Community: Dynamics of the Teller, the Tale, and the Audience." *Signing the Body Poetic: Essays on American Sign Language Literature*. Ed. H-Dirksen L. Bauman, Jennifer L. Nelson, and Heidi M. Rose. Berkeley: U of California P, 2006. 21–50.
Bailey, Richard W. *Speaking American: A History of English in the United States*. Oxford: Oxford UP, 2012.
Bakhtin, Mikhail. *Rabelais and His World*. Trans. Helene Iswolsky. Bloomington: Indiana UP, 1984.
Ballin, Albert. *The Deaf Mute Howls*. Washington, DC: Gallaudet UP, 1998.
Barkan, Elazar, and Ronald Bush. Introduction. *Prehistories of the Future: The Primitivist Project and the Culture of Modernism*. Ed. Barkan and Bush. Stanford: Stanford UP, 1995. 1–19.
Barthes, Roland. "The Death of the Author." *Image/Music/Text*. Trans. Stephen Heath. New York: Hill and Wang, 1978.
Bass, Eben. "Meaningful Images in *The Sound and the Fury*." *Modern Language Notes* 76.8 (1961): 728–731.
Bauman, H-Dirksen L. "Body/Text: Sign Language Poetics and Spatial Form in Literature." *Signs and Voices: Deaf Culture, Identity, Language, and Arts*. Ed. Kristin A. Lindgren, Doreen DeLuca, and Donna Jo Napoli. Washington, DC: Gallaudet UP, 2008. 163–176.
———. "Getting out of Line: Toward a Visual an Cinematic Poetics of ASL." *Signing the Body Poetic: Essays on American Sign Language Literature*. Ed. Bauman, Jennifer L. Nelson, and Heidi M. Rose. Berkeley: U of California P, 2006. 95–117.
———. "On the Disconstruction of (Sign) Language in the Western Tradition: A Deaf Reading of Plato's *Cratylus*." *Open Your Eyes: Deaf Studies Talking*. Ed. Bauman. Minneapolis: U of Minnesota P, 2008. 127–145.
———, ed. *Open Your Eyes: Deaf Studies Talking*. Minnesota: U of Minnesota P, 2008.
Baxandall, Michael. *Painting and Experience in Fifteenth-Century Italy: A Primer in the Social History of Pictorial Style*. Oxford: Oxford UP, 1988.

Baynton, Douglas C. *Forbidden Signs: American Culture and the Campaign against Sign Language*. Chicago: U of Chicago P, 1996.

———. "A Silent Exile on This Earth: The Metaphorical Construction of Deafness in the Nineteenth Century." *The Disability Studies Reader*. 2nd ed. Ed. Lennard J. Davis. New York: Routledge, 2006. 33–48.

Beasley, Rebecca. *Ezra Pound and the Visual Culture of Modernism*. Cambridge: Cambridge UP, 2008.

Bec, Louis. "Life Art." *Signs of Life: Bioart and Beyond*. Ed. Eduardo Kac. Cambridge: MIT P, 2007. 83–92.

Bell, Alexander Graham. *Memoir upon the Formation of a Deaf Variety of the Human Race*. Washington, DC: Alexander Graham Bell Association for the Deaf, 1969.

Bergson, Henri. *Laughter: An Essay on the Meaning of the Comic*. New York: Arc Manor, 2008.

Berman, Marshall. *All That Is Solid Melts into Air: The Experience of Modernity*. New York: Penguin, 1988.

Bersani, Leo. *Intimacies*. Chicago: U of Chicago P, 2010.

———. "Is the Rectum a Grave?" *AIDS: Cultural Analysis / Cultural Activism* 43 (1987): 197–222.

Blackmur, R. P. *Language as Gesture: Essays in Poetry*. New York: Harcourt Brace Jovanovich, 1952.

Bloom, Harold. Introduction. *The Complete Poems of Hart Crane: Centennial Edition*. Ed. Mark Simon. New York: Liveright, 2001.

Bradshaw, Melissa. *Amy Lowell: Diva Poet*. Aldershot, UK: Ashgate, 2011.

Bragg, Bernard. "Flowers and Moonlight." YouTube. Updated 16 July 2010. http://www.youtube.com/watch?v=MHDO8d6url4. Video.

Breslin, James E. "William Carlos Williams and Charles Demuth: Cross-Fertilization in the Arts." *Journal of Modern Literature* 6.2 (1977): 248–263.

Brueggemann, Brenda Jo. *Deaf Subjects: Between Identities and Places*. New York: New York UP, 2009.

Brunner, Edward J. *Splendid Failure: Hart Crane and the Making of "The Bridge."* Urbana: U of Illinois P, 1985.

Burke, Seán. *The Death and Return of the Author: Subjectivity in Barthes, Foucault, and Derrida*. Edinburgh: Edinburgh UP, 1998.

Burnett, Gary. *H.D. between Image and Epic: The Mysteries of Her Poetics*. Ann Arbor, MI UMI Research Press, 1990.

Burton, Stacy. "Rereading Faulkner: Authority, Criticism, and *The Sound and the Fury*." *Modern Philology* 98.4 (2001): 604–628.

Cameron, Sharon. *Impersonality: Seven Essays*. Chicago: U of Chicago P, 2007.

Carr, Helen. *The Verse Revolutionaries: Ezra Pound, H.D. and the Imagists*. London: Jonathan Cape, 2009.

Caso, Pere Borrell del. *Boy Escaping Criticism*. 1874. Banco de España, Madrid.

Cavarero, Adriana. *For More than One Voice: Toward a Philosophy of Vocal Expression*. Stanford: Stanford UP, 2005.
Chaplin, Charles. *My Autobiography*. New York: Simon and Schuster, 1964.
Chen, Mel Y. *Animacies: Biopolitics, Racial Mattering, and Queer Affect*. Durham: Duke UP, 2012.
Churchill, Winston. "Everybody's Language." *Collier's* 26 October 1935. Rpt. *The Essential Chaplin: Perspectives on the Life and Art of the Great Comedian*. Ed. Richard Schieckel. Chicago: Ivan R. Dee, 2006. 205-214.
Clark, John Lee, ed. *Deaf American Poetry: An Anthology*. Washington, DC: Gallaudet UP, 2009.
Clarke Schools for Hearing and Speech. Home page. 2013. http://www.clarke-schools.org/.
Collier, John, Jr. *Visual Anthropology: Photography as a Research Method*. Albuquerque: U of New Mexico P, 1986.
Condillac, Étienne Bonnot de. *Cours d'instruction du Prince de Parme*. Vol. 1. Parma, 1793.
Conley, Willy. "Salt in the Basement: An American Sign Language Reverie in English." *Deaf American Poetry: An Anthology*. Ed. John Lee Clark. Washington, DC: Gallaudet UP, 2009. 195-197.
Connor, Rachel. *H.D. and the Image*. Manchester: Manchester UP, 2004.
Cook, Peter, and Kenneth Lerner. "Poetry." *Signing the Body Poetic: Essays on American Sign Language Literature*. Ed. H-Dirksen L. Bauman, Jennifer L. Nelson, and Heidi M. Rose. Berkeley: U of California P, 2006. DVD.
Cornia, David, Ursula Bellugi, and Judy Reilly. "Neuropsychological Studies of Linguistic and Affective Facial Expressions in Deaf Signers." *Language and Speech* 42.203 (1999): 307-331.
Courtin, Cyril. "The Impact of Sign Language on the Cognitive Development of Deaf Children: The Case of Theories of Mind." *Journal of Deaf Studies and Deaf Education* 5.3 (2000): 266-276.
Cowley, Malcolm. "The Dilemma of *The Waste Land*." *The Waste Land: A Norton Critical Edition*. Ed. Michael North. New York: Norton, 2001. 163-166.
Crane, Hart. "At Melville's Tomb." *The Bridge. The Complete Poems of Hart Crane: The Centennial Edition*. New York: Liveright, 2001. 33.
———. *The Bridge. The Complete Poems of Hart Crane: The Centennial Edition*. New York: Liveright, 2001. 42-108.
———. "The Broken Tower." *The Complete Poems of Hart Crane: The Centennial Edition*. Ed. Marc Simon. New York: Liveright, 2001. 161-162.
———. "Episode of Hands." *The Complete Poems of Hart Crane: The Centennial Edition*. Ed. Marc Simon. New York: Liveright, 2001. 173.
———. "General Aims and Theories." *Hart Crane: Complete Poems and Selected Letters*. Ed. Langdon Hammer. New York: Library of America, 2006. 160-164.
———. "A Letter to Harriet Monroe." *Hart Crane: Complete Poems and Selected*

*Letters*. Ed. Langdon Hammer. New York: Library of America, 2006. 165–169.

———. *O My Land, My Friends: The Selected Letters of Hart Crane*. Ed. Langdon Hammer and Brom Weber. New York: Four Walls Eight Windows, 1997.

———. "Voyages." *The Complete Poems of Hart Crane: The Centennial Edition*. Ed. Marc Simon. New York: Liveright, 2001. 34–40.

———. "The Wine Menagerie." *The Complete Poems of Hart Crane: The Centennial Edition*. Ed. Marc Simon. New York: Liveright, 2001. 23–24.

Crawford, James. *At War with Diversity: US Language Policy in an Age of Anxiety*. Clevedon, UK: Cromwell, 2000.

Crosby, Harry. "Aeronautics." *Transition: A Paris Anthology*. New York: Doubleday, 1990. 90–92.

Davidson, Michael. *Concerto for the Left Hand: Disability and the Defamiliar Body*. Ann Arbor: U of Michigan P, 2008.

Davis, Lennard J. *Bending Over Backwards: Disability, Dismodernism, and Other Difficult Positions*. New York: New York UP, 2002.

———. "Constructing Normalcy: The Bell Curve, the Novel, and the Invention of the Disabled Body in the Nineteenth Century." *The Disability Studies Reader*. 2nd ed. Ed. Lennard J. Davis. New York: Routledge, 2006.

———. *Enforcing Normalcy: Disability, Deafness, and the Body*. London: Verso, 1995.

———. Introduction. *The Disability Studies Reader*. 2nd ed. Ed. Davis. New York: Routledge, 2006. xv–xviii.

Dean, Tim. "Hart Crane's Poetics of Privacy." *American Literary History* 8.1 (1996): 83–109.

Demuth, Charles. *I Saw the Figure 6 in Gold*. 1929. Oil on composition board. Alfred Stieglitz Collection, Metropolitan Museum of Art, New York.

Descartes, René. *Discours de la method*. 1636. *Oeuvres de Descartes*. Vol. 5. Ed. Charles Adam and Paul Tannery. Paris: Cerf, 1913. 57–58.

Dickie, Margaret. *On the Modernist Long Poem*. Iowa City: U of Iowa P, 1986.

Diepeveen, Leonard. *The Difficulties of Modernism*. New York: Routledge, 2003.

Doyle, Laura, and Laura Winkiel, eds. *Geomodernisms: Race, Modernism, Modernity*. Bloomington: Indiana UP, 2005.

Dresser, Charlotte Elizabeth, and Fred Rafferty. *Spirit World and Spirit Life: Automatic Writing*. New York: J. F. Rowny, 1922.

Duchamp, Marcel. *Nude Descending a Staircase, No. 2*. 1912. Oil on canvas. 147 cm × 89.2 cm. Philadelphia Museum of Art, Philadelphia.

Eliot, T. S. "The Metaphysical Poets." *Selected Prose of T. S. Eliot*. Ed. Frank Kermode. San Diego: Harcourt, 1975. 59–67.

———. "Tradition and the Individual Talent." *The Sacred Wood and Other Essays*. Mineola NY: Dover, 1998. 27–33.

———. "The Waste Land." *T. S. Eliot: The Complete Poems and Plays, 1909–1950*. New York: Harcourt Brace, 1950. 37–55.

———. *The Waste Land: A Facsimile and Transcript of the Original Drafts Including the Annotations of Ezra Pound*. Ed. Valerie Eliot. San Diego: Harcourt Brace, 1971.

Ellmann, Maud. *The Poetics of Impersonality: T. S. Eliot and Ezra Pound*. Cambridge: Harvard UP, 1987.

Esmail, Jennifer. "The Power of Deaf Poetry: The Exhibition of Literacy and the Nineteenth-Century Sign Language Debates." *Sign Language Studies* 8.4 (2008): 348–368.

———. *Reading Victorian Deafness: Signs and Sounds in Victorian Literature and Culture*. Athens: Ohio UP, 2013.

Faulkner, William. "Class Conferences at the University of Virginia." March 13, 1957. *The Sound and the Fury: Norton Critical Edition*. Ed. David Minter. New York: Norton, 1994. 234–237.

———. "Interview with Jean Stein vanden Heuvel." *The Sound and the Fury: Norton Critical Edition*. Ed. David Minter. New York: Norton, 1994. 232–234.

———. *The Sound and the Fury*. New York: Vintage, 1990.

Fay, E. A. "Tabular Statement of American Schools for the Deaf, 1889." *American Annals of the Deaf and Dumb* 35 (1890).

Ford, Ford Maddox. "Foreword: 'Those Were the Days.'" *Imagist Anthology 1930*. New York: Covici-Friede, 1930. 13–21.

Forster, E. M. *Aspects of the Novel*. New York: Harcourt, Brace and World, 1954.

Foucault, Michel. *The Birth of the Clinic*. 3rd ed. New York: Routledge, 2003.

———. "Friendship as a Way of Life." *The Essential Works of Michel Foucault: Ethics, Subjectivity and Truth*. Ed. Paul Rabinow. New York: New Press, 1994. 135–140.

———. "The Social Triumph of the Sexual Will." *The Essential Works of Michel Foucault: Ethics, Subjectivity and Truth*. Ed. Paul Rabinow. New York: New Press, 1994. 157–162.

———. "What Is an Author?" *Aesthetics, Method, and Epistemology*. Ed. James D. Faubion. Trans. Robert Hurley et al. New York: New Press, 1994. 205–222.

Fox, Margalit. *Talking Hands*. New York: Simon and Schuster, 2007.

Frank, Joseph. "From *Spatial Form in Modern Literature*." *Theory of the Novel: A Historical Approach*. Ed. Michael McKeon. Baltimore: Johns Hopkins UP, 2000. 784–802.

Friedman, Susan Stanford. "Periodizing Modernism: Postcolonial Modernities and the Space/Time Borders of Modernist Studies." *Modernism/Modernity* 13.3 (2006): 425–443.

Galow, Timothy W. *Writing Celebrity: Stein, Fitzgerald, and the Modern(ist) Art of Self-Fashioning*. New York: Palgrave Macmillan, 2011.

Gannon, Jack R. *Deaf Heritage: A Narrative History of Deaf America*. Silver Springs, MD: National Association of the Deaf, 1981.

Garber, Randy. "Conversing and Reversing." *Contemporary Impressions* 10.2 (2002): 2–5.

———. *Made in Translation*. 2011. Copper wire on copper panel.
Gee, J. P. , and Walter J. Ong. "An Exchange on American Sign Language and Deaf Culture: J. P. Gee and Walter J. Ong." *Language and Style: An International Journal* 16.2 (1983): 231–233.
Gilbert, Helen. "Dance, Movement and Resistance Politics." *The Post-Colonial Reader*. Ed. Bill Ashcroft, Gareth Griffiths, and Helen Tiffin. London: Routledge, 1995. 341–345.
Glass, Loren. *Authors Inc.: Literary Celebrity in the United States, 1880–1980*. New York: New York UP, 2004.
Goldman, Jonathan. *Modernism Is the Literature of Celebrity*. Austin: U of Texas P, 2011.
Goldwater, Robert. *Primitivism in Modern Art*. New York: Belknap, 1986.
*The Great Dictator*. Dir. Charlie Chaplin. Charlie Chaplin Studios, 1940. DVD.
Groce, Nora Ellen. *Everyone Here Spoke Sign Language: Hereditary Deafness on Martha's Vineyard*. Cambridge: Harvard UP, 1985.
Hammill, Faye. *Women, Celebrity, and Literary Culture between the Wars*. Austin: U of Texas P, 2010.
Haselstein, Ulla. "Gertrude Stein's Portraits of Matisse and Picasso." *New Literary History* 34.4 (2003): 723–743.
H.D. "Hermes of the Ways." *Complete Poems 1912–1944*. Ed. Louis L. Martz. New York: New Directions, 1983. 37–39.
———. *Notes on Thought and Vision*. San Francisco: City Lights Books, 1982.
———. *Palimpsest*. New York: New Directions, 1998.
———. "Review of John Gould Fletcher's *Goblins and Pagodas*." *Egoist* 3 (1916): 183.
———. "Sea Rose." *Complete Poems 1912–1944*. Ed. Louis L. Martz. New York: New Directions, 1983. 5.
———. "Sheltered Garden." *Complete Poems 1912–1944*. Ed. Louis L. Martz. New York: New Directions, 1983. 19–21.
———. *Tribute to Freud*. New York: New Directions, 1974.
———. *Trilogy*. 1946. New York: New Directions, 1998.
Heidegger, Martin. "The Nature of Language." *On the Way to Language*. Trans. Peter D. Hertz. New York: HarperCollins, 1971. 57–108.
———. "The Origin of the Work of Art." *Poetry, Language, Thought*. Trans. Albert Hofstadter. New York: HarperCollins, 1971. 15–76.
Hilder, Jamie. "'After All One Must Know More than One Sees and One Does Not See a Cube in Its Entirety': Gertrude Stein and Picasso and Cubism." *Critical Survey* 17.1 (2005): 66–84.
Hintz, Evelyn J. "Hart Crane's 'Voyages' Reconsidered." *Contemporary Literature* 13.3 (1972): 315–333.
Hollenberg, Donna Krolik. "Introduction: 'A Whole Deracinated Epoch.'" *Between History and Poetry: The Letters of H.D. and Norman Holmes Pearson*. Ed. Hollenberg. Iowa City: U of Iowa P, 1997. 1–15.

Homer. *The Iliad*. Trans. Richmond Lattimore. Chicago: U of Chicago P, 1951.
———. *The Odyssey*. Trans. Robert Fagles. New York: Penguin, 1996.
Hughes, Glenn. "Note." *Imagist Anthology 1930*. New York: Heinemann, 1929. 12.
Huyssen, Andreas. *After the Great Divide: Modernism, Mass Culture, Postmodernism*. Bloomington: Indiana UP, 1986.
Irigaray, Luce. "The Path toward the Other." *Beckett after Beckett*. Ed. S. E. Gontarski and Anthony Uhlmann. Gainesville: UP of Florida, 2006. 39–51.
Jaffe, Aaron. *Modernism and the Culture of Celebrity*. Cambridge: Cambridge UP, 2005.
Jarrell, Randall. *Kipling, Auden and Co.: Essays and Reviews, 1935–1964*. New York: Farrar, Straus and Giroux, 1980.
Jay, Martin. *Downcast Eyes: The Denigration of Vision in Twentieth-Century French Thought*. Berkeley: U of California P, 1993.
Jones, Steve. *The Language of Genes*. New York: Doubleday, 1995.
Joyce, James. *Dubliners: A Norton Critical Edition*. Ed. Margot Norris. New York: Norton, 2006.
Kac, Eduardo. *Genesis*. March 2014. http://www.ekac.org/geninfo2.htmlKac.
———. "Life Transformation—Art Mutation." *Educating Artists for the Future: Learning at the Intersection of Art, Science, Technology and Culture*. Ed. Mel Alexenberg. Bristol, UK: Intellect Books, 2008. 203–216.
Kantanski, Amelia V. *Learning to Write "Indian": The Boarding School Experience and American Indian Literature*. Norman: U of Oklahoma P, 2007.
Kenner, Hugh. *The Pound Era*. Berkeley: U of California P, 1973.
Kern, Stephen. *The Culture of Time and Space, 1880–1915*. Cambridge: Harvard UP, 2003.
*King Kong*. Dir. Merian C. Cooper and Ernest B. Schoedsack. Perf. Fay Wray and Robert Armstrong. Warner Brothers, 1933. Film.
Kittay, Eva Feder. "Dependency, Equality, and Welfare." *Feminist Studies* 24.1 (1998): 32–43.
———. *Love's Labor: Essays on Women, Equality, and Dependency*. New York: Routledge, 1998.
Kleege, Georgina. *Sight Unseen*. New Haven: Yale UP, 1999.
Krentz, Christopher. "The Camera as Printing Press: How Film Has Influenced ASL Literature." *Signing the Body Poetic: Essays on American Sign Language Literature*. Ed. H-Dirksen L. Bauman, Jennifer L. Nelson, and Heidi M. Rose. Berkeley: U of California P, 2006. 51–70.
———. *Writing Deafness: The Hearing Line in Nineteenth-Century American Literature*. Chapel Hill: U of North Carolina P, 2008.
Kroeber, Karl. *Retelling/Rereading: The Fate of Storytelling in Modern Times*. New Brunswick: Rutgers UP, 1990.
Leick, Karen. *Gertrude Stein and the Making of an American Celebrity*. New York: Routledge, 2009.

Lemke, Sieglinde. *Primitivist Modernism: Black Culture and the Origins of Transatlantic Modernism.* Oxford: Oxford UP, 1998.
Leonardo da Vinci. *Treatise on Painting.* Vol. 1. Trans. Philip McMahon. Princeton: Princeton UP, 1956.
Levinas, Emmanuel. *Entre Nous: On Thinking-of-the-Other.* Trans. Michael B. Smith and Barbara Harshav. New York: Columbia UP, 1998.
———. *Humanism of the Other.* Trans. Nidra Poller. Urbana: U of Illinois P, 2006.
Lewontin, Richard, and Richard Levins. *Biology under the Influence: Dialectical Essays on Ecology, Agriculture and Health.* New York: Monthly Review P, 2007.
Lilly, Paul R., Jr. "Caddy and Addie: Speakers of Faulkner's Impeccable Language." *Journal of Narrative Technique* 3.3 (1973): 170–182.
Lowell, Amy. "Preface to *Some Imagist Poets.*" *Norton Anthology of Modern and Contemporary Poetry.* 3rd ed. Vol. 1. Ed. Jahan Ramazani, Richard Ellmann, and Robert O'Clair. New York: Norton, 2003. 926–927.
———. "Spring Day." *The Complete Poetical Works of Amy Lowell.* Boston: Houghton Mifflin, 1925. 145–147.
Mao, Douglas, and Rebecca L. Walkowitz, eds. *Bad Modernisms.* Durham: Duke UP, 2006.
Marinetti, Filippo Tomaso. "The Founding and Manifesto of Futurism 1909." *Modernism: An Anthology of Sources and Documents.* Ed. Vassiliki Kolocotroni, Jane Goldman, and Olga Taxidou. Chicago: U of Chicago P, 1998. 249–253.
Masters, Edgar Lee. *Spoon River Anthology.* 1915. New York: Dover, 1992.
McCabe, Susan. *Cinematic Modernism: Modernist Poetry and Film.* Cambridge: Cambridge UP, 2009.
McCaskill, Carolyn, Ceil Lucas, Robert Bayley, and Joseph Christopher Hill. *The Hidden Treasure of Black ASL: Its History and Structure.* Washington, DC: Gallaudet UP, 2011.
McGann, Jerome. *Black Riders: The Visible Language of Modernism.* Princeton: Princeton UP, 1993.
McRuer, Robert. *Crip Theory: Cultural Signs of Queerness and Disability.* New York: New York UP, 2006.
Mencken, H. L. *The American Language: An Inquiry into the Development of English in the United States.* 4th ed. New York: Knopf, 1984.
Mesch, Johanna. *Tactile Sign Language.* Washington, DC: Gallaudet UP, 2002.
Meyer, William E. H., Jr. "Faulkner, Hemingway, et al.: The Emersonian Test of American Authorship." *Journal of American Culture* 21.1 (1998): 35–42.
Miller, Joshua L. *Accented America: The Cultural Politics of Multilingual Modernism.* Oxford: Oxford UP, 2011.
Mitchell, David T., and Sharon L. Snyder. *Narrative Prosthesis: Disability and the Dependencies of Discourse.* Ann Arbor: U of Michigan P, 2000.

Mitchell, W. J. T. *Picture Theory: Essays on Verbal and Visual Representation.* Chicago: U of Chicago P, 1995.

———. "Preface: Utopian Gestures." *Signing the Body Poetic: Essays on American Sign Language Literature.* Ed. H-Dirksen L. Bauman, Jennifer L. Nelson, and Heidi M. Rose. Berkeley: U of California P, 2006. xv–xxviii.

*Modern Times.* Dir. Charlie Chaplin. United Artists, 1936. DVD.

Morrison, Toni. *Lecture and Speech of Acceptance, upon the Award of the Nobel Prize for Literature, Delivered in Stockholm on the Seventh of December, Nineteen Hundred and Ninety-Three.* New York: Knopf, 1993.

———. *Playing in the Dark: Whiteness and the Literary Imagination.* New York: Vintage Books, 1993.

Myklebust, Helmer R. *Psychology of Deafness: Sensory Deprivation, Learning, and Adjustment.* New York: Grune and Stratton, 1957.

National Human Genome Research Institute, National Institute of Health. "Human Genome Project." March 2014. http://report.nih.gov/NIHfactsheets/ViewFactSheet.aspx?csid=45&key=H#H.

New, Elisa. "Hand of Fire: Crane." *The Regenerate Lyric: Theology and Innovation in American Poetry.* Cambridge: Cambridge UP, 1993. 182–263.

Nietzsche, Jane Chance. *The Genius Figure in Antiquity and the Middle Ages.* New York: Columbia UP, 1975.

North, Michael. *The Dialect of Modernism: Race, Language and Twentieth-Century Literature.* Oxford: Oxford UP, 1994.

———. *Novelty: A History of the New.* Chicago: U of Chicago P, 2013.

———. *Reading 1922: A Return to the Scene of the Modern.* Oxford: Oxford UP, 1999.

Oliver, Kelly. "Subjectivity as Responsivity: The Ethical Implications of Dependency." *The Subject of Care: Feminist Perspectives on Dependency.* Ed. Eva Feder Kittay and Ellen K. Feder. Lanham, MD: Rowman and Littlefield, 2002. 322–333.

Oppen, George. "Of Being Numerous." *George Oppen: Selected Poems.* Ed. Robert Creeley. New York: New Directions, 2001. 83–109.

Padden, Carol. *Interaction of Morphology and Syntax in American Sign Language.* New York: Garland, 1988.

Padden, Carol, and Tom Humphries. *Deaf in America: Voices from a Culture.* Cambridge, Harvard UP, 1990.

———. *Inside Deaf Culture.* Cambridge: Harvard UP, 2005.

Perloff, Marjorie. *The Poetics of Indeterminacy: Rimbaud to Cage.* Evanston, IL: Northwestern UP, 1999.

Peters, Cynthia. *Deaf American Literature: From Carnival to the Canon.* Washington, DC: Gallaudet UP, 2000.

Peucker, Brigitte. *Incorporating Images: Film and the Rival Arts.* Princeton: Princeton UP, 1995.

Plato. *Cratylus.* Trans. C. D. C. Reeve. Indianapolis: Hackett, 1998.

Poizner, Howard, Edward S. Klima, and Ursula Bellugi. *What the Hands Reveal about the Brain*. Cambridge: MIT Press, 1987.
Pound, Ezra. *The Cantos*. New York: New Directions, 1996.
———. "Date Line." *Literary Essays of Ezra Pound*. Ed. T. S. Eliot. New York: New Directions, 1918. 74–87.
———. "Hugh Selwyn Mauberly." *Norton Anthology of Modern Poetry*. 3rd ed. Ed. Jahan Ramazani, Richard Ellmann, and Robert O'Clair. New York: Norton, 2003. 354–366.
———. "In a Station of the Metro." *Norton Anthology of Modern Poetry*. 3rd ed. Ed. Jahan Ramazani, Richard Ellmann, and Robert O'Clair. New York: Norton, 2003. 351.
———. *The Letters of Ezra Pound to Margaret Anderson: The Little Review Correspondence*. Ed. Thomas L. Scott and Melvin J. Friedman. New York: New Directions, 1988.
———. "A Retrospect." *Literary Essays of Ezra Pound*. Ed. T. S. Eliot. New York: New Directions, 1918. 3–14.
Powell, Charles. "So Much Waste Paper." *Manchester Guardian* 31 October 1923: 7.
Pro-Tactile: The DeafBlind Way. Home page. 2013. http://www.protactile.org/.
Rainey, Lawrence. *Institutions of Modernism: Literary Elites and Public Culture*. New Haven: Yale UP, 1998.
Rée, Jonathan. *I See a Voice: Deafness, Language, and the Senses—A Philosophical History*. New York: Metropolitan Books, 1999.
Rennie, Debbie. "Missing Children." *Signing the Body Poetic: Essays on American Sign Language Literature*. Ed. H-Dirksen L. Bauman, Jennifer L. Nelson, and Heidi M. Rose. Berkeley: U of California P, 2006. DVD.
Riddel, Joseph. "Hart Crane's Poetics of Failure." *ELH* 33.4 (1966): 473–496.
Rives, Rochelle. *Modernist Impersonalities: Affect, Authority, and the Subject*. New York: Palgrave Macmillan, 2012.
Rony, Fatimah Tobing. *The Third Eye: Race, Cinema, and Ethnographic Spectacle*. Durham: Duke UP, 1996.
Roosevelt, Theodore. "Americanism." *Works of Theodore Roosevelt: Memorial Edition*. Vol. 20. New York: Scribner, 1926. 464–465.
Rose, Heidi M. "The Poet in the Poem in the Performance: The Relation of Body, Self, and Text in ASL Literature." *Signing the Body Poetic: Essays on American Sign Language Literature*. Ed. H-Dirksen L. Bauman, Jennifer L. Nelson, and Heidi M. Rose. Berkeley: U of California P, 2006. 130–146.
Rose, Phyllis. *Jazz Cleopatra: Josephine Baker in Her Time*. New York: Random House, 1989.
Rosner, Mary, and T. R. Johnson. "Telling Stories: Metaphors of the Human Genome Project." *Hypatia* 10.4 (1995): 104–129.
Rousseau, Jean-Jacques, and Johann Gottfried Herder. *On the Origin of Language*. Trans. John H. Moran and Alexander Gode. Chicago: U of Chicago P, 1986.

Rubin, Joan Shelley. *Songs of Ourselves: The Uses of Poetry in America*. Cambridge: Harvard UP, 2007.

Russell, Emily. *Reading Embodied Citizenship: Disability, Narrative, and the American Body Politic*. New Brunswick: Rutgers UP, 2011.

Sacks, Ethan. "Coca Cola's 'America the Beautiful' Super Bowl Commercial Angers Conservative Pundits." *New York Daily News* 3 February 2014. http://www.nydailynews.com/entertainment/tv-movies/coca-cola-super-bowl-ad-angers-conservatives-article-1.1600849.

Sacks, Oliver. *Seeing Voices*. New York: Random House, 2000.

Sanchez, Rebecca. "'Human Bodies Are Words': Towards a Theory of Non-verbal Voice." *College English Association Critic* 73.3 (2012): 32–46.

Sartre, Jean-Paul. "On *The Sound and the Fury*: Time in the World of Faulkner." *The Sound and the Fury: A Norton Critical Edition*. 2nd ed. Ed. David Minter. New York: Norton, 1994. 265–271.

Saussure, Ferdinand de. *Course in General Linguistics*. Ed. Perry Meisel and Haun Saussy. Trans. Wade Baskin. Peru, IL: Open Court, 1972.

Schepp, James W. *Shepp's New York City Illustrated*. Chicago: Globe Bible Publishing Company, 1894.

Schmitz, Neil. "Gertrude Stein as Post-Modernist: The Rhetoric of 'Tender Buttons.'" *Journal of Modern Literature* 3.5 (1974): 1203–1218.

Shakespeare, Tom. "The Social Model of Disability." *The Disability Studies Reader*. 3rd ed. Ed. Lennard J. Davis. New York: Routledge, 2010. 266–273.

Shakespeare, William. *Macbeth: Folger Edition*. New York: Simon and Schuster, 2003.

"Shantih, Shantih, Shantih: Has the Reader Any Rights before the Bar of Literature?" *Time* 3 March 1923: 12.

Siebers, Tobin. *Disability Theory*. Ann Arbor: U of Michigan P, 2008.

Sitney, P. Adams. *Modernist Montage: The Obscurity of Vision in Cinema and Literature*. New York: Columbia UP, 1990.

Smith, Edward P. *Annual Report of the Commissioner of Indian Affairs to the Secretary of the Interior*. Washington, DC: United States Bureau of Indian Affairs, 1874.

Snyder, Charles. "Clarence John Blake and Alexander Graham Bell: Otology and the Telephone." *Analysis of Otology, Rhinology, and Laryngology* 83.4 (1974): 30.

Snyder, Sharon L., and David T. Mitchell. *Cultural Locations of Disability*. Chicago: U of Chicago P, 2006.

Solomon, Bill. "The Novel in Distress." *Novel* 43.1 (2010): 120–131.

*Sound and Fury*. Dir. Josh Aronson. Docurama, 2002. DVD.

Sowell, James William. "The Oralist." *Deaf American Poetry: An Anthology*. Ed. John Lee Clark. Washington, DC: Gallaudet UP, 2009. 88.

Stein, Gertrude. *The Autobiography of Alice B. Toklas*. 3rd ed. New York: Vintage, 1990.

———. "Composition as Explanation." *Stein: Writings 1903–1932*. New York: Library of America, 1998. 520–529.

———. *Everybody's Autobiography*. New York: Exact Change, 2004.

———. *Picasso*. New York: Dover, 1984.

———. "Portraits and Repetition." *Stein: Writings 1932–1946*. New York: Library of America, 1998. 287–312.

———. *Tender Buttons*. *Stein: Writings 1932–1946*. New York: Library of America, 1998. 313–355.

———. "A Transatlantic Interview." *The Norton Anthology of Modern and Contemporary Poetry*. 3rd ed. Vol. 1. Ed. Jahan Ramazani, Richard Ellmann, and Robert O'Clair. New York: Norton, 2003. 987–993.

Sterne, Jonathan. *The Audible Past: Cultural Origins of Sound Reproduction*. Durham: Duke UP, 2003.

Stewart, George R. "'Each in Its Ordered Place': Structure and Narrative in 'Benjy's Section' of *The Sound and the Fury*." *American Literature* 29.4 (1958): 440–456.

Stokoe, William. *A Dictionary of American Sign Language on Linguistic Principles*. Washington, DC: Gallaudet UP, 1965.

———. "Syntactic Dimensionality: Language in Four Dimensions." Paper presented at the New York Academy of Sciences, 1979.

Suarez, Juan A. "T. S. Eliot's *The Waste Land*, the Gramophone, and the Modernist Discourse Network." *New Literary History* 32.3 (2001): 747–768.

Sweeney, Carole. *From Fetish to Subject: Race, Modernism, and Primitivism, 1919–1935*. New York: Praeger, 2004.

Taylor, Alan. *Writing Early American History*. Philadelphia: U of Pennsylvania P, 2006.

Thompson, Rosemarie Garland. *Extraordinary Bodies: Figuring Physical Disability in American Culture and Literature*. New York: Columbia UP, 1997.

———. Introduction. *Freakery: Cultural Spectacles of the Extraordinary Body*. Ed. Thompson. New York: New York UP, 1996.

———. *Staring: How We Look*. Oxford: Oxford UP, 2009.

Tocqueville, Alexis de. *Democracy in America*. New York: Penguin, 2003.

U.S. Bureau of the Census. *Historical Statistics of the United States, Colonial Times to 1970*. Washington, DC: U.S. Bureau of the Census, 1975.

Valli, Clayton. "Dew on a Spiderweb." Signed by Ella Mae Lentz. *ASL Poetry: Selected Works of Clayton Valli*. San Diego: Dawn Pictures, 1995. DVD.

———. "Tears of Life." *ASL Poetry: Selected Works of Clayton Valli*. San Diego: Dawn Pictures, 1995. DVD.

Valli, Clayton, Ceil Lucas, and Kristin J. Mulrooney. *Linguistics of American Sign Language: An Introduction*. 4th ed. Washington, DC: Gallaudet UP, 2005.

Veditz, George. "The Preservation of Sign Language." Trans. Carol Padden and Eric Malzkuhn. *Deaf World: A Historical Reader and Sourcebook*. Ed. Lois Bragg. New York: New York UP, 2001. 83–85.

Whitehouse, David. "Scientists Hail New 'Map of Life.'" BBC News. 20 November 2003. http://news.bbc.co.uk/2/hi/science/nature/3223318.stm.

Whitman, Walt. *Leaves of Grass 1855*. *Walt Whitman: Complete Poetry and Collected Prose*. New York: Library of America, 1982. 27–145.

——. "A Song of the Rolling Earth." *Walt Whitman: Complete Poetry and Collected Prose*. New York: Library of America, 1982. 362–368.

Widdemer, Margaret. "The Legend of Amy Lowell." *Texas Quarterly* 2 (1963): 193–200.

Williams, William Carlos. *The Autobiography of William Carlos Williams*. New York: New Directions, 1967.

——. "The Great Figure." *Selected Poems*. Ed. Charles Tomlinson. New York: New Directions, 1985. 36.

——. *Paterson*. New York: New Directions, 1992.

Wilson, James C. "(Re)Writing the Genetic Body-Text: Disability, Textuality, and the Human Genome Project." *Cultural Critique* 50 (2002): 23–39.

Wilson, Sarah. *Melting-Pot Modernism*. Ithaca: Cornell UP, 2010.

Woll, Bencie. "Perspectives on Linearity and Simultaneity." *Simultaneity in Signed Languages: Form and Function*. Ed. Myriam Vermeerbergen, Lorraine Leeson, and Onno A. Crasborn. New York: John Benjamins, 2007. 337–344.

Woolf, Virginia. *Mrs. Dalloway*. San Diego: Harcourt, 1981.

——. "Pictures." *The Essays of Virginia Woolf: 1925–1928*. Ed. Andrew McNeillie. London: Hogarth, 1994. 243–247.

Yeats, W. B. "Among School Children." *The Collected Poems of W. B. Yeats*. 2nd ed. Ed. Richard J. Finneran. New York: Scribner, 1989. 215–217.

——. *A Vision*. New York: Kessinger, 2003.

Yingling, Thomas. *Hart Crane and the Homosexual Text: New Thresholds, New Anatomies*. Chicago: U of Chicago P, 1990.

——. "*Winesburg, Ohio* and the End of Collective Experience." *New Essays on Winesburg, Ohio*. Ed. John W. Crowley. Cambridge: Cambridge UP. 1990. 99–128.

Zenders, Karl F. "Faulkner and the Power of Sound." *PMLA* 99.1 (1984): 89–108.

# Index

Adorno, Theodor, 66–67
African Americans, Africanist presence, 4; exploitation of, 162n48; primitivism and, 65, 69; segregated schools, 70–71, 77
Aiken, Conrad, 43, 161n29, 168–169n13
Aiken, Edward A., 115
American Sign Language (ASL), 3, 170n19; embodiment and, 25, 68, 151, 166–167n62; history of, 7–8, 21, 165n24; linguistics, 16, 18, 32–33, 92, 96, 98–101, 109, 162n42, 163n73, 170n25, 170n27, 174n24; literature, 4, 23–24, 28, 31, 36, 44–48, 51, 56–61, 126–131, 146, 175n25, 175n29; other forms of manual communication and, 157n58; role shifting, 46, 58–59, 162n42; Tactile ASL, 45, 154n9, 169n21, 170n21; translation of, 23–24, 49, 162n41, 174–175n28; vision and, 30, 109, 121–122, 133, 139
Americans with Disabilities Act, 5
Anderson, Sherwood, 101, 162n45; *A New Testament* and *Mid-American Chants*, 31, 36, 48–56, 58, 60, 150; *Winesburg, Ohio*, 32, 71, 79–91, 144;
Andrews, Austin, 127
Appelbaum, David, 68
Armstrong, Tim, 62, 66, 92

Bahan, Ben, 56–57, 161n35
Bailey, Richard, 10

Baker, Josephine, 32, 63–64, 68–69, 71, 77
Bakhtin, Mkihail, 70–80
Barkan, Elazar, 65
Barthes, Roland, 39
Bass, Eben, 177n71
Baynton, Douglas, 71
Beasley, Rebecca, 29
Bec, Louis, 147, 151
Bell, Alexander Graham, 19–21, 67–68, 157n65, 158n68, 158n70, 165n19
Bellugi, Ursula, 18, 98
Bergson, Henri, 74
Berman, Marshall, 124
Bersani, Leo, 50–51, 162–163n50
Blackmur, R.P., on Crane, 102; *Language as Gesture*, 77–79, 101
Bloom, Harold, 102, 10
boarding schools, 12, 13–14, 20–22, 32; segregation of, 69–71, 77
Bradshaw, Melissa, 40–41, 42, 161n28
Bragg, Bernard, 33, 127–129, 146, 151, 174–175n28
Braidwood, Thomas, 17
Breslin, James E., 115–116, 119
Brueggemann, Brenda Jo, 8, 15, 153n7
Brunner, Edward, 102
Bulwer, John, 15
Burton, Stacy, 143
Bush, Ronald, 65

Cameron, Sharon, 37

Cavarero, Adriana, 122–123
Chaplin, Charles, Churchill on, 76–77, 165n28; *Modern Times*, 32, 71–75, 79, 88, 91, 144
Chen, Mel, 152
Churchill, Winston, 75–77, 165n28
Clerc, Laurent, 17–18, 69
communicative norms, 26–27, 32, 66, 68, 71, 73–74, 79–84, 87–88, 90–91, 144
Condillac, Étienne Bonnot de, 16
conformity, 9, 12, 13, 20, 26, 32, 42, 67, 69, 72, 74, 80, 82, 84, 86, 88, 90, 91. See also standardization
Conley, Willy, "Salt in the Basement," 22–25, 46, 101, 150
Connor, Rachel, 133, 176n47
Cook, Peter, 31, 36, 46–48, 55, 58
Cowley, Malcolm, 43, 168–169n13
Crane, Hart, 43, 141, 162–163n50, 169n14, 170n34; embodied language and, 32–33, 119, 121; "Episode of Hands," 27–29; genetic text and, 148; indeterminacy and, 95, 113; "Voyages," 100–108
Crosby, Harry, 138
cubism, 29–30, 63, 108–111, 115, 117, 125, 142

Davidson, Michael, 46, 175n29
Davidson, S.G., 70
Davis, Lennard, 2, 6, 159; norm, 67–68
Deaf, 153n7; community, 9, 17, 155n11, 155n22, 161n35; culture, 3, 8, 17, 19, 21, 28, 32, 34, 146, 149, 166n62, 166–167n62, 174n24; education, *see* boarding schools; epistemology, 3, 24, 30, 33, 62, 119, 146, 149, 152, 153n8; gain, 153n8, 161n38; history, 3, 9, 19–22, 57, 61, 69–71; studies, 4, 7, 9, 31, 34, 66, 153n8, 154n10, 161n38; theory, 2–4, 31, 44
DeafBlind 45, 154n9, 161, 169n21
Dean, Tim, 162–163n50, 170n34
Demuth, Charles, 33, 109, 115–120, 121
Descartes, René 15
Dickie, Margaret, 125–126, 177n61
Diepeveen, Leonard, 93, 96
difficulty, 1–2, 23, 27, 29, 40, 44, 52, 75, 77, 82, 105, 126, 144, 155n25; modernist aesthetics of, 8, 31–33, 34, 43, 91–96, 102–103, 109, 112, 115, 117, 119, 142, 148, 149, 161n29, 169n14, 170n34
disability, 81, 87, 91, 165n13, 178n4; insight, 31, 92; interdependence and, 49–51; medical model of, 6–7, 75, 178n4; relationship to deafness, 154n11; regulation of, 67, 69, 88; representations of, 92, 120, 142–144, 156n44, 167–168n4; social model of, 6–7, 166n56; studies, 4–5, 34, 149
Doyle, Laura, 66
Duchamp, Marcel, 111
Dudley, Leis, 70

Einstein, Albert, 65
Eliot, T.S., 27, 167n2; difficulty and, 93, 102, 119, 132, 161n29, 169n14; impersonality and, 31, 47–48, 55; "Tradition and the Individual Talent," 36–39, 139; *The Waste Land*, 43–44, 93–96, 115, 168n13
Ellmann, Maud, 37–38
embodiment, 2, 6–7, 25–26, 30, 52–53, 55, 64, 65–66, 78–79, 89, 90, 92–93, 96, 101–103, 106–109, 113–114, 117, 121, 147–148, 150–152, 155n21; ASL as embodied language, 3, 5, 8, 25–28, 30, 31–33, 34, 38, 45–46, 48, 59, 68–71, 92, 97–101, 129, 154n9, 162n42, 163n73; embodied impersonality, 31, 35–36, 39–41, 43–44, 48–49, 56, 61; normative, 5, 68–69, 71–72, 74–77
epic, 58, 136, 146; definition of, 126, 177n72; relation to imagism, 31, 33, 132–134, 146, 149
epistemology, 30, 35; crip, 3, 92, 153n6; Deaf, 3, 24, 30, 33, 62, 119, 146, 149, 152, 153n8
Esmail, Jennifer, 57–58, 154n10, 165n23
eugenics, 20, 69, 158n70, 158–159m85, 165n23

Faulkner, William, *The Sound and the Fury*, 33, 121, 141–146, 177n72, 177n74, 178n77
Ford, Henry, 11–12, 62
Ford, Maddox Ford, 132
Forster, E.M., 85
Foucault, Michel, 6, 28, 39, 51, 60, 123, 163
Fox, Margalit, 98, 107
Frank, Joseph, 132
Friedman, Susan Stanford, 66

Gallaudet, Edward Miner, 19
Gallaudet, Thomas Hopkins, 17–18, 69
Gallaudet University, 19, 70; affiliation of William Stokoe, 126

Galow, Timothy, 40–41, 160n21
Garber, Randy, 1–2, 150
Garrett, Emma, 79, 165n19
Gee, J.P., 166–167n62
genetics, 17, 178n3, 178n4; genetic art, 33, 147–152, 178–179n9; language and, 103
gesture, 15–16, 18, 20, 69–74, 76–79, 101, 151–152, 169n20
Gilbert, Helen, 28, 159n91
Goldwater, Robert, 63–64

Haselstein, Ulla, 112, 172n76
H.D., 174n20; imagism and, 33, 121, 125, 131–141, 176n38; *Notes on Thought and Vision*, 35, 37; palimpsest and, 138–141, 145–146; *Sea Garden*, 134–138, 176n54
Heidegger, Martin, 175–176n35
Hilder, Jamie, 111
Hintz, Evelyn J., 104
Homer, 37
Hull, Susan E., 70
Human Genome Project (HGP), 33, 147–149, 178n1
Humphries, Tom, 21
Huyssen, Andreas, 94, 159n2, 168n8

image, the, 3, 8, 25, 29–34, 40, 46, 49, 58–60, 101, 103, 105–107, 109, 110–112, 114–120, 121–142, 146, 151, 152, 173n2, 174n20, 175n29, 176n57, 177n71, 179n12
imagism, 25, 31, 33, 108, 121–123, 131–136, 139, 141–142, 149, 175n29, 176n37, 176n38
impersonality, 8, 30–31, 34, 35–39, 43, 45, 47–48, 49, 54, 56, 61, 149, 152, 160n14, 162n45, 168n9
indeterminacy, 2, 31, 33, 92, 93, 95–96, 100–101, 105–106, 109–111, 113, 114, 115, 119, 121, 130–131, 133, 138, 141, 146, 149, 150–152, 175n35, 179n12
Indigenous Americans. *See* Native Americans
interdependence, 48–50, 52, 54, 59, 60
interpenetration, 31, 37, 48–52, 55–56
Irigaray, Luce, 51

Jay, Martin, 29, 124–125, 159n96, 173n7
Jarrell, Randall, 132
Johnson, T.R., 178n1
Jones, Steve, 178n3
Joyce, James, 172n77

juxtaposition, 31–32, 92–94, 96, 100–101, 108–109, 111, 115–119, 142, 149

Kac, Eduardo, 150–152, 178n8, 178–179n9
Kantanski, Amelia V., 22
Kern, Stephen, 65
*King Kong*, 65
Kittay, Eva, 49, 162n48,
Kleege, Georgina, 155n31, 173n1
Klima, Edward, 98
Krentz, Christopher, 154n10, 174n24
Kroeber, Karl, 85–86

language politics, 8–25, 30, 66, 71, 90–91, 154n9, 156n36, 174n25
Lemke, Sieglinde, 62
Leonardo da Vinci, 15
Lerner, Kenny, 31, 36, 46, 58, 164n78
Levinas, Emmanuel, 56–57
Levins, Richard, 148–149
Lewontin, Richard, 148–149
lipreading, 20, 22, 24
Lowell, Amy, 40; embodiment and, 41–43, 160n27; imagism and, 131–132

Mao, Douglas, 66
Marinetti, Filippo Tomaso, 62–63
Martha's Vineyard, 17–18
McRuer, Robert, 153n6, 167n67
Meyer Jr., William E.H., 141–142
Miller, Joshua A., 12, 66, 167n1
Minkowski, Hermann, 65
Mitchell, David, 5, 34, 92, 143, 155n31, 156n44, 167–168n4
Mitchell, W. J. T., 121, 129–130
Morrison, Toni, 4, 21–22
Myklebust, Helmer, 18

Native Americans, 9, 12–14, 20, 22
New, Eliza, 102
norm, 7, 13, 28, 43, 63, 67, 86, 167n67; communicative, 26–27, 32, 66, 68, 71, 73–74, 79–84, 87–88, 90–91, 144; normative, 5–7, 12, 21–22, 55, 69, 72, 75, 80–81, 83, 89, 108, 113, 155n21, 159–159n85
North, Michael, *The Dialect of Modernism*, 27, 167n2; *Reading 1922*, 30, 125; *Novelty*, 155n26, 164n3

Oliver, Kelly, 50
Ong, Walter J., 166–167n62

Oppen, Geroge, 58
oralism, 20–22, 69–71, 86–87, 89–90, 158n68

Padden, Carol, 21, 98, 170n25
Perloff, Marjorie, 95, 105
Plato, 15, 136, 157n52
Poizner, Howard, 98
Pound, Ezra, 27; difficulty and, 102; Eliot and, 43, 94, 168n9, 168n10; epic and, 126, 177n72; imagism and, 122–124, 127, 131–135, 160n27, 175n29, 176n38; impersonality and, 38; "make it new," 54, 164n3
Powell, Charles, 43
Pratt, Richard Henry, 13, 21
primitivism, 8, 27, 31, 32, 34, 62–66, 69–71, 75, 77, 84–86, 90, 149

queer, 4, 31, 50–51, 106–107, 158n75

Rainey, Lawrence, 43
Regnault, Felix-Louis, 69–70
Rennie, Debbie, 31, 36, 58–60, 164n78, 164n80
rhetorical sovereignty, 21–25
Riddel, Joseph, 102
Rives, Rochelle, 38
Roosevelt, Theodore, 12–13
Rose, Heidi M., 45, 47
Rose, Phyllis, 63
Rosner, Mary, 178n1
Rousseau, Jean-Jacques, 16

Sartre, Jean-Paul, 144–145
Saussure, Ferdinand de, 96–98
Schmitz, Neil, 109
Shakespeare, Tom, 7
Shakespeare, William, 143, 178n77
Siebers, Tobin, 6–7, 155n21
simultaneity, 16, 17, 30, 32, 35, 37, 38, 53–54, 59, 60–61, 77, 81, 96–100, 105, 108–110, 111, 112, 115, 116–117, 119, 142, 149, 152, 157n58, 169n20, 169n21
Simultaneous Communication, 17, 157n58
Sitney, P. Adams, 29
Smith, Edward P., 13
Snyder, Sharon, 5, 34, 92, 143, 156n44, 167–168n4

Solomon, Bill, 84, 85
Sowell, James William, 21
Stamp Act, The, 9
standardization, 9, 16, 18, 21, 26–28, 32, 40, 67–68, 74–76, 79–80, 85, 87–89, 108, 137, 167n1, 169n19; assimilation and, 10–11, 13–14, 19–20, 22, 27. *See also* conformity
Stein, Gertrude, 27, 40, 121, 142, 174n20; "Composition as Explanation," 128, 145, 172n76; impersonality/personality and, 31, 33, 38, 41–42; "Portraits and Repetition," 29, 101, 170n30, 173n14; *Tender Buttons*, 109–114, 135; visual image and, 30, 115, 117, 119, 124, 125
Sterne, Jonathan 19–20
Stewart, George R., 142, 177n74
Stokoe, William, 7, 126, 155n23
storytelling, 31–33, 48–49, 52–57, 59, 79–81, 84–90, 161n35, 162n42, 166–167n62
Suarez, Juan A., 25
Sweeney, Carol, 63–64

Thomson, Rosemarie Garland, 113, 158–159n85
Tocqueville, Alexis de, 9–10

Valli, Clayton, 33, 100–101, 111, 119, 129–130, 137, 146, 151, 170n29, 174n24, 176n36
Veditz, George, 15, 122
voice, 2, 25, 42, 47, 54, 59–60, 68, 72–73, 76, 143, 164

Walkowitz, Rebecca L., 66
Whitman, Walt: *Leaves of Grass*, 54, 102, 103; "A Song of the Rolling Earth," 25–26
Widdemer, Margaret, 42–43
Williams, William Carlos, 33; "The Great Figure," 109, 115–121, 172n88; *Paterson*, 122
Wilson, Edmund, 43–44, 161n32
Wilson, James C., 147–148, 178n4
Wilson, Sarah, 27, 66, 167n1
Winkiel, Laura, 66
Woolf, Virginia, 29, 167–168n4, 172n88

Yeats, W.B., "Among School Children," 44–45; automatic script, 38, 160n15
Yingling, Thomas, 86–87, 106–107

## About the Author

Rebecca Sanchez is Assistant Professor of English at Fordham University.